Praise for *The Millionaire Mystique*

"Dr. Jude Miller Burke is a pioneer, studying women millionaires and the personality traits and work styles that propelled them from unremarkable and challenging beginnings to astonishing success. No professional woman should work another day without it!"

—**Kim Kiyosaki,** Co-owner The Rich Dad Company. Author of *Rich Woman: A Book on Investing for Women* and *It's Rising Time!: What It Really Takes To Reach Your Financial Dreams.*

"Wow! I wish I had this treasure years ago. Full of jaw-dropping epiphanies . . . a must-read for smart women who want it all. Through years of research talking to millionaires, Jude Miller Burke breaks the code of how women build wealth while also enjoying a flourishing family life."

—**Teri Gault,** a self-made millionaire and Founder, GroceryGames.com

"Dr. Jude Miller Burke draws a compelling and well-researched map to wealth. This book is full of wisdom for everyone looking to break from old paradigms surrounding money and unlock the secret to financial freedom."

—**Emily Bennington,** bestselling author of *Who Says It's a Man's World: The Girls' Guide to Corporate Domination*

"As a data-driven businesswoman, I appreciated Dr. Miller Burke's solid, scientific research as the basis of her insights to *The Millionaire Mystique*. The stories in her book highlight that many wealthy working women are simply women who translated childhood adversity into the resiliency, focus, and drive that fueled their professional and personal success. This book should encourage all women to believe that yes . . . they can have it all."

—**Dr. Archelle Georgiou,** President Georgiou Consulting and KSTP-ABC Medical Consultant

"Jude's book is the story of women doing well by doing good work for their organizations and communities. Her book is based on a three year research project of high-achieving women, which provides insights and advice on how to overcome obstacles and be successful. Jude's years of experience in management and as a leader add to the veracity of her book. A copy of this book should be on every businesswoman's desk!"

—**Dr. Edward Bergmark,** Founder and Former CEO, OPTUM, United Healthcare

"Executive coach Burke sets out to learn what makes super successful women (in this case, self-made millionaires) different from the rest of us, and discovers that her subjects have much in common with each other: many grew up in middle-class or poor families and had to overcome some kind of childhood trauma.

Burke shares insights from a number of these superstars in the hopes that their journeys will help others, with discussion of work styles, personality characteristics, relationship skills, mentors, leadership techniques, life detours, and the importance of resiliency.

Readers will find sage advice for overcoming challenges, achieving goals, and maximizing opportunities."

—**Publishers Weekly**

The
MILLIONAIRE
Mystique

How Working Women Become Wealthy—
And How You Can, Too!

Jude Miller Burke, Ph.D.

NICHOLAS BREALEY
PUBLISHING

BOSTON • LONDON

First published by Nicholas Brealey Publishing in 2014.

20 Park Plaza, Suite 610
Boston, MA 02116, USA
Tel: + 617-523-3801
Fax: + 617-523-3708

3-5 Spafield Street, Clerkenwell
London, EC1R 4QB, UK
Tel: +44 (0)20 7239 0360
Fax: +44 (0)20 7239 0370

www.nicholasbrealey.com

www.themillionairemystique.com

Printed in the United States of America

20 19 18 17 16 15 14   1 2 3 4 5 6 7 8 9 10

ISBN: 978-1-85788-621-4
E-ISBN: 978-1-85788-983-3

Library of Congress Cataloging-in-Publication Data
Burke, Jude Miller.
The millionaire mystique : how working women become wealthy—and how you can, too! / Jude Miller Burke.
pages cm
Summary: "Fifty years ago The Feminine Mystique uncovered the hidden world of the unhappy 50's housewife. In The Millionaire Mystique EAP psychologist Jude Miller Burke looks at today's self-made female millionaires and how they successfully manage career and family life. What can struggling women learn from them? Miller Burke backs up her findings using results from her scientific research study of millionaire businesswomen."— Provided by publisher.
ISBN 978-1-85788-621-4 (paperback) — ISBN 978-1-85788-983-3 (ebook) 1. Businesswomen—United States. 2. Women millionaires—United States. 3. Self-employed women—United States. 4. Wealth—United States. 5. Success in business—United States. I. Title.
HD6054.4.U6B87 2014
332.024'010820973—dc23
2014010514

Contents

A Note from the Author   vii

Introduction: Who Wants to Be a Millionaire?   ix

Chapter 1   Living the *Millionaire Mystique* Life   1

Chapter 2   Were You Born to Be a Millionaire?   15

Chapter 3   The Millionaire Personality   45

Chapter 4   The Millionaire Work Style   69

Chapter 5   Are You a Social Influencer?   93

Chapter 6   The Millionaire Way: Leading with Grace   109

Chapter 7   Choose to Be Resilient   139

Chapter 8   Great Kids, Great Work Life: The New
             American Dream?   165

Chapter 9   The Unspoken Obstacles for Aspiring
             Millionaires   189

Chapter 10   For Your Greater Good: Earning Satisfaction   209

Conclusion: Becoming a Millionaire . . . Your Own Way   221

Appendix: The Research Behind the Book   223

End Notes   247

Acknowledgments   259

Index   263

A Note from the Author

Over the past few years, I've studied a group of women and men who are among the most successful in the country, all self-made millionaires and multimillionaires. I embarked on this study because I was curious about the super-successful women I had met in my professional and community work as well as the high-achieving women I read about in the media. These women seemed to have a lot in common—suprisingly, many of them came from middle-class or poor families and quite a number even suffered some kind of childhood trauma. (You'll find the details about their backgrounds and characteristics in the appendix at the end of this book.) Yet they had figured out how to achieve admirable levels of success. They shared intimate details of their childhood backgrounds, work experiences, psychological makeup, and strategies for success.

I hope you will profit by their experience. Throughout this book they share their insights and provide you with a roadmap that will ease your way to the top. There are specific personality and work style traits you'll want to develop, leadership skills to practice, education and training to receive, obstacles to overcome, and techniques to learn for balancing work with the most important job: raising the next generation of children. Let's get to work.

Introduction: Who Wants to Be a Millionaire?

"There are no limits unless we see ourselves as limited."

—*Cionne McCarthy, multimillionaire,*
Russ Lyon Sotheby's Realty

I live in one of the wealthiest zip codes in the country, a place of multimillion dollar homes and manicured lawns. Considering where I began, in an agricultural community in rural Minnesota, no one could be more surprised than I am that my life has brought me the kind of breakthrough success that has allowed me to live in this wealthy neighborhood. Looking back, I realize it was a bit like Dorothy arriving from Kansas to the Emerald City wondering—how did all these people get to this beautiful place? As I started talking to people here and making friends, I realized that self-made women millionaires were all around me. They had made their money on their own through business ownership or corporate leadership, combined with good financial planning. As a psychologist, my curiosity was piqued: How had men and women in areas like these around the country—especially the women—achieved so much?

In fact, today, it is much more likely than ever for a woman to command a healthy six-figure income and to become a millionaire—or even a multimillionaire. There are about three million millionaires and multimillionaires in the U.S., and of that group, about one million are women, 15 percent of whom are self-made.[1] These women are not only supporting themselves and their families but are also reaching new heights both professionally and financially—heights that were unimaginable even a decade or two ago. Women have indeed come a long way, baby. Or have they?

Just over fifty years ago, Betty Friedan identified "the problem that has no name" in *The Feminine Mystique*, published in 1963.[2] The problem she identified was society's expectation that women would be content to stay at home, support their husbands and children, and never want anything more. That assumption was then blown away by generations of women who decided they wanted the same opportunities as men to have a satisfying and well-compensated work life. Problem solved, right? Well, not exactly, as working women well know.

Today it seems that we have developed a new problem with no name. Despite a workforce filled with talented, motivated women, only a small percentage reach high levels of success. Some women accomplish astonishing breakthrough achievements through work—becoming self-made millionaires and multimillionaires—while most women never attain anything near that level. Women like me, who grew up in the "women's lib" era, are pretty surprised that women are still so uncommon in the upper echelons of big business and national nonprofits, and are still in the minority on corporate boards, even though they now comprise more than half of college graduates. A mere 15 percent of Fortune 500 corporate officers are female, as are fewer than 4 percent of Fortune 500 CEOs.[3] Somehow we thought that, fifty years on, being a woman would no longer derail anyone's chance to make it big.

What I refer to as the *Millionaire Mystique* is really my shorthand for the qualities that a certain rare breed of women possesses. Women who have these qualities impress us with their ability to have it all—wealth, career, happy family—and to carry it off with what appears to be a minimum of sweat. But they are still so rare.

In fact, there seems to be a real divide between the two groups of women. As an employee assistance psychologist and executive coach, I've seen firsthand how some women—successful, smart, motivated, capable women—struggle to meet their dual goals of meaningful work and a happy, healthy family. The rare breed of female millionaires and multimillionaires, on the other hand, seem to have found the secret to mastering both roles and thrive as working parents. I began to wonder what distinguished these two groups of women and was especially curious about the ultra-successful women I saw in corporate settings or as business owners, the majority of whom also had thriving families. How had they gotten where they were? And what practical advice would they give to make the journey easier for women who want to follow their path?

What I discovered is that little scientific research exists about this group of women. To discover how they did it all—to uncover their mystique—I decided to study them in-depth, using quantitative and qualitative measures.[4] I interviewed female millionaires and multimillionaires who worked for corporations or owned their own medium or large businesses. I asked them probing questions about:

- The work styles that led to their success,
- Essential personality characteristics,
- Relationship skills,
- Mentors,
- Effective leadership techniques, and
- Recommendations for overcoming obstacles to truly impressive success.

In addition, they completed an in-depth survey about their:

- Family backgrounds,
- Life satisfaction,
- Health,
- Paths to success,

- Failures,
- Detours,
- Methods for negotiating family and work responsibilities, and
- Tools for becoming more resilient.

And for comparison, I included a large group of millionaire and multimillionaire men.

The *Millionaire Mystique* study, on which this book is based, was born from this work. I wanted to let both men and women in on the secrets that this exclusive group of self-made wealthy people shared with me. I believe that this book has insights to offer to anyone who wants to achieve at a high level. And I particularly hope that readers who have the ability to mentor women will help them step on an upward trajectory. Studies have shown that having a mentor, male or female, is very significant in the work lives of women who achieve significant financial success.

The New Feminine Mystique: Having It All

The stories and advice the *Millionaire Mystique* women share in upcoming chapters should help anyone looking for a happier work life and home life, emotionally and financially.[5] Sending your kids to fine colleges, living comfortably, and retiring without worry are worthy goals that every woman—and the men who love them—should pursue.

And yet, for *Millionaire Mystique* women, success is about so much more than just money. They do work that rouses their passions, fully utilizes their natural talents, and allows them to feel satisfied about their personal lives. *Millionaire Mystique* women often named the following achievements in their lives:

- An ambitious career
- A satisfying relationship

- Thriving children
- Enjoyable hobbies
- Rewarding community work
- A general *sense of well-being*

How are these women able to "have it all" when so many other women (and men) around them never achieve that level of personal and professional success? What is that mysterious *something* that certain women possess that seems to allow them to reach the pinnacles of success while maintaining happy lives at the same time?

Friedan pointed out, quite reasonably, that a woman could spend years trying to adjust to her feminine role or she could "listen to her own inner voice to find her identity in the changing world. Once she asks herself 'What do I want to do?' she begins to find her own answers."[6]

Women today still struggle to hear that inner voice, only now, societal expectations pull them in a multitude of directions. Some women who want to be successful in their work find that the discrepancy between what women want to do with their lives and the feminine role modeled by family and society continually undermines their sense of success. A clean house, home-cooked meals, sex appeal, and a happy marriage are still, to an unfortunate degree, the measures of a woman. In addition, role conflicts at work and corporate policies (written and unwritten) toward women may toss obstacles in the way of the most ambitious woman on a corporate career path. Is it any wonder that women with promising careers—or who want to launch promising careers or businesses—feel tired, cranky, and confused sometimes?

The upshot of all these remnants of female social conditioning is that women may be *personalizing* both their successes and their failures too much. Every day, women may feel like they are struggling and fighting to achieve, but not making as much progress as their peers. Women can feel like it is their fault if they are not able to easily have it all, as the most accomplished women seem to be able to do this with ease. Echoing Friedan, it is almost certainly *not* a woman's fault if she is not yet in the C-suite—but she can do something about it.

What You Can Expect

Do you have what it takes to become a millionaire or even a multimillionaire? Can you do it through your own efforts, rather than inherited privilege, and have a fulfilling work life? How about creating a fulfilling family life at the same time—a partner and kids if you want them? In other words, is it possible for women to have it all?

My research showed that you have to be thoughtful, determined, and resilient on your way to the top if you are going to have a hope of having it all. This book will help you develop the personality traits, work styles, and leadership acumen you need to achieve professional and personal success. It identifies the building blocks of the *Millionaire Mystique* and provides insights from some of the women who have reached the top. It highlights the success factors you will want to enhance and coaches you on how to reach your individual goals. You will learn how to spot and diminish troubling personal and work-life drawbacks. My goal is not to give you "right answers" but to provide you with thoughtful, candid, and, at times, uncomfortable food for thought. (Aren't we over sexism yet? No, and it could derail your high-flying career.) I hope to help you generate new perceptions and understanding of women in the workplace. And, unlike most career-oriented books, we'll discuss how to find (or mold) helpful personal relationships that will contribute to your success. You'll also receive tips on how to overcome gender-related obstacles and strengthen your personality assets.

Throughout the book, you will hear stories and case studies of women who possess the *Millionaire Mystique*—women who overcame the odds against them and achieved beyond their wildest dreams. Among them are Pat Petznick, who overcame dyslexia and poverty; Jamie Thorsen, who had no funds or support to go to college, but did anyway; Angie Hallier, who overcame domestic violence; and Candyce Williams, who surmounted prejudice and discrimination. All are self-made multimillionaires.

The *Millionaire Mystique* study has opened my eyes to the traits that multimillionaire women have in common with women who never achieve that high level of success. As a result, I believe that most women have the potential to be wealthy and to have it all. This book will help you identify the essential traits that you can develop to find your own place at this rich banquet table.

You'll learn:

- Why starting "at the bottom" isn't a disadvantage and how you can build on your childhood and early career circumstances, whatever they are;
- How childhood adversity can create the framework for success at work;
- What personality factors wealthy working women have in common and how to develop them yourself;
- What work styles and habits millionaires have in common and how you can incorporate those habits into your life;
- How to develop the two most critical traits for overcoming obstacles to success;
- How to become a more compelling leader; and
- How to manage the guilt as you balance your responsibilities at both work and home.

Whether you are unexpectedly stalled in your career, are a mid-level manager who is ready for the next step, are considering a career change, or are launching your own business (or are in the process of building one), this book will improve your chances of becoming financially, personally, and professionally successful. With the tools I offer here, you should be able to achieve greater recognition at work, make more money, and, ideally, achieve balance at home and work.

The *Millionaire Mystique* Women

As noted, after working with hundreds of successful career women, I decided to take a closer look at women who were effectively blending lucrative work lives with a home and children. These business owners and executives had discovered ways to be successful, overcome obstacles, and be great mothers, partners, coworkers, bosses, and, at times, entrepreneurs. In this study of high-achieving women and men, I focused on the lives of more than one hundred noteworthy female millionaires and multimillionaires. For the most part, wealthy self-made women like these want nothing to do with being studied and probed. They are too busy pursuing business and life goals. But I made it clear that I wanted to explore their experiences in a way that would enlighten and empower up-and-coming working women to reach the highest levels. The women and the men I studied were very willing to share what they had observed and what had worked for them over decades of pursuing their life goals. Surveys and questionnaires were completed anonymously, although some of the women and men gave me permission to use their names.

My *Millionaire Mystique* research study was conducted over three years and included more than 300 participants, at all professional levels. We also studied more than sixty male millionaires and multimillionaires, especially for insights about women's success and limitations in the world of work.

My fellow researcher, Mark Attridge, Ph.D., of Attridge Consulting, and I designed the research study and asked our social networks and colleagues to recommend potential study participants. We then asked the participants questions about their families, personalities, work strategies, workplace and personal hardships, gender-specific work difficulties, leadership styles, and how they became so successful and wealthy. Our questionnaire included more than seventy-five items that allowed us to compare the participants with non-millionaires and look for gender similarities and differences. Twenty of the questions allowed participants to give advice on work, leadership, families, and personal strategies to manage both ordinary and extraordinary life challenges. When I reached out to potential participants, interest in the topic was so high that the response rate was 60 percent—*far* higher than most research studies.

The result was lots of statistically significant data—data that cannot be attributed to chance. In other words, we can trust that these results are meaningful and can provide guidance for women and men who want to imitate the work and family paths of the women we studied.

In many ways, the results were astonishing and offer insights for anyone who aspires to follow in their footsteps. For instance, a large percentage of *Millionaire Mystique* women were successful in their work life in spite of difficult, even abusive childhoods. That was a revelation to me. I was also surprised that most of them did not live in wealthy homes growing up, nor did they go to private schools or take expensive vacations with their families. In fact, a full 75 percent of *Millionaire Mystique* women came from middle-class or low-income backgrounds. And, while there is a stereotype of the college-dropout-turned-successful-entrepreneur, 59 percent of the women in my study had graduate degrees, compared with only 10 percent of the general population. Most gratifyingly, as it turns out, they did not typically give up a satisfying family life in order to succeed.

Millionaire Mystique women did not define success in a single way, however. It wasn't simply net worth, or salary, or yearly earnings. In evaluating their level of happiness, these women also considered factors like personal life satisfaction, work accomplishments, achieving leadership positions—*and* giving back to their communities or the nation. In the same way, your own definition of success may differ from that of a coworker or colleague. But I am going to assume that the closer you can get to "having it all" while maintaining your health and emotional well-being, the more successful you will consider yourself to be.

Who Am I to Talk?

Along with the voices of millionaires and multimillionaires that you'll hear in this book, you'll also hear quite a lot of advice from me. I believe I offer several useful perspectives. First, I achieved breakthrough success myself—which is very uncommon in the field of psychology—capping my corporate career as vice president of operations at Optum, a subsidiary of UnitedHealthcare, that provided twenty-four hour access to counselors and social workers for any kind of work or personal problem.[7]

In addition, I am a business-oriented psychologist and an executive coach. I have helped hundreds of people, both men and women, overcome the barriers that were standing in the way of their success and helped them go on to lucrative work lives. The advice that you will see here has been proven "in the field" through my consulting and coaching and is also based on sound scientific research.

But perhaps the most valuable insights I bring to this come from the fact that I never expected to be as financially successful as I am. As a college graduate in the field of psychology, I began my career as a part-time night crisis hotline manager. I simply wanted to help people and earn enough to keep a roof over my head and food in the refrigerator. Psychologists don't go into the field with the expectation of becoming wealthy.

But after I became the program director of the center nine years later, I was encouraged to apply for a job managing the employee assistance department at a large Minneapolis-based division of Honeywell, a Fortune 100 company. Honeywell put me on a fast track that provided me with management and financial training and experience. There I got the opportunity to manage an employee assistance program for 6,000 employees and had my first chance to teach classes on how to fight fairly at home, on how to balance work and family, and on leadership development. So I was ready when the opportunity came along to help start a brand-new division from scratch at UnitedHealthcare. This became Optum, which, fifteen years later and with expanded services, now serves sixty-one million people. Yet for a while, there were only three of us running it.

I had my children while I was working at Optum (UnitedHealthcare was very supportive), but I resigned when my husband needed to move to Phoenix. While there, I finished my Ph.D. and started my executive coaching business, which I have pursued while completing the research studies that became *The Millionaire Mystique*. At the same time, I also created and delivered an executive leadership coaching program at the University of St. Thomas. I believe I've discovered a lot of secrets to stellar success that will be useful to women (and men) looking to have more satisfying home lives and more lucrative work lives. After all, through hard work and luck, I was able to become successful and wealthy myself.

Shall we begin?

Living the *Millionaire Mystique* Life

We put all of our money into the business and I had
to make it a success. Women should know that they
can do it, too.

—*Sandy Brue, Founder and former owner, Sandicast*

What Does the *Millionaire Mystique* Life Look Like?

Picture this for a moment: Women and men are competing for high-
level positions or business customers and nobody notices their gender. Talent, drive, ideas, and hard work are the only attributes that
are considered in choosing who wins the job or the business. Women
and men are equally represented at every level of every business,
including the C-suite and the boardroom. And at home, children are
growing up happy and confident, getting plenty of parental attention and concern. This is still mostly a fantasy, but it is gradually
changing. To begin, let's take a look at two real-life multimillionaires.
Later, we'll examine some of the hurdles and stereotypes you may
encounter, and then highlight the behaviors you can cultivate to
achieve your own success.

Sandy's Story: Starting a Business

Sandy Brue never expected to own a business that grossed nearly $20 million in its best year. Especially since it all came about because of a challenge issued by her husband when he lost his job: Find a way to bring in $10,000 more each year to help support their four kids. She was already working from home as a freelance designer, and she knew that the local openings for full-time designers were few and far between, although she did get several offers that didn't fit her desire for flexibility. Then she saw an ad seeking people who could make animal sculptures from clay. She made a sample in her garage, felt certain it hit the mark, and submitted it, but she still didn't get the job.[1]

At the same time, she knew she had found something she could do to bring in that $10,000. She started molding baby animal figurines in her garage. The business was so successful she had to double her space six months later and triple it to a warehouse space by her second anniversary. Sandicast, which began with molds of a bunny, puppy, squirrel, and fawn based on her original designs, made millions for twenty-five years and spread her artwork to more than forty-two countries worldwide. In 2005, she sold the business and retired in comfort.

How did she achieve such success with little more than a quirky idea and a determination to make that $10,000 for the family? She decided to sell her creations at wholesale to her favorite local gift shop, the Mole Hole in La Jolla, California. The first sales call didn't start auspiciously—the owner made her wait an hour and then forgot about her. But Sandy decided, while she was cooling her heels, that she wasn't going to leave the store without a sale:

> "If you're not getting results," I thought to myself, "you need to change (tactics)." Once she noticed me again, I started flattering her, saying that I came to her store first because it was my favorite and I knew why my animals would sell there. And I did come away with a sale. I never looked back.

Sandy created an ever-changing line of lifelike purebred dog sculptures and other animals that became more popular with each passing year. By focusing on what customers loved about their own animals, she kept refining her sculptures, and expanding the business, almost until the very end.

I tell Sandy's story because she is a perfect example of a woman who is living the *Millionaire Mystique* life by starting her own successful business. She focused on a talent she loved, sold her products with passion, multiplied her efforts through expansion, and then sold out at the right time for an astonishing profit, especially considering where she started.

Fran's Story: Corporate Climbing

You can also, of course, achieve millionairedom in the more conventional way, by rising to the top in the corporate world. Fran Jacques, former strategic communications director for a business unit of Motorola that was subsequently acquired by military contractor General Dynamics, became wealthy traveling that route. General Dynamics bought her division, which specialized in radio communications software, just one month before 9/11 and as a result, she spent thirteen years on what she calls a "wild ride." Fran was constantly busy supporting the company's efforts to get bug-free radio software to soldiers in the field. "Soldiers cannot call a help desk when something goes wrong, so it's your patriotic duty to get it right."[2]

During Fran's tenure at General Dynamics, her division went from 1,300 employees to 10,000, another source of adrenalin and intensity. She says she only noticed she was on the corporate fast track when she found herself being asked to high-level meetings and given rides on the corporate jet.

> Most raises surprised me because I didn't focus on moving up the corporate ladder. I'm a broadcast journalist by training, so I just focused on doing the jobs I loved—the ones that allowed me to tell a good story and find the "Wow factor." It's just way too much trouble to plot your next move.

In fact, Fran's story symbolizes the paradox underlying the *Millionaire Mystique* for many of our millionaires and multimillionaires. A significant proportion of them told me that they did not pursue millionairedom, *per se*. What they did was pursue a passion that happened to be well-compensated (or could be made so, like Sandy Brue's animal sculptures).

"Work hard" is a theme that will come up more than once as you read the advice of our millionaires and multimillionaires. But Fran Jacques and the others understand that "work hard" is just shorthand for another concept: "Find the best way to get the job done." In Fran's case, it led to a brilliant insight that surely helped her get those unexpected raises. "I focused on the intent of the CEO—I listen well to what's needed. And I am always thinking about what's keeping the CEO up at night."

Other advice Fran offers to those building careers in corporations is equally useful:

- Anticipate the next day's questions before you go home at night. Your brain will work out answers and give them to you in the morning if you listen for them.
- Get in early and stay late. Exercise before that. (Look for Fran at 4:45 a.m.)
- If you want to stay alive in the corporate world, do what they want you to do. Just do it more effectively than the next person.
- Rehearse every important conversation aloud. A broadcast journalist knows that your words will sound different when spoken aloud, than how they sound in your head. Talk out every possibility and scenario.
- Remember what success looks like: When you are in a bad situation or facing a big project, it's easy to lose sight of what you are fighting for.

Fran left General Dynamics in 2013, realizing that layoffs were coming and not wanting to be caught up in them. "I've never been laid off from any job," she laughs triumphantly. She has now, in her words, "followed her heart home" to health care at West Hills Hospital and Medical Center (now owned by HCA), where she started her career and is now the vice president of marketing and PR. Because she had ample savings in the bank, she was able to take her time to find the perfect job. The extra time was particularly important because many employers didn't understand how military contracting translated into health care. "I needed to be able to navigate my own course," she says. "If you have the financial resources personally, you do not have to acquiesce to not being in charge." Money gives you freedom and choice.

Myth or Reality? Having It All

Sandy Brue never valued the trappings of luxury as she was building her business. Instead, she was living the true *Millionaire Mystique* life by investing all of her spare cash into the business. Yet she felt like she was "having it all": a thriving business, customers who thought she was a rock star, loyal employees, and a loving family. In fact, before she sold the business, one of her sons was in charge of operations for the company. Life was good.

The same was true for Fran Jacques. She says she barely noticed when her life became comfortable enough to stop worrying about having money. It was probably when she was able to pay her mom back for the money her father had lent her to buy a house. Or perhaps when she was recently able to provide funds to her son for a business that required a significant investment. She notes, "I like being able to help my family like my dad did for me. I want to be able to help them while I'm still in my earning years." To her, having a *Millionaire Mystique* life is also about being able to set a firm, early retirement date: "I want to retire at fifty-nine-and-a-half and play golf!" Fran also plans to assist charities that help kids succeed. She says, "I love reading stories about people who give up corporate gigs and work for good causes for pennies." Clearly, both Sandy Brue and Fran Jacques believe they are having it all.

Unfortunately, the idea that women cannot have it all—a successful work life, healthy children, happiness—has been endorsed in several prestigious places lately, most notably in a widely discussed article called "Why Women Still Can't Have It All," by Princeton professor Anne-Marie Slaughter, published in *The Atlantic Monthly* in 2012.[3] "Having it all," she said, "was not possible in many kinds of jobs . . . the minute I found myself in a job that is typical for the vast majority of working women (and men), working long hours on someone else's schedule, I could no longer be the parent and the professional I wanted to be." Even Facebook COO Sheryl Sandberg, in her wonderful book, *Lean In*, explains the low numbers of women in the C-suite and boardrooms by noting that there is a "leadership ambition gap" in which more men aspire to senior leadership positions than women do. She challenges them to continue to "lean in" throughout their careers and believe that they can get there.[4]

Both see things somewhat differently than I do. Slaughter, who assessed her own experience as a long-distance commuter and White House staffer, believes that rising to the top means accepting working conditions that would drive anyone crazy, not just women. Sandberg, on the other hand, could have provided more specific steps on overcoming the obstacles that women have to overcome on the way to the top, although I agree that to be in the best spot, women need to "lean in" as hard as possible before they have children. Ultimately, I believe that, with the right toolbox of skills, you can live the *Millionaire Mystique* life and make it to the top sane, with well-adjusted children. The millionaires and multimillionaires of the *Millionaire Mystique* prove it.

What did my research show about having it all? For one thing, many of the *Millionaire Mystique* women reported that healthy relationships had helped them scale the corporate wall, start businesses, and acquire wealth. I saw case after case of this new twist on the achievement myth. Specifically, "behind every successful man there is a woman at home" has now become "for most successful women, there's a heavily contributing husband or partner at home."

The Importance of Perseverance

Unfortunately, there are still many institutional obstacles to having it all, like a lack of flextime in some companies and insane demands on both women and men. Betty Friedan would not be pleased, although she wouldn't be surprised, either.

Both men and women in my study agree that working women frequently experience prejudice and discrimination, making it more difficult to get ahead. In the corporate setting, many women are challenged in terms of the amount of help they receive (or, more specifically, do not receive) in moving up the corporate ladder and the amount of prejudice they experience. Similarly, women business owners reported more difficulty getting loans and competing for customers, simply because they were women. Just 6 percent of the men reported experiencing sexism that interfered with their jobs, compared to 50 percent of the women. In addition, female executives and business owners reported being in charge of family responsibilities *ten times more often* than the men, although a significant number of the *Millionaire Mystique* women were also the primary breadwinners in their families.

And, flying in the face of stereotypes about the rich, the vast majority of the *Millionaire Mystique* women have not led charmed lives that eased them into financial success without a great effort on their part. Far from it. Many of the *Millionaire Mystique* women grew up in poverty, had alcoholic parents, and experienced abuse or health problems. But they had the one quality that separates them from less-successful people: They persevered. They overcame whatever was thrown their way.

Stereotypes, Barriers, and Myths

As I'll show you later in detail, millionaire women also turned out to have common personality traits, work behaviors, and leadership styles that separated them from the average person. On the personal level, they reported significantly higher life satisfaction than the general population. But perhaps most surprising of all is that high-achieving men and women are far more similar to each other than they are different.

In fact, this group exhibited *none* of the gender stereotypes we have been led to believe about women: Women lack the drive and work engagement to succeed; women are reactive to others or passive; women are more emotional than men; women are less analytical than men; women don't care about money as much as men; women gossip more than men; women are not as competitive as men; women are uncomfortable with their power; and women are not willing to move for their jobs. Let me repeat: These stereotypical behaviors *do not exist* among the *Millionaire Mystique* group.

I believe that certain myths about women still undercut their efforts to achieve the corner suite, where many of them belong. They are myths that we need to combat, individually and as a society, before a majority of women can even hope to live the *Millionaire Mystique* life. The *Mystique* women have had to overcome these myths—and you may need to as well.

First and foremost, of course, is the fact that women have been held back by society's continuing inability to recognize the contribution women make by having children. In many workplaces, if you are not willing to work seventy-hour weeks and jump to fulfill every request that comes in on the weekend, you are not fast-track material. Fortunately, this is changing in many companies. Today, many management teams have begun to understand that when they are unwilling to help families find time to nurture their children, they are driving away valuable resources. As more women join the leadership ranks, I believe such flexibility will become more the norm. Even men are starting to demand more time with their families, a very good sign.

As noted earlier, there is also a belief that women are less ambitious than men. True, many women are quieter about their ambition. You'll witness few women at dinner parties talking about the promotion they hope to get or their plans to take over their departments. Smart women, instead, are quietly planning their paths to the top and persistently executing them, even in the face of setbacks. Yet not enough of these women are effective at making their triumphs known. In fact, making sure people in power know about your achievements is essential to achieving *Millionaire Mystique* status. Bragging can draw hostility, but you should remember to subtly work your achievements and plans for the future into conversations or take advantage of social media to casually highlight your successes.

Women are also labeled by men in many workplaces as "too serious." I encourage you to let your natural humor show through at work as much as possible: *Millionaire Mystique* participants declared it to be an essential skill and the key to a happier life. Everybody loves a good laugh, so humor bridges all kinds of barriers. Trust me, you won't be perceived as less serious about your work if you can laugh about it. It's strange, but the perception of you as a threat diminishes as you become a more gender-neutral friend through humor.

Do you need to work twice as hard as a man to achieve the *Millionaire Mystique* life? No, I don't think so. In fact, if you spend countless hours at work, higher-ups may perceive that you are incompetent because you can't get your work done during regular hours. I often (often!) took work home, especially when I ran Optum operations for UnitedHealthcare, but I tried to never leave the impression that I was scrambling to catch up. Rather, I would casually highlight how much I achieved the previous day, even though I left work early to be at a soccer game. You need to keep your boss informed about how much work you are actually accomplishing; this will ensure that schedule changes are less of an issue. Managing the perceptions of others can be as subtle as comments in the coffee room, especially if you keep it lighthearted.

Women are also said to be too emotional at work, but this is a reflection of the differing responses to stress that women and men have. Men express plenty of emotion, but their stress is frequently manifested as irritation or anger. Women tend to experience negative emotions at work as distress or sadness, which if not expressed appropriately can be seen as unprofessional. Most women can definitely cope with work stresses without breaking down to cry because they already handle the stress of work, kids, parents, home, and social life. And while *Millionaire Mystique* women don't report better health than average women, they do report very good to excellent health, a good indication that the stress of their jobs doesn't affect them too negatively.

Another myth is that women don't support other people at work. The reality is just the opposite. Perhaps surprisingly, very few of the wealthy women in my study embodied what is sometimes called "Queen Bee Syndrome,"[5] the desire to have a say in every little decision their employees make. Successful women would rather delegate. In the long run, leadership comes easier to those who rehearse the process of delegation. Delegation is harder than it looks, especially for people with a high need for perfection. You can practice now by letting go of a project that has consequences; delegate it to someone really good. But be sure to check back regularly so you can reassure yourself that progress is being made.

Another insidious and damaging perception also persists: that women bosses cannot motivate employees and therefore don't belong in leadership. Nonsense. Both men and women among the *Millionaire Mystique* group are good at building relationships. The women can also tell heroic stories to facilitate understanding and motivate employees to higher achievement. Such behavior may not work well in an autocratic company, but it will come to be valued in companies where everyone feels invested in the mission of the company.

Dispelling the Myths: A Closer Look at Sandy Brue, Creator and Business Guru

As we've discussed, there is also a myth that women who start out with basically nothing cannot become multimillionaires. Yet Sandy Brue proved that to be untrue when she formed her animal sculpture company. She started the business with, essentially, nothing except a good idea and the motivation to help her family out of a tight spot. To outsiders, she might have looked like an overnight success, but she operated on certain principles from the beginning that other aspiring multimillionaires can also use.

Ask for Feedback

Once Sandy had convinced several local stores to carry her animal sculptures, she decided she needed to know more about distribution, so she could expand. She approached the buyer at a Hallmark store at a mall in San Diego and made an irresistible offer: "Let me take you to lunch and I won't try to sell you a thing." Instead she simply asked for feedback on her order form. "I thought it would be much harder to say no to me if we were meeting in person. I also learned over the years that many people will help you if you just listen, take notes, and be thankful."

Honor Clients

Sandy was eventually asked to present her animal sculptures to Disney Tokyo. Their only requirement was a personal meeting with her. Sandy had the good sense to have part of her catalog and her business card translated into Japanese. "They were impressed that I did that," she remembers. "I was apparently the only vendor who thought to do that. Frankly, I was very surprised that no one else had thought to make it easier for the Japanese. I wouldn't have considered doing it any other way." She got the business.

Create Solid Relationships

Throughout the years she owned the business, one of Sandy's main goals was to create solid relationships with people who could sell her creations throughout the world. She'd throw dinners at trade shows, inviting the best dealers for an evening of insider information about the gift industry, or take anyone to lunch, any time. She explains,

> Of course, I was picking their brains at the same time about what was working in my product line and what wasn't. In the process, I gained the loyalty of thousands of dealers. And I paid close attention so when I came out with a new product, I could say, "You asked for this."

Personal relationships—and a real talent for creating realistic animals—made Sandy richer than she ever dreamed when she first told her husband she'd try to contribute $10,000 a year to the family finances. She became a multimillionaire when she sold the business. The only surprise, she says, was seeing how much wealth could be created by owning your own business. "I never thought I would be in business," she says. "What I would like to tell women and men is: Seriously assess your talents and what you'd like to sell, then tap someone in the same business to evaluate your potential. If it's a good match, go for it!"

Sandy also passed along other tips that helped her succeed. This advice will help other women, even if they never start their own businesses.

- Create the kind of business you'd like to work in. Sandy's company was made up of people who made her creations by hand. She rewarded at least one employee per month with lunch and a tour of a customer facility. Often they would see an animal they had personally created and have an "I made that!" moment. Once you become a leader or supervisor, you need to help employees have those gratifying moments. Personal attention and recognition for employees are among the qualities that mark you as an effective leader with a future.

- Recognize people for their ideas. Sandy rewarded all kinds of ideas—even if they were impractical—which encouraged her employees to supply more. "We even rewarded complaints," Sandy says, "because they gave us a good idea of where quality problems might be occurring." Rewards were especially important for her immigrant workforce, who initially valued compliance and routine over innovation.

- Confess your problems. If a leader is willing to be utterly transparent about both triumphs and problems, employees will be too. Sandy required all of her department heads to report mistakes annually—how much they cost, what was learned, and what changes were made to prevent the problem in the future. She did the same with company finances and developments. As long as confession is not punished, you'll learn valuable information that allows your company or department to continually improve.

Sandy, the daughter of an Italian immigrant mom, did not grow up in wealth and privilege. In fact, her mom spent some of her own childhood in an orphanage. But she credits her mom with teaching her about taste and quality. Sandy adds, "And she taught me never to give up and to be creative about finding solutions to problems." The *Millionaire Mystique* women share that attitude with Sandy, and in many cases their positive attitudes began in childhood. How your family helps or hurts your chances for success—and what you can do about it—is where we'll go next to begin explaining how you can put yourself on the fast track, accelerating your path to a leadership position.

Mystique Lessons for Aspiring Millionaires

Chapter 1: Living the *Millionaire Mystique* Life

» Adopt a growth mindset. Multimillionaire Sandy Brue could have remained a starving artist in her garage, creating ceramic animals by herself. Instead, she adapted to challenges, grew, and let others manufacture her designs. In this way, she multiplied herself into a multimillionaire.

» Never take "no" for an answer. Think of new ways to overcome the resistance you encounter, but don't reinvent the wheel. Observe how successful people get to yes.

» Choose a field or business that fits your personality and that you are curious about. It will keep you committed and creative, especially in the face of inevitable problems.

» Recall that male and female millionaires have more similarities than differences. The main difference is in the amount of household and childcare duties women are responsible for. Choose an egalitarian spouse or negotiate with your current partner to share responsibilities.

» Never let them see you sweat. Perform at a high level even if you have to take work home, but don't complain about how hard you work. Keep emotions in check.

» Don't brag about your achievements but rather use them as examples of success stories other people could emulate.

» Let go of little things. Delegate and don't overreact.

» Build relationships with everyone to strengthen motivation throughout your group. Give recognition and credit to others for good ideas and work done.

» Treat your business or work with the seriousness it deserves and you will be rewarded. But don't be afraid to enjoy work and laugh, too.

CHAPTER 2

Were You Born to
Be a Millionaire?

The greatest discovery of all time is that a person
can change his future by merely changing his
attitude.

—*Oprah Winfrey*

Oprah Winfrey, one of the richest women in the world, came
from an intensely challenging, painful childhood in rural Mis-
sissippi and rough urban Milwaukee. Chan Laiwa, a Chinese real
estate mogul, is twice as wealthy as Oprah, and grew up even poorer.[1]

Obviously, growing up in a wealthy or nurturing background
is not required if you want to be financially successful. So where
does this myth come from? People who are successful in life often
give the impression that their achievement was easy, something
they expected all along. As a result, we assume that their ambition
to succeed was planted early in childhood and carefully nurtured
while they were growing up. "They must have come from a wealthy
background," we think, "or their parents must have had the means
to send them to the best colleges. At the very least, they had to have
experienced stable home lives and had a lot of support growing up.
Surely, they had to have some terrific advantages in life to rise so
high."

In many cases, that's not true at all. In fact, a majority of the millionaires and multimillionaires (75 percent) in the *Millionaire Mystique* study grew up in poor to middle-class families. Most also experienced at least two traumatic events in their childhoods. But you'd never know it upon meeting them. You only find out the truth once you get to know them.

When I first moved to a wealthy suburb of Phoenix fifteen years ago, while still an executive for UnitedHealthcare, the wealthy people I met presented their life stories as tidy and perfect. Straight shot to the top, silver spoon from birth: that's how their lives looked. But after sharing a lot of dinners and glasses of wine, these new friends started revealing the real stories of what they overcame to achieve success. These multimillionaires, men and women, told me about the pain of poverty, lack of parental support, and outright abuse they had experienced as children. Even if they hadn't experienced any outright trauma, their paths to success from their family beginnings were rarely a given.

The juxtaposition of their groomed lawns and huge homes with the struggles they had endured was remarkable. I knew that there was power in what these successful people had discovered: You can embrace what is useful in your family background, nurture your own talents, and develop coping skills to overcome the negatives. The millionaires and multimillionaires in my study had created their own high level of achievement. One female high achiever told me, "Even as a small child, I always believed that I could find a way to get something done. I had no money, but I had a strong work ethic and motivation."

Your family background—whatever it is—doesn't have to hold you back. Oprah took her ambition to overcome the difficulties of her childhood and used it as a motivation to build a successful enterprise, Harpo Productions. Many of our most successful participants, including those who started out in professions like law and medicine, were compelled to either join large, profitable companies or create thriving businesses, just like Oprah did. The key is to look past whatever you didn't like about your family to find the beliefs and behaviors that made you what you are today. You can consciously choose to capitalize on the positive aspects of your childhood, and you can work to extinguish long-held habits of mind that could sabotage you. And remember, we've all seen spectacular failures emerge from environments that "should" have given them every advantage. The power to rise above your childhood belongs to you.

What Your Family Teaches You

Whether we want to admit it or not, our perspectives, our values, and our limitations (positive or negative) are determined by where and who we came from. You can't begin to consider the drive for success without understanding the powerful impact of nature (genes) and nurture (parental role models). The luckiest children have parents who are always supportive of their ambitions, take the time to give them positive feedback, and act as positive role models of successful people. But what's the chance of that happening? Almost everyone emerges from childhood with attitudes that need reshaping in order to achieve the highest possible level of success.

Early life experiences influence our adult lives more than we are generally willing to admit. A large-scale ongoing study by Keith J. Karren, Ph.D. and his colleagues, reported in their book *Mind/ Body Health: The Effects of Attitudes, Emotions, and Relationships*, emphasized the vital importance of upbringing to future success. "The way parents treat their children," noted Karren, "determines in large part the way the children feel about themselves—while they are children and when they become adults. Parents can endow them with a healthy self-image or engender feelings of low self-esteem."[2] There is a lot of "do as I say" in families, but the most important factor is "do what I do."

For instance, parents can tell their children not to be selfish and yet constantly exhibit petty, selfish behaviors, like cutting in lines and getting angry when they do not get their own way. This negative "behavioral modeling" has a tendency to make it harder for the children to succeed. Behavioral modeling can also be a positive influence on success, of course. This is particularly true when children witness their parents take substantial risks that pay off, such as starting a major business.

I witnessed my dad struggle to build a large excavating company when I was growing up. My siblings and I heard him say almost every night how he wanted more for himself and his family. We witnessed all of the ups and downs, successes and failures, and the day-to-day challenges my parents faced. Would they be able to meet payroll during a downturn in business? Could they afford to buy another piece of heavy equipment? Would a new supplier try to gouge them? No matter what, though, my parents showed us through their reactions to challenges that giving up was not an option—they always found a way to move forward, like great white sharks. In my own life, that has translated into an absolute refusal to give up. I have been able to recognize and grab opportunities because I witnessed my parents' hard work, tenacity, resilience, and optimism. Even when I was a teen, my parents expected me to work hard without complaining and have a positive attitude toward my job. I started working as an administrative assistant in the family business at age fifteen and have never really stopped working since.

How to Succeed If Your Childhood Was "Rotten"

Please do not assume that if your parents were not good role models, you are disqualified from being successful. Most of the women and men in my study told me they had very strong self-esteem and confidence in their own abilities, significant factors in high achievement. But only a third of them claimed that those feelings came from their parents. One fifty-five-year-old law firm partner said, "I probably had [high self-esteem] from childhood since I had to be independent from an early age." Her parents were immigrants and didn't speak English. In her case, the need to be *self-reliant* and an advocate for her parents created a confidence in her skills both as a child and as an adult.

Repeatedly in the *Millionaire Mystique* study, we interviewed women and men who emerged ambitious and hard-charging from environments that were quite dysfunctional. An amazing 80 percent of female millionaires and multimillionaires in our study had experienced at least one "adverse event" while growing up, including abuse. (Fifty percent experienced two to eight serious childhood events.) Just like people in the general population, the childhoods of our highly successful group included the serious illness or death of family members (35 percent), an alcoholic parent (22 percent), domestic violence (18 percent), parents who divorced (21 percent), low income or poverty (17 percent), or childhood abuse (20 percent). Yet they were able to move past it—and even gain strength from these events. The question is: "How did they overcome childhood challenges when less-accomplished people possibly did not?"

My *Millionaire Mystique* study did not specifically address the developmental problems of less-successful people. But research suggests that those who capitalize on challenging experiences in childhood are those who develop a strong drive to escape the situation they grew up in. Malcolm Gladwell, in his book *David and Goliath*, tells the story of a Hollywood mogul whose father put him to work in his Minnesota scrap metal business at an early age. "It was awful. It was dirty. It was hard . . . I think, looking back, that my father wanted me to work there because he knew that if I worked there, I would want to escape. I would be motivated to do something more."[3]

That story vividly reminds me of my own early experiences working for my father's construction business. I learned the value of hard work, accuracy, conscientiousness, and what it meant to earn a living. But I also learned that I did not want to work in construction. I believe that people who are defeated by their childhoods become convinced that their efforts will never succeed, so they stop trying.

A recent study of minority groups in America has shown that three traits propel success: a superiority complex, insecurity, and impulse control. "It's odd to think of people feeling simultaneously superior and insecure," noted the study's authors, Yale Law School professors Amy Chua and Jed Rubenfeld. "Yet it's precisely this unstable combination that generates drive: a chip on the shoulder, a goading need to prove oneself. Add impulse control—the ability to resist temptation—and the result is people who systematically sacrifice present gratification in pursuit of future attainment."[4]

The ability to overcome childhood adversity is related to the personality structure called "hardiness." This concept was first introduced by psychologist Suzanne C. Kobasa of the University of Chicago thirty years ago, based on a study of people in stressful occupations.[5] Your hardiness is what allows you to deal with the stress of solving personal or work problems. The hardy person is able to stay positive under difficult circumstances.

Case in Point: Pat Petznick

One of the most admired, financially successful, and hardy women I know had a very challenging childhood. Pat Petznick is the cofounder (with her sister, Beverly Stewart) of Fresh Start Women's Foundation, the largest women's resource center in the country.[6] Its goal is to help women overcome obstacles in life and achieve at the highest level possible with counseling, career assessments and preparation, parenting and financial classes, legal services, support groups, and other resources for displaced women. (Full disclosure: I'm on the board of directors of Fresh Start.) Pat launched Fresh Start after a career that included working as a regional sales director at Revlon and owning her own large, upscale salon. But her early life was not so promising—she grew up in a remote two-bedroom house in rural Arizona while her father pursued his own entrepreneurial dreams.

Her father started working at age twelve when his father died of tuberculosis; his widowed mother lived in the back of a grocery store where she worked during the day and took in ironing at night to help her family survive. He eventually became Arizona's largest cattle and hay broker, a business Pat's husband and son run today. "I marvel that my dad built his first company into a multimillion-dollar business with only a sixth-grade education," Pat says today.

Pat herself also struggled with school, due to what she now knows is dyslexia. She learned what she could from listening to the lessons but was never able to read well or do math; to get by, she learned to charm those around her with intuitive people skills. Like her father, who she also suspects was dyslexic, she developed a knack for connecting with those around her and took pride in her appearance. Without formal training, she began working as a model and makeup artist after high school.

Her magnetic personality, a coping strategy to induce teachers to ignore her inability to do schoolwork, was soon recognized by Revlon, which gave her a position to introduce their makeup line in Phoenix, Arizona. But when she was required to travel to New York, she had to leave her husband and kids back home in Arizona, so she decided to start a business from scratch, with absolutely no experience. "I built a [business] because I knew how to network with the local Saks, the Ritz-Carlton, and the local television stations," Pat explained to me. "I never said no to any of their requests—I knew how to make customers happy." Those skills, she says, came from her father. "My dad had great people skills, was charismatic, an entrepreneur, and was a legend in his own time."

Pat's story is an excellent example of a high achiever embracing her inborn talents—hardiness, confidence, love of beauty, and ability to connect with others—and the values endorsed by her family to succeed. "You take on your weaknesses and overcome them," she advises. "When God takes you down an unexpected path, you use your family as your anchor. Love takes care of a lot of things." Pat was able to achieve as much as she has in life because she was able to capitalize on those things she was good at—persuading people, enhancing beauty—while minimizing the impact of traumatic events on her outlook. No, she has never gotten over the dyslexia. She simply concentrates on those areas of her life and work where she feels the best about herself: building her businesses and Fresh Start into successful enterprises.

Both Pat and her sister Bev credit their family with giving them some of the motivation to overcome the problems they experienced growing up. "Drive is a funny thing," says Bev. "We're kind of a driven family, I guess. Thinking back, I don't know if it comes from Dad or Mother. I can't say we're pushy, but we will make things happen one way or another."

Focus on Islands of Competence

Physician Kenneth Ginsburg, author of *Building Resilience in Children and Teens: Giving them Roots and Wings*, refers to sources of personal accomplishment and pride, like Pat's, as "islands of competence," and he urges parents to build them up in order to help their children sail through life.[7] Finding your islands of competence is possible as an adult, too, and you should concentrate on those if you have experienced a less-than-perfect childhood.

People who have experienced a traumatic incident early in life are likely to end up at one of two extremes if they reflect back on their childhood—they'll either gravitate toward negative memories or try to deny painful family history. Avoid both of these traps and try to see your past as a chance to identify your islands of competence. Be honest with yourself. What have you always been good at? What have people admired you for? If your work trajectory is currently floundering, perhaps because of an overreaction to childhood or adolescent problems, consider changing gears to an island of competence like Pat Petznick did. It's not too late.

Making the Best of the Past: The Four A's

Although we cannot go back in time to change our childhoods to give ourselves the best chance of achieving our dreams, we *can* reframe what we learned from our families—to make a choice to rewrite the complexity of our family background with all its wonder and warts. In executive coaching, I often suggest that people use the "Four A's" to profit from whatever background they bring to the table.

Step 1: Awareness

The first step in rewriting your script is to develop an *awareness* of the behaviors your mom and dad bequeathed to you. You need to become aware of the values, actions, and choices you admired about each of your parents and those things you did not like. If you really want to dig into this, take the time to write out (or record) the full story of your family upbringing. Or just think about what your parents did that influenced you. Maybe your mother propped up your self-esteem like mine did. My mother devoted herself to our well-being and made each one of us feel special. And my father was industrious and a risk taker. At the same time, my mom was shy, and my father had problems communicating with his children. All of our parents did things we would have wanted them to change. Acknowledge those behaviors, both positive and negative, by going through the exercise of writing them down or talking them out. Let's look at a few examples first.

Examples of Influential Family Behaviors

Positive

1. Hard-working
2. Fun-loving
3. Entrepreneurial

Negative

1. Unsupportive of education
2. Angry
3. Unable to budget

Think back on the themes that popped up time after time in your childhood. Which of them came from your parents' behaviors and their attitudes toward life and their kids?

Your Family's Behaviors

Positive

1.
2.
3.
4.
5.

Negative
1.
2.
3.
4.
5.

Step 2: Assessment

Next, *assess* which of your behaviors—both positive and negative—remind you of your parents' behaviors. The truth is, whether we like it or not, we can unconsciously take our parents' behaviors and attitudes as our own. To what extent do you "see" your mom in the mirror when you get dressed for work or "hear" your dad talking when you criticize an employee? Take the time to think of incidents when your behavior or thinking has reflected your parents' influence. Make another list of the behaviors you are repeating. Also list the behaviors you are consciously rejecting. We all have some of those.

Your Parents' Positive Behaviors That You Are
Choosing to Adopt
1.
2.
3.
4.

Your Parents' Negative Behaviors That You Reject
1.
2.
3.
4.

Step 3: Acceptance

Once you've become aware of the role that your childhood has played in developing the person you are today, it's time for *acceptance*.

Accepting in a conscious way that you are a mix of both parents, with their good and bad qualities, allows you to select which qualities you want to carry forward. Rewriting your story is vital if you want to capitalize on whatever positive influences come from your childhood and prevent the negative ones from undermining your success. When I was younger, I never wanted to think that I was like my dad, but now I accept that he is part of who I am. I take it as a positive that I learned dogged persistence, entrepreneurship, how to have fun, and a huge capacity for work from him. Concentrate on accepting the positives in your background and consciously letting go of the negatives.

What Are the Family Issues You Struggle to Release?
1.
2.
3.

Step 4: Action

Finally, you must take *action*. Think about the list of behaviors or story you wrote in the first step. Are there any positives that have come out of your negative experiences? How can you carry the positives forward in your own life? Allow yourself to see the strengths of what you have learned from your parents and grandparents. Also, be aware that some of your behaviors involve reactions that may be directly linked to your upbringing. For example, if you had a fearful mother, then you might be unreasonably fearful yourself in some situations. Or you may have perfectionistic tendencies as a result of having overly critical parents. Negative family-influenced behaviors—which could be getting in the way of your success—may begin to diminish when you simply become aware of them.

What Negative Behaviors Also Had a Positive Element?
1.
2.
3.

The remainder of this chapter outlines specific actions you can take to overcome bad childhood influences and enhance positives on your way to achieving millions.

Family Values That Work

Each family is a microculture that is determined by the parents. Many of the millionaires in my study, both women and men, credited their parents with modeling the values and behaviors that contributed to their ability to aim high in life. If your parents had deficits in any of these areas, it will require active work on your part to overcome negative tendencies that will otherwise get in your way. But even if you had parents who were good role models, there is almost always room for improvement. Here are the four key skills you will want to focus on:

1. Social connection
2. Emotional discipline
3. Moral judgment and integrity
4. Outsmarting the world

All of these skills are best learned at home, but can be acquired at any time with concerted effort. Each of the four major sections to come explores these "Dimensions of Success" in detail. Let's take a closer look at each of them.

First Dimension of Success—Social Connection

People in the top echelons of the business and nonprofit world—either corporate officers or business owners—almost always display high levels of skills that allow them to connect with others:

- Caring
- Charisma
- Commanding presence

- Humor
- Professional appearance

If you are lucky enough to have had parents who modeled these behaviors on a consistent basis, as I did, you will have a head start to success. If you did not—or such skills were on display only sporadically—you can still develop them. Here are some examples of what to do.

Display Sincere Caring

It is very difficult to succeed if you don't genuinely care about others. Yes, the charming sociopath succeeds for a time, and I can think of some companies that are led by executives who care little for anything but profit. However, this never works out in the long run.

Instead, people who hope to achieve long-term success must learn to display sincere caring. Sometimes people consciously take on a reserved demeanor at work in order to be perceived as intellectually more accomplished. However, this is actually counterproductive. As a coach, I am often asked to work with people *because* they come across as cold and emotionless. Their careers are in danger of becoming derailed because their leaders and coworkers find them unapproachable. When we first meet, their demeanors sometimes remind me of those terrible experiments in the 1950s where newborn monkeys were given "mothers" made of wire.[8] In a few weeks, the baby monkeys with these cold mothers had withdrawn into themselves and could not be comforted when frightened or stressed.

My intervention is important with these executives because effective leadership is based on caring for others. Your employees may certainly appreciate rewards like financial bonuses or increased creative responsibilities, but if you can't show you care about them, then on some fundamental, unconscious level they won't like working for you. In fact, eventually they are very likely to leave. The "St. Paul Fire and Marine Insurance Study" of 28,000 employees in the

1990s was one of the first to show that employees are most motivated and happy when they have a caring and flexible boss.[9]

In coaching sessions, I counsel executives with this issue to start small in reaching out to others. Simply inquiring about the well-being of others (without interrogating) will greatly boost their perception of you as someone who cares. Say good morning to everyone. Say thank you more than you think you should. Ask people about their family or weekend, even if you feel you are too busy. It doesn't take much effort or time. And make it sound as sincere as possible.

Truly analytical people (think engineers and accountants) will have to convince themselves to be more caring because it's part of their jobs. But it is likely to also enhance their own well-being at work and their career development. Over time it becomes a habit and makes *everyone's* work lives more pleasant.

Project Charisma

I consider charisma to be the reflection of confidence in yourself and your abilities. Charismatic people believe in their worth to such an extent that they want to enthusiastically share their dreams and hopes with others. Charismatic leaders are able to describe their visions so vividly that others can also see the future they envision and become excited about it and dedicated to achieving it. But you do not have to be a leader of a big organization or the president of a country to be charismatic. You just have to believe in the larger purpose of what you are doing, feel enthusiasm about what you plan to achieve, and be willing to share your enthusiasm with others. Charismatic people also pay careful attention to what their listeners are prepared to hear and believe. They present their arguments not in terms of "I want" but "this is what we need to do." See the difference? Explain exactly what your vision means and why it will be beneficial to others personally to help you achieve it.

At the other extreme, people who lack charisma are not at all interested in interacting with others in a positive or an inspiring way. As children they may have internalized the message that if they don't say anything, they won't be punished or ridiculed. These people bore others whenever they speak. Some can also be insincere, verbose, irritable, and unwilling to engage with other people.

If you need to develop charisma, start with a small project where the cooperation of others will help you reach greater heights. Choose a small group of people you think might be interested in helping if you present it right. Analyze the factors that make this an important project in the first place. Then share that enthusiasm with others, either alone or in groups. Skip the PowerPoint, and make sure the connection is personal. Your words and commitment (belief in the project) alone must convince them to follow your lead.

You may not be successful the first time out, because the people whom you approach may need a while to warm up to the prospect of taking on more work. Just keep talking and trying out ways to show your passion for your idea. Keep telling it to others and sharing the dream. Eventually, your obvious love for the project—and your ability to define specific tasks that will help achieve it—will draw people to lend a hand.

Even if you never feel that charisma is your strongest attribute, you can continue to take steps to exude confidence that your projects are important. Each time, make sure you are clear and prepared. A depth of knowledge and sincerity will go far in convincing people to follow your lead.

Develop a Commanding Presence

You've seen it happen. When successful individuals walk into a room and start greeting people, they command attention. What is it about them that draws the eye? One factor is their directness. They look you in the eye, shake hands with everyone, and seem to be genuinely interested in meeting everyone in the room. Yet, while you are talking to them, you feel like you are the only person in the room. You are enveloped in their skill for active listening, aware that they are paying attention to what you are saying and questioning you appropriately. Their eyes are not wandering the room looking for a more important person to talk to, either. These are the traits you will want to develop and project to others.

But how does active listening mesh with sharing your message with others? They seem almost polar opposites. But this is why it works: Listening makes you more knowledgeable about others' beliefs, so you can tailor your message to them. Tailored messages are always perceived as more powerful than generic messages that could be directed at anyone.

The key to developing a commanding presence is (1) to be clear about what you truly believe and (2) to share it with others in a personally-tailored way. It is a given that children who are encouraged to develop their own beliefs, who feel listened to, and whose words are respected will develop a confidence in their interactions with others that will continue on into their work lives. However, even if you did not have these positive experiences as a child, it is not too late to develop your listening and sharing skills now.

Laugh at Yourself

Being able to laugh at yourself is good both for you and for your business. Of course, I am not talking about high-energy, slay-'em-in-the-aisles, standup-comedian-level humor. And you should be aware of the quality of humor, too; ethnic and sexist humor have no place in the workplace. You could even be offending people with banter that is perceived as too personal. Try to let your humor arise out of situations you face rather than the people you meet.

Your family heavily influences what you are going to find funny. A negative humor style, such as merciless teasing, is brought directly from home. As at home, humor can be a power play at times, particularly practical jokes and sexual innuendo. Be sure to avoid these mistakes.

To enhance your humor gene, start by relaxing and then observe what makes you and others laugh at work. (You may not need to do this if you can already sling humor far and wide, but this does not come naturally to most people.) Give yourself permission to be lighthearted. Women, especially high achievers, sometimes feel so much pressure at home and at work that they miss opportunities to develop better working relationships with others by just sharing a laugh with them. Because that's what humor is: the glue that helps connect people and makes it more fun to come back to work every day. Best of all, you may find yourself developing better solutions to problems if you just laugh off your serious self and allow yourself to think more freely.

Second Dimension of Success: Emotional Discipline

Are you strong enough emotionally to handle the highs and lows involved in becoming a millionaire? Many people are not, particularly those who grew up in chaotic households where emotions ran wild. Many of the respondents to the *Millionaire Mystique* survey noted that they were the children of entrepreneurs (51 percent— much higher than expected), so from an early age they probably witnessed the emotional highs and lows related to owning a business. The following components of emotional discipline are all essential for high-level achievement:

- Managing your energy level
- Problem-solving efficiently
- Managing your emotions

Let's look at how you can break away from your family's influence in each of these areas.

Manage Your Energy Level

You will have absorbed from your family ideas about appropriate amounts of work to produce. For instance, an influential family member could have role-modeled idleness. Did your mom or dad relax in front of the TV most of the time? If so, you may struggle to put in the amount of time necessary to rise to the top. You may stay at work extra hours when you need to, but your mind would rather have you jumping on the elevator at 5 p.m., so you don't get a lot accomplished. Or you may have the opposite problem. If you are really frenetic and nervous about getting things done, and spending a tremendous number of hours at work to the neglect of your outside life, at least one of your parents probably acted the same way.

Neither of these extremes is a pathway to success—and either can distract you from your goals by getting in the way of your efficiency at work. The ideal solution for both extremes of energy use is to explicitly use the "4A" strategy outlined earlier: be aware, assess, accept, and act. In this case, be aware of the energy level you naturally possess, assess its appropriateness for your work environment, accept the outcomes you can't change, and act to change the rest. Take sleep, for instance. So many *Millionaire Mystique* survey participants responded that they had little need—or perhaps little ability—for sleep. And, indeed, some people thrive on four or five hours of sleep per night and use energy reserves to power through each day. Are you one of them?

The best test for whether you need more sleep for peak performance was developed by Stanford sleep researcher William C. Dement.[10] Here's his experiment.

1. Choose a time when you are feeling fairly rested.
2. Sit down in a comfortable, darkened room for twenty minutes with no distractions (nothing to read, no phone, no computer).

If you are still awake and bored after twenty minutes, you are getting enough sleep. If you can't stay awake that long, you really need to take steps to get more sleep. You will accomplish a lot more if you are well rested; you may just need to more efficiently spend the time you are awake. (Get rid of your TV!)

Problem-Solve Efficiently

Problem solving, at its most fundamental level, is learned (or not learned) at home. Some families take a very analytical approach to solving problems, considering all the alternatives and selecting the best one. At work, it's similar to a manager making a decision to reorganize without considering employees' feelings of ownership about their current jobs or pride in their teams. Emotionless problem-solving can create more problems than it solves.

Other families, including my own, are emotional about everything in life. Happy was very happy in our home; sad was very sad. In emotional families, decisions are made with the gut. What "seems right" at the time is the solution selected, whether it is right or not. However, if you rely on emotional decision making at work, you can suffer the consequences. For instance, you may decide to not downsize the workforce because you are fond of the employees, only to find that you exceed the budget each month, which harms the organization.

A third category of families is not good at either analytical or emotional decision making. They are experts at ignoring problems until they become major crises. At that point, it is often too late to fix the problem or the emergency solution results in higher costs.

Where was your family on this continuum of decision making? If your mother and father had different decision styles, who was the person who ultimately controlled most decisions? What style did they employ? How successful were those decisions? I believe that in almost all cases, those who use an analytical approach combined with an awareness of their emotions about their decisions come up with better solutions. I have often been surprised at the number of people who come to me for executive coaching who believe they can get by with trusting their gut or ignoring problems. You can't. A high number of *Mystique* millionaires rely on an analytical thinking style. If you are not already using analytical thinking to solve problems, you will go further if you apply it to most of your business decision making. (It also works at home.) The well-known four-step system for applying analytics to decisions is so effective that it is taught in business schools:

1. State the problem.
2. Discuss possible solutions.
3. Identify obstacles.
4. Make an action plan.

Sounds simple, right? It is not. The temptation to jump to a gut-based decision or avoid a decision altogether is always strong. I suggest you always write out the steps as you are discussing them, including any preliminary conclusions you come to. For complex work problems, allow several days for this process or suggest that it be part of a corporate retreat.

Manage Your Emotions

Have you ever wanted to cry at work or throw your computer across the room in frustration? I actually saw a sales director throw his computer once. It didn't help his career. In fact, showing too much emotion at work is a really bad idea if you want to get ahead. Women in the *Millionaire Mystique* study manage their emotions much better than people in general. In fact, 50 percent of them told me that emotional intelligence and self-awareness are critical to their leadership success. You will find that people admire you when you can handle the emotional situations that arise in any work situation, especially when you are the one helping others put their emotions in perspective.

Managing emotions well is a skill that children can learn in their families, as long as the parents are very empathetic and take the time to help their children cope with emotions they are too young to handle. However, there is a high chance that you did *not* learn this skill at home. Perhaps you are one of the many people who experienced trauma in childhood, as many of the *Millionaire Mystique* participants did. You may even find that the jealousy or insecurity that you experienced in a sibling relationship rears its head again in work relationships, tempting you to replay old, unworkable patterns in a new setting. If you've had any of these experiences, or if you grew up with people yelling or crying in your home, then you must recognize that you are not going to be able to self-manage without some effort or even counseling.

I teach people to manage emotions at work. Some of the ways people adapt to emotional crises are healthy: prayer, meditation, play. Some are maladaptive: drugs, alcohol, outbursts. Other people are helpless when it comes to dissipating destructive emotions. For instance, many people watch television to relax, but research has shown that people may actually end up more tense after watching television than before.[11] Perhaps it is because television and the Internet simply prevent us from thinking for a while but do nothing about the underlying emotions. Or maybe too much time with our screens is keeping us from getting restorative sleep that would actually relax us and help us keep our emotions under control.[12]

I try to get people to modify their emotional responses through Dialectical Behavior Therapy (DBT), developed in theory and practice by psychology professor Marcia Linehan of the University of Washington,[13] which has had great applicability when I coach executives. In essence, this involves:

1. Learning to tolerate distress,
2. Focusing on the present, also called mindfulness,
3. Becoming aware of your emotions and observing them, and
4. Communicating verbally and nonverbally to express your beliefs and needs.

In other words, you rewrite the script of your reaction to a serious emotional crisis before it can escalate further. Once again, as with decision making, this requires you to become analytical when you might prefer to wallow in emotions. Keep your eye on the prize. If you want to get ahead, you'll reflect on the troubling emotions that may be interfering with your performance. That's how the *Mystique* millionaires did it. As one female multimillionaire told me, "I grew up in an emotionally based home where every decision was based on how you felt with no acknowledgement about the subjective and fleeting nature of emotions. As a result, I developed an acute awareness of when my emotional reaction at work was overpowering, learned to step back, let the emotions subside, and develop a rational plan of action."

Third Dimension of Success: Integrity
and Moral Values

When we look at the scandals and reprehensible behavior of executives in the news, it can be hard to remember that most successful executives have sound moral compasses. The ones who get in trouble—who fail so spectacularly—are actually exceptions proving the rule. In the short run, you may look like a winner when you cut corners and do whatever it takes to beat others, but in the long run you will not succeed by flouting common decency and fairness. This should be good news for women executives in particular, because they often express their commitment to fairness and integrity at work.

Professors Linda Carli and Alice Eagly, in their book *Through the Labyrinth: The Truth About How Women Become Leaders*, write that

> [W]omen, more than men, disapprove of unethical business practices such as the use of insider information, although this sex difference is smaller among managers than non-managers. Women are also less accepting than men of unscrupulous negotiation tactics, such as misrepresenting facts, feigning friendship to gain information, and making promises with no intention of honoring them.[14]

The traits most likely to help you get ahead at work are honesty, humility, and respect for others, which are values that many of us first learned at our mother's knee. All of them get harder to put in practice in the corporate setting, though, as we rise through the ranks, simply because there are too many people who (due to stress) are willing to cut corners to get ahead. And business owners will discover that at least a few of their competitors have little or no scruples about doing anything necessary to get a competitive edge. But *Millionaire Mystique* women overwhelmingly showed that it was possible to succeed in a better way: by being honest, being humble, and winning respect.

Practice Honesty

Lots of people lie out of fear. It takes courage, for instance, to tell your staff that a layoff is coming. But you'll lose credibility if you tell even a little white lie. If an employee has done a bad job at a meeting, saying she did a good job does not enhance your standing *even with that employee*. Telling the truth in difficult situations is why executives and business owners get the big bucks, of course, because the biggest problems, the ones that require the most truth telling, rise to the top. In fact, the *Millionaire Mystique* study shows that more than 70 percent of the millionaires value integrity and honesty as critical to ensuring their employees will follow their leadership to success.

Study after study has shown that honesty is something that is learned in families. If your family tolerated or even rewarded lying, you need to realize that telling the truth is a core leadership value. If you were brought up in an environment where lies were considered acceptable, you may have to struggle with your natural inclinations to not always be truthful in your work and home life.

Of course, that doesn't mean that a bald-faced truth is always the best approach. Successful leaders walk a fine line between tact and truthfulness, an approach that will help ensure that you don't ruin morale. The bottom line is that you must think through the consequences if you are considering even shading the truth.

Sometimes you will be rewarded for telling the truth. For example, I used to have town hall meetings at Optum UnitedHealthcare where I would pull anonymous questions out of a hat. My willingness to do that—to answer every question, even sensitive ones—seemed to make people very comfortable with my leadership.

Be Humble

The leaders that the world respects most are those who are the most humble. Dave Thomas, founder of Wendy's, came across as the regular guy he was and did not brag about his achievements. He just went about his business. He advised, "Give everyone a chance to have a piece of the pie. If the pie's not big enough, make a bigger pie."[15] The person who always seeks to gain attention or take credit for a team's effort is likely compensating for poor self-esteem.

Self-esteem—how you feel about yourself when you are home alone—is influenced by your parents in their tone of voice and the words they used to talk to you. If your parents treated you negatively, you may be motivated to "prove them wrong" through success at work. That's healthy. You just have to make sure you don't become obnoxious about your ambition. Quiet ambition that doesn't sing its own praises—coupled with real achievements—is most likely to be rewarded at work. To enhance everyone's self-worth, make sure your team always gets the proper credit for accomplishments both in praise from you and in public announcements: "We all did this—we all won this contract."

Win Respect

Your "natural" ability to win respect at work (and at home) critically depends on how your parents treated each other and you. If your opinions were listened to and your personal choices were considered when you were a child, you probably have an easy time winning respect at work. You expect to be listened to and to earn rewards for your effort. You respect others, as role-modeled at home, and they pick up on your deeply ingrained sense of self-worth and reflect it back to you.

But what if you didn't grow up in that kind of supportive environment? Many successful women in the *Mystique* study, including Pat Petznick and me, grew up watching as the women in our mothers' generation were oppressed by the burden of expectation and responsibility to please their husbands and children. We learned, intellectually, that you do not gain respect by trying to please everyone. But we still tend to fall into habits of being accommodating to every request until we burst at the seams and do everything badly for a little while. As pleasers, we then lose our sense of being a great mother, for a time. Worse still, we sometimes earn the label of "incompetent about the world of work."

Respecting yourself enough to rationally order your priorities is one of the better ways to earn respect. You can't do everything or please everyone, so deciding what tasks will advance your work life or make a happy home life is critical. Respect yourself enough to say "no" to everything else. Sometimes saying no is the hardest thing you can do, but it can also be the most important. It is especially hard to say no to a boss who wants you to take on a job that doesn't serve your long-term goals or is below your pay grade. In that case, you won't want to bluntly say no, but you should sit down and try to figure out together how to get the job done—or whether it needs to be done at all.

Fourth Dimension of Success: Outsmarting the World

Intelligence is innate. This dimension is more about honing your natural intelligence for the greater good. Jamie Thorsen, recently retired head of foreign exchange products and executive managing director at BMO Harris Bank in Chicago, debated with her dad every day when she was growing up about current affairs and personal decisions.[16] As a result of the daily debates as a child, she felt able to handle anything her competitors threw at her when she grew up.

Outsmarting the world requires education, creativity, curiosity, and tenacity, all of which can either be nurtured or squelched at home. Fortunately, you can take steps to enhance any elements of this dimension of success that you did not learn as a child.

Continue Your Education

My parents married at eighteen and never had a chance to go to college. Yet they emphasized the importance of education to all their children. The vast majority of the millionaires and multimillionaires (85 percent) in the study had at least a college degree. In fact, *Millionaire Mystique* women were much higher than the average person in education, with 59 percent having a graduate degree. In most cases their parents were much better educated than the norm, even if they were not able to capitalize on it to move out of a middle- or lower-middle-class life themselves. Research by UC-Davis sociology professor Rand Conger and colleagues has shown that successful individuals seem to have learned from their families the importance of education. In particular, mothers who are more educated or successful in their own careers can be a positive role model for their children, leading them to have higher expectations for educational and career success.[17]

Even if your parents didn't feel education was important, you shouldn't put off attaining the highest level of education you can in order to compete for the highest-paying jobs. To the vast majority of employers, having an advanced degree signifies that you are persistent and able to delay gratification if necessary. Also, many good jobs these days, particularly in manufacturing and health care, are going unfilled because people with technical skills are not readily available. These jobs are often the first stepping stone for those with the ambition to aim high. I started as an unpaid intern in a nonprofit crisis center and, through education and tenacity, was able to succeed beyond my wildest dreams.

Value Creativity

Wealthy people, including those in the *Millionaire Mystique* study, are very high on the personality trait of openness, much more than the average person. That means they are open to new experiences and want to try new things. By extension, they tend to be creative. Many people are more creative than they realize; a well-crafted budget is an art form in itself.

You can become wealthy without being creative, of course, but it may be more challenging. At the very least, you need to value creativity and make sure to have some creative people on your team. The person who seems to always be saying, "Why can't we do it a different way?" should be valued as innovative rather than annoying.

Creative people tend to use assignments to better themselves, even if the tasks are intrinsically boring. They will go beyond the scope of the project to learn important aspects of the field or will suggest new approaches they think may accomplish project goals most efficiently. They may be shot down by a noncreative or busy boss, but at least they will have become more skilled at applying creative thought processes to problems.

Of course, creativity also needs to be harnessed so that idea-oriented employees don't waste time on unworkable ideas. Ask creative employees to commit promising ideas to paper and work out the kinks. Then commit yourself to implementing the workable ones.

Creative children in families tend to be the troublemakers, so your creativity may have been suppressed as you were growing up. It is so sad to watch children who start out as bright and curious kindergartners approach their teen years sullen and beaten down. Often, that is a result of a home or school life where none of their ideas were taken seriously or were even punished for being disruptive. (Note to parents: Are you allowing your kids' natural creativity to flow? Are their teachers?) If you need some help in the creativity department, try tuning into your ideas in quiet moments: while exercising, showering, or daydreaming on the train. And learn to value the ideas you get while sleeping—you'll often think of a creative solution to a problem the minute you wake up. Write down whatever pops into your head during these quiet times!

Become Curiouser and Curiouser

If your parents wanted you to be seen but not heard (13 percent in the *Mystique* study), you may have to work to bring out your natural curiosity. Don't fall for the voice in your head that says you're too busy to learn more about something that fascinates you. The luckiest children were challenged intellectually at the dinner table. They were expected to keep up on current affairs and be able to discuss them. Having a sharp curiosity about the world helps you conquer that world. You can make better decisions about where to profitably operate or what innovations you should pursue. Reading widely and in a variety of fields also helps separate successful people from the rest: You can see connections between ideas that other people will not see.

You also don't want to seem ignorant of the world around you at work. You will be faced with ever more complex and intellectually challenging conversations as you rise to the top. Therefore, be sure to never stop reading and learning for pleasure because it will make you more compelling as a person, and encourage more complex thinking, which in turn improves your decision making.

Show Your Tenacity

Another quality that our female and male millionaires exhibited is tenacity—similar to when a puppy gets a child's toy in its teeth and just won't let go. Tenacity was demonstrated in their responses to questions that were aimed at teasing out their staying power in personal and career paths. Tenacity, sometimes called "grit," is the persistent and ongoing pursuit of small and medium goals in spite of obstacles, detours, and failures. Regardless of experiences, tenacious people don't give up for any length of time. Maybe for awhile, but not for long.

Tenacity is nurtured by childhood experiences, good and bad. If you had challenges and got through them without giving up, you were rewarded for persisting. The more of these experiences you had, the more likely you are to respond to challenges in your life by looking for solutions instead of wilting. This possibly explains why so many of our *Millionaire Mystique* women succeeded despite having childhood traumas.

This grit that the male and female millionaires exhibited helped them become more quietly strong and confident as they weathered heartbreaking experiences, even the loss of a spouse or child. Tenacity can be detected by coworkers even though you may not recognize the quality in yourself initially. But, over time, it results in high respect and regard, encouraging others to follow you.

Leaving Your Family Behind?

We never escape our upbringing, but that doesn't mean we have to be trapped by it. You are the composite of all the good and bad from your parents—take the good and run with it. Acknowledging that your family background probably includes both positives and negatives is a way to profit from all aspects of it. Thinking through the negative aspects, perhaps with the help of a therapist if the issues are severe enough, allows you to put those troubles behind you. In my twenty years of management and executive coaching experience, I saw that the people who find the climb to the top easiest are the ones who are clearest-eyed about their pasts. They are the people who can consciously take on board what their families did to positively shape them. And then they leave the rest behind.

Mystique Lessons for Aspiring Millionaires

Chapter 2: Were You Born to Be a Millionaire?

» You do not have to grow up in a wealthy household to become wealthy yourself.

» A stressful and difficult childhood need not hold you back. A vast majority of *Millionaire Mystique* study participants had at least two traumatic events in their childhoods.

» Choose to build upon those aspects of your youthful experiences that were positive for later achievement and consciously rebuild the rest.

» It's important to learn to display a caring attitude, charisma, and a commanding presence. And don't forget to charm people by laughing at yourself.

» You will want to develop the discipline to manage your energy level and emotions, as well as organize your thoughts.

» You do not have to sacrifice morality or ethics to be highly successful. Be honest and humble. Respect yourself and others. Earn the respect of others.

» It's essential to receive as much education as you can and then use it creatively. If you remain curious about the world, you are more likely to have a breadth of knowledge to generate the good ideas necessary to achieve millionairedom.

» As you look back on your childhood, use the best of your upbringing to inform your future success and let go of the negative.

CHAPTER 3

The Millionaire Personality

*The minute I let those insecurities go, ninety-nine
percent of the time I find success.*

*—Apryl Allen, CFO, Allen+Philp Architects
and President, Songwriter, ADA*

Psychologists describe personality as the temperament, traits,
and characteristics that make us unique, the one and only. Yet
we also have general personality traits in common with a lot of
other people. Do you share personality characteristics with millionaires and multimillionaires? Almost certainly. When we look at
people who are super successful in their work (and, usually, in life),
a combination of key biological and environmental factors accounts
for that success. In fact, a few core aspects of personality, such as
conscientiousness, self-confidence, extraversion, self-esteem, competence, and others we'll discuss, are all strongly associated with
work mastery.

In the *Millionaire Mystique* study, I wanted to tease out how the
personalities of female millionaires and multimillionaires differed
from the average woman—and the average man. Does a woman
really have to work twice as hard to be considered the peer of the
average man? I especially wanted to know if the *Millionaire Mystique*
gave high-earning women greater self-esteem than other women and
whether that self-esteem led to their success or was a *result* of it.

To answer these questions, I asked the millionaires and mul- timillionaires about the personality traits that had contributed to their success. None of them claimed to have ideal personalities for breakthrough success, at least in their own minds. And all readily admitted that they had both positive and negative personality traits and challenges (at times) with self-esteem. What I found exception- ally inspiring, though, was that almost all personality types have a potential for success if we learn to cope with the traits that may be holding us back. I believe that women (and men) with the *Millionaire Mystique* have been able to do that exceptionally well.

It's very difficult to change your basic personality traits, but understanding which personality traits are associated with suc- cess will give you a chance to enhance certain characteristics and downplay others. One fifty-seven-year-old Arizona multimillionaire business owner even told me that she still worries others are going to "find out" she really is not competent and reject her for it. "My best qualities are my honesty, caring, and trustworthiness. But while I am attractive and highly successful, I always feel self-conscious and like something is lacking in me. The qualities that make me endearing to some in the workplace, to others [might make me] an easy target."

One of my goals in writing this book is to show people, women in particular, that you never should be afraid to show your real self and to be authentic. The multimillionaire woman I just quoted uses so many positive words to describe herself—*attractive, honest, caring, trustworthy, endearing*—and yet she feels like the vultures would come out if she allowed her true personality to completely emerge. What I'm suggesting is that you can consciously strive to enhance your positive personality traits and minimize the negative while remaining true to yourself. Learn to be comfortable with yourself. The difference is in the amount of "mindfulness" (conscious aware- ness) with which you approach personality enhancement. If you remain aware of what you are doing—and why—you will not need to second-guess yourself like that multimillionaire is still doing, long after she achieved financial success.

What Is Your Personality Saying About You?

While there are many different ways to analyze personality, I decided to use the classic and reliable "Big Five Personality Factors"—conscientiousness, extraversion, agreeableness, openness, and neuroticism—as part of my study of millionaires and multimillionaires.[1] A similar study of the personalities of super-wealthy women has never been done, to my knowledge, and it resulted in a number of significant insights. The Big Five has shown that there is a strong correlation between individual personality characteristics and success in work and leadership.

Think about how your personality fits into each of the factors:

1. **Conscientiousness** includes being self-disciplined, well-organized, and dependable. The higher you rank on the conscientiousness scale, the more likely you are to honor commitments and plan in advance. A highly conscientious person is often described as efficient, organized, and thoughtful. A less conscientious person may be known by the words *easygoing* or *careless*. If you need to plan exactly where you are going to be every minute of your vacation, you rank on the high end of conscientiousness. A person who goes on vacation without a single hotel reservation is on the opposite end of the spectrum.
2. **Extraversion** points to strong social skills. Extroverts tend to be talkative (sometimes excessively so), positive, energetic, and optimistic. Someone high on the extraversion scale has a strong drive to be in the company of others, while someone on the other end of the spectrum equally craves time alone to decompress. Interestingly, people with high extraversion experience less anxiety over negative feedback. They are also naturally assertive and tend to have strong relationships with many people. Introverts, on the other hand, have strong relationships too, but with fewer people.
3. **Agreeableness** describes you if you are considered cooperative, trusting, gentle, modest, and trustworthy. People with high

agreeableness value affiliation and avoid conflict; they tend to view the world and the people in it with compassion. As a result, they have a tendency to take on more work than they should and have a hard time delegating. People low on agreeableness tend to be suspicious and aggressive at work and at home. They are often the office grouch and the jealous spouse.

4. **Openness to experience** is the descriptive trait for those who are naturally creative, imaginative, insightful, curious, and flexible. Individuals high in this trait are emotionally responsive and intellectually curious. They appreciate the arts and sciences and intellectual pursuits—the ability to learn and reason. If you have a lot of ideas and are excited by trying anything new, or if you have flexible attitudes and imagination, you are high in openness. If you are disturbed by changes in routine or more comfortable focusing on just one area, you are probably low in openness.

5. **Neuroticism** is considered high if you tend to view the world through a negative lens. If you find yourself constantly worrying/ruminating about issues at work to the point where it affects your sleep or weekend activities, you may be higher in neuroticism. We all worry about work some of the time, but most successful people in the business world are on the low end of the neuroticism spectrum. In fact, if you often experience emotions like anxiety or depression at work, you may be experiencing a higher-than-normal level of neuroticism.

Do high-achieving men and women bring different personality traits to the business world? Does that explain why there are still so few female CEOs in the Fortune 500? Almost certainly not. The *Millionaire Mystique* study found no substantial gender differences in any of the Big Five personality factors among male and female millionaires and multimillionaires. However, the personality traits of both wealthy women and men differed to a great degree from the traits of the average person.

Where you fall on the spectrum of each of these personality traits—and you probably realize where you fall just by reading the descriptions of each one—to some extent determines your ability to achieve stellar success. But, although your personality undoubtedly plays a powerful role in your work and personal life, unless you are extremely neurotic, your personality traits are not predestined to stand in your way. If you are aware of the personality traits of high-achieving people, you should be able to enhance your personality to give yourself a better chance of success. Here are some ideas on how to achieve your best work personality.

Trait #1: Tap into the Power of Conscientiousness

The personality trait most closely linked with high-level work achievement in the *Millionaire Mystique* study (and confirmed in other research) is conscientiousness, and millionaires and multimillionaires display it at a much higher level than less-successful people.[2] I specifically asked women in my study to tell me how being reliable, thorough, and consistent (all factors in conscientiousness) helped them find significant success at work.

One female CEO of a social service agency and multimillionaire told me that "(those) are qualities that are not that evident in the work world, so when they are applied, they are extremely visible, notable, and appreciated. I use these attributes as my hallmark and ensure that colleagues can count on me in this way." A multimillionaire owner of a real estate law firm said, "My personal traits of thoroughness, detail orientation, and organizational skills contributed greatly to my business. Perseverance and honesty are also key factors in what I do." A health care executive said simply, "My conscientiousness has been a key driver of my success."

Perhaps it shouldn't be surprising, really, that conscientious people are rewarded at a higher level than others. They are self-disciplined, concerned about following through, dependable, and well-organized. Conscientious people do not need external motivation to perform; their motivation comes from within. They complete any necessary task and are constantly looking for ways to be more effective at their work. Although this trait may be linked in popular imagination to the nerdy accountant or fussy librarian, it is a key determinant of success. Conscientiousness is also the *most* important personality trait associated with being a strong leader. If your employees can count on you, they'll follow you anywhere.

What does conscientiousness really look like at work? At its simplest, it is doing what you said you'd do, when you said you'd do it. An up-and-coming attorney hoping to make partner, for instance, comes to work early, stays current with developments in her field, double-checks case law even though she suspects she has already reviewed all the necessary information, and stays late to prepare for staff meetings.

Conscientiousness requires working a little bit harder, going a little bit further, and being a little bit better than others in your company and your industry. It also requires thinking about the impact of what you do on others. One female multimillionaire who is a CEO of an education and training firm told me:

> To me, being conscientious is about self-awareness and your ability, through thoughts and actions, to change the outcome of a situation for the better. This requires me to be aware of the needs of others—employees, employers, family, etc.—or others you serve expecting you to deliver on your promise . . . whatever that may be.

Even if you were not born extremely conscientious, you can improve on this dimension. Finding your own organizational style, so that you can be more reliable and get more done, is important and doesn't have to be done according to some established norm. A person with a messy office who is nevertheless productive about getting work done is organized in a way that works for her.

For women with children, support systems are paramount. We can have it all, but not if we try to do it all alone. Work with your support system to develop an organizing system that works, particularly a group calendar, selectively visible to everyone in your family and work group, as appropriate, which is so easy to create today with smartphones and tablets. And have a way for everyone to track their progress toward their goals. A high achiever is further uplifted by productive employees and supportive family members who also know what they want and where they are going.

Conscientious people reap rewards because they are the least likely to let their lives spin out of control when a crisis happens. They plan carefully, execute their plans, and reap the self-esteem that comes from keeping their promises and working at a high level. They are also the most likely people to get noticed for keeping their heads and focusing on the job when all about them are losing theirs. That kind of outstanding performance in the face of difficulty is what can put them on the path to success at the upper reaches of the business world.

You are much more likely to exhibit conscientious behaviors if you had parents who role-modeled this for you. If you watched your parents rise early, dress appropriately, work extra hard to meet deadlines, and happily rush out the door to work, you will see that as normal. If you didn't learn that at home, or if you are not naturally conscientious, it can help to select highly placed conscientious people as role models. You don't even have to let your role models know that you are trying to emulate them. Select people you interact with often enough to observe their work habits. Be careful, though, not to choose people whose conscientiousness veers into the obsessive. Conscientiousness with a sense of humor about it strikes a good balance.

Trait #2: Find the Right Career Fit for Your Extroverted/Introverted Traits

Both extroverts and introverts are well represented among my study participants. Although more were extroverts, the wealthy women in *Millionaire Mystique* were not *extremely* extroverted. Many of our female millionaires had realized the necessity of improving their people skills and had *learned* how to make connections in professional settings.

Natural introverts may do well to emulate one of the most skilled women I have ever met when it comes to relationship building. Angie Hallier, the owner of the mid-sized and profitable family law firm of Hallier & Lawrence PLC in Phoenix, is a natural extrovert.[3] In meetings of almost any size, Angie will greet every individual who enters the room, ask each person a personal or work question, make appreciative comments, and acknowledge work well done. She'll take steps to send participants off with a clear idea of next steps and responsibilities for tasks, and then, before they leave, thank everyone warmly. In other words, she initiates contact with new people comfortably and leaves a positive lasting memory. Rewards of all kinds tend to come to those who can create bonds with others.

The fact that Angie does all this relationship building without conscious effort does not mean that natural introverts have no chance of developing similar warm connections. No matter your place on this spectrum, you can join the ranks of high achievers. *Mystique* millionaires know that people remember you for how you make them feel.

Extroverts are talkative, assertive, energetic, and seek excitement and social attention. Introverts are self-reflective, need quiet time alone, are not socially dominant, and can blend into a group. The key to high achievement is to find a job match with your natural extrovert/introvert tendencies. Don't fight them. Many people seek executive coaching for the very reason that their jobs do not match their personality traits. Given that many of us "fell into" what we are doing now, people who want to succeed will give careful consideration to exploring career change with a counselor if their daily work life seems ill-fitting.

With that in mind, there are always exceptions to this rule. For instance, an introvert who is a salesperson has chosen a job where it is necessary to interact with people, go to many social events, and ask for business. Some introverts are very good at this because they quietly build strong business relationships, or they like to win so much that they find it easy to sell services or products. However, other introverts in a job that asks them to be outgoing will suffer on a daily basis. They'll find they are irritable, reluctant to perform the tasks required, lacking energy, and often thinking of the solitary activities that nourish them.

Still, even a natural introvert can be an effective leader. Steve Jobs, Mother Teresa, and Albert Einstein were all self-admitted introverts, yet they also had the ability to inspire and change people. You must be able, as a leader, to provide firm direction while maintaining positive relationships.

If you are not a natural connector, keep in mind that you can practice reaching out to others until it feels comfortable and natural. Make a point to thank someone every day, for example. Do it every hour if you can. And take time to make personal connections. If you can't remember the people whom you encounter any other way, use the classic salesperson's trick and write down every detail you know about them. Yes, even their dog's name. Then review your notes before you meet again. I've learned that what Maya Angelou has said is true: "People will forget what you said, people will forget what you did, but people will never forget how you made them feel."[4]

Trait #3: Agree to Be Agreeable

A stereotype I often encounter centers around the idea that a person who rises to the top cannot be kind, gentle, trusting, or cooperative. That is a myth. The female and male millionaires and multimillionaires in my study actually scored *significantly* higher on agreeableness than national averages. But agreeableness means more than being easy to get along with. High agreeableness means people can cooperate with others to achieve goals and tend to think other people have honorable motives for doing things. They are the classic "team players."

A female executive I coached had a serious problem with agreeableness. She would come into work and not communicate with anyone; she was elusive about what she was working on and not cooperative. When her boss would ask for last-minute help, like on a case going to court the next day, she would refuse, preferring to continue with the project she was working on. I helped her become aware of how her behavior looked to others, how it was affecting perceptions of her, and how it made her seem less like a team player and, therefore, less promotable. Together, we identified how she could be cooperative and build better work relationships—how she could be more agreeable. New behaviors included saying 'yes' to more requests, so when her boss needed help, she said, "Of course." This was not easy for her, but the changes she made created a positive change in her work prospects.

Even if they are high-powered, busy executives, highly agreeable people are positive and get along with others—they tend to say "yes" to the things they are asked to do on a daily basis. People who are agreeable are more successful because they tend, by their actions, to gather a support system around them. If you often say to your colleagues, "Sure, I can help you with that," you are likely to be surrounded by people who will help you when you run into trouble. (If they won't help in an emergency, you are surrounded by a group of exploiters who are taking advantage of you—get a new group!)

The potential to be overworked is, of course, one of the pitfalls of excessive agreeableness. There is also the problem of the twenty-four-hour day. If you say yes to everything, you will constantly disappoint someone, and your support system will eventually crumble. Agreeable people who agree to things they can't deliver are perceived as incompetent rather than accommodating. So, you need to be selective. You can *choose* when to be agreeable. Build warm work relationships, but when it comes to helping others with their work, make sure it occurs only in situations when you can deliver on your promises. Then you'll avoid the stress and embarrassment of failing to come through.

If you want to become more agreeable, ask for feedback about how you've interacted with employees and peers. Are you keeping all important projects to yourself because you don't trust other people? If so, you'll never build the trust you need to create a cohesive team. You have to trust people—and give them a chance to succeed and fail. They will trust you more if you show them kindness even if they try hard to achieve goals and still fall short. Are your employees afraid of you? I once worked with a senior executive who everyone feared. To change their perception of her, I assigned her the task of giving someone a genuine compliment on his or her work. I truly believe that practicing random acts of kindness like this can change how you are perceived at work. And then when real problems crop up—whether it's losing customers or exceeding budgeted expenses—employees will trust you more and cooperate with your efforts to solve the problems.

The agreeable person is also fundamentally honest. People who are agreeable are most likely to value honesty and demonstrate it strongly in their daily lives.

Trait #4: Create Openness

The high-earning women in the *Millionaire Mystique* displayed the trait of openness at a significantly higher level than the average person. This means that they tend to be creative, resourceful, emotionally responsive, and flexible. They are also intellectually curious and appreciate novelty. Openness is linked with leadership, too, because people who score higher on this trait tend to be open to taking on the challenge of being "the boss." Or any other challenge, for that matter. Rigid, novelty-fleeing personalities, on the other hand, are less likely to be able to adapt to today's rapidly changing economic conditions and work environment.

The naturally open person has no issue seeing problems in a new light and saying yes to innovative solutions. Many times, though, creative people are not particularly realistic about whether a particular approach is actually practical or will work. That is why I think that the *Mystique* study ended up showing that the personalities of highly successful people combine openness with conscientiousness. Having those two traits (or developing them as strongly as you can) actually helps to mitigate the grandiosity that sometimes comes with too much openness, as well as the niggling over details that can derail an extremely conscientious person. It is as if combining these two traits brings out the best in both of them.

What if you don't consider yourself to be creative enough? My first suggestion is to embrace every new experience that is offered to you, no matter what you think the outcome will be. Becoming successful is often a matter of saying yes more than no to the world.

For example, when I was newly divorced, I was asked by a friend to go to the opera. I had not been a fan of opera but I decided to say yes. I ended up enjoying myself immensely—and learned a new appreciation for music, as well as meeting so many creative and interesting people who like the arts.

I've also tried to be open to new experiences on the job. At Honeywell, I was offered the management of the medical department in addition to managing the employee assistance program, and, as a result, had to learn a wide range of technical skills I thought were beyond my scope as a psychologist. But I decided to be open to the experience—and open to the possibility of failure. I was quite surprised when I learned all I needed to know in a fairly short period of time, successfully met all the goals of the department, and provided high-quality service for the employees. I discovered that if you succeed when you are open to experience, you feel a great deal more confident than you did before about taking on challenges. And even if you fail, at least you had an experience that you will be able to draw on the next time you are in a similar situation.

Now, I make it a policy to try something radically new at least once a month. I recommend it highly.

The key to enhancing your creativity, resourcefulness, relationships, and flexibility is to learn to respect your impulses. Almost always, when you are in need of an idea, your brain will present you with one (or several). Unfortunately, it almost never happens when you are sitting at your desk waiting for it. I know people who get their best ideas when they first wake up in the morning, in the shower, while exercising, or during their commute. The people perceived as most creative by their peers are the ones who always carry something to record their brainstorms, because if they are not captured immediately, they are gone. These days, there's no excuse not to have a simple recording app on your phone, such as SoundNote (for iPhone) or Tape-a-Talk (for Droid). Hop out of the shower if you must to record that brilliant thought. You probably won't remember it if you wait until you dry off.

Creativity is also enhanced by having a "beat." Just like a journalist, you'll be more readily able to identify really good new ideas if you are thoroughly versed in your subject. Angela Elbert, a Chicago attorney who practices insurance policy-holder law, has made a conscious effort to become an expert in the new field of cyber insurance.[5] She is constantly reading articles in the field, attending conferences, speaking about the subject, and writing articles. As a result, she can instantly spot a true innovation in the field where others might overlook it. She is also able to reject ideas that have already proven to be unworkable. She finds it exciting to go to work because she's motivated to help others adopt her ideas.

It can also help your creativity to engage in a variation of the familiar *Sesame Street* game: "One of these things is not like the others." Start by thinking of two things that couldn't be more different, such as personalized counseling and the busy customer service desk. How could you create an organization that combined the two? Twenty years ago no one had thought about social workers and psychologists providing work and personal counseling over the phone, 24/7. Everyone assumed it had to be face-to-face during business hours. But we implemented it at UnitedHealthcare, despite serious questions that it would work, and it is now a fairly widespread concept that allows more people to get access to the help they need on their own schedule. This is the kind of divergent thinking that can result in truly unexpected ideas—and enhance your openness if it becomes second nature through regular practice.

Trait #5: Become Less Neurotic

While the first four of the Big Five personality traits are clearly positive, the last one has more negative connotations. In popular culture, the neurotic person is often mocked for being overly nervous, fussy, or just tiresome to be around. In reality, even the most positive people are at least a little neurotic about something. When you feel negative, fearful, or blue, the neurotic part of your personality may be asserting itself.

Perhaps not surprisingly, *Millionaire Mystique* women exhibit very low levels of neurotic traits. They have a higher than average ability to view the world through a positive lens in the face of personal and business stressors. They are also less likely to experience free-floating anxiety, guilt, or anger to the extent that it interferes with their ability to perform to their highest abilities. One sixty-two-year-old executive director in the service industry, a Chilean-American, told me that she almost never experiences any neurotic feelings. She said, "Life, for me, is an adventure and a place and time for me to learn. In good times or in bad times, I always believe [life] is perfect. I've lived great difficulties and life-changing events, and I'm convinced that they are opportunities to learn about my existence on earth. I love life."

Few of us are that relentlessly positive at all times, though. Our level of neuroticism is more pronounced at times of stress. For example, during a business merger, it is prudent to be hyper-vigilant about what is going on around you and natural to feel anxious about your future. Indulging in negative emotions on a regular basis, however, is likely to harm your upward mobility. Imagine you are a manager of a department during a reorganization. If you act depressed and hopeless, the impact on your staff will be profoundly negative. We all enjoy being around people who are relaxed, confident, and hopeful. Your employees will appreciate your efforts to remain upbeat in the face of difficulty, even while your personality may be telling you to curl up in a ball and pull the blankets over your head.

If you have a tendency to be a worrier, you need to acknowledge it, so that it doesn't get in the way of your success. For instance, if you have a conflict at your workplace, people who are not high on the neuroticism scale will be likely to argue the issue to closure and then walk away, considering it a healthy exchange of views. The person with neurotic tendencies, on the other hand, will fret about it long after—even if she got the upper hand in the argument. She will stew over questions like, "Did I make an enemy? Will she try to sabotage me next time? Will my competitor try to destroy my business?" Women, unfortunately, get into these self-blame cycles much too often, and much more frequently than men do. If you get feedback from someone about your conflict, just accept it as useful information and move on. Obsessing over it will just get in your way.

An internal "jangling of nerves" is also a symptom of excessive neuroticism. If you always feel tense and wired, even if you don't consciously realize that you are worried, you need to find ways to soothe yourself. I've found that journaling can help a great deal to identify the "cue," or the stressor, that is causing the jangling. You may want to create a specific work journal. (Just be sure to keep it at home. Never create one on electronics you would ever take to work!) Your goal here is to identify the false thoughts that dominate your mind in these situations and the unhelpful, negative feelings that result. These are fuel for the fire that keeps your engine racing.

For example, let's say your boss has told you he wants to make you CFO (the cue) but promotes someone else instead, prompting (1) false thoughts that you are a failure and (2) real feelings, including anger, shock, and frustration. Your work journal can help you identify those thoughts and feelings, as well as how you reacted in the moment and the behaviors you want to *choose* to enact in the future. Journaling can help you think through how you are going to respond to the disappointment in order to stay centered, be professional, and move toward the next opportunity. Bonus: Journaling really keeps the jangling nerves in check.

A person who gives in to her neurotic personality traits simply makes life unnecessarily hard for herself and others around her. Her mind will tell her things that aren't true. Turning that off can give you the clarity of thought to move forward and achieve great things. In addition to journaling, you can combat neuroticism if you meditate, exercise, pray, relax in nature, make time for friends, volunteer, or do good deeds for others. All of these techniques bring you out of your head and encourage you to put your problems in perspective. The neurotic person tends to think that "It's all about me," when it almost never is. That promotion you didn't get? Look at it as an opportunity. Who would want to work for that guy anyway?

Personality Traits in Action

One of the women I admire most is a great example of a person who makes her personality traits march in formation. Jamie Thorsen, recently retired head of foreign exchange products and executive managing director at BMO Harris Bank in Chicago, parlayed a talent in math and a stellar personality into a high-flying work life she enjoyed immensely.[6] "Most people last only five years in investment banking," she said. "I got my dream job and stayed at it for twenty-five years!"

Jamie started at the bank as one of forty management training recruits. Quite soon, she was a trader in her own right and the only woman on the bank's executive committee. But she was unafraid to threaten to take a job at a competitor when she found out that, instead of getting a promotion to head a division, management wanted her to train a younger male she had been supervising for the position. "It is essential that you know your worth at work to ensure you get compensated well," she said. After several days of negotiations, she was offered the promotion and decided to stay with BMO Harris for the rest of her career.

Jamie's experience reflects how she put her personality traits to work:

- **Conscientiousness.** Jamie knew she would have to work long hours to succeed and routinely clocked sixty-hour work weeks. Completing every assignment to the best of her ability was a given. She displayed her conscientiousness early and wouldn't let anything stand in her way. She started working at a drugstore at sixteen. When her father refused to pay for her college education (saying, "I won't compromise my retirement fund to send a girl to college"), she applied for enough loans, grants, and scholarships to cover the cost. She even completed a semester of college in London, paving the way for a future working in foreign exchange. Her persistence in negotiating in the face of discrimination also shows high conscientiousness.
- **Extraversion.** Jamie is highly verbal, comfortable meeting people, and witty. She is also comfortable arguing a point with anyone. These personal qualities served her well when she was named as one of only two women in the New York Foreign Stock Exchange. Jamie is confident when meeting others and never hesitates to speak her mind. She is the person you notice at a dinner party who piques your curiosity.

• **Agreeableness.** Often our friends and family are the best judges of our levels of agreeableness. (Just ask them!) Jamie's friends describe her as "kindhearted, loyal, and generous." She also finds time in her busy schedule to give to others, without expectation of a return, which is another strong marker of agreeableness. As a board member of Dennison University, she works to ensure that "people of all shapes, sizes, and colors have access to education based upon their willingness to work and on their abilities." She was key in the development of a program where underprivileged Dennison students could room with others from their high school in order to have friends to rely upon during their adjustment. Jamie understands the importance of a support system.

• **Openness to experience.** Jamie's decision to pursue a career in the traditionally male field of investment banking, particularly in the 1980s, demonstrates her openness to experience. People in the financial industry must always take calculated risks, and Jamie rose to the challenge. She is a strategic thinker, has an ability to juggle several issues at one time, and makes connections between disparate ideas to come up with sometimes startlingly innovative approaches.

• **Neuroticism.** Jamie scores low on the neuroticism scale and is able to take most stresses in stride. She thrives in a male-dominated, highly aggressive, conflict-ridden work environment and does not take conflict or insult personally. She credits much of her well-adjusted nature to her father, who constantly challenged her to argue about current affairs, including abortion and women's rights. While the rest of the family refused to "fight" with him, Jamie learned to hold her ground and assert herself. Her own personality, honed and strengthened, allowed her to thrive in the cutthroat world of foreign exchange trading.

Jamie Thorsen, in fact, is an excellent example of a strong, psychologically healthy woman who made it to the top in her field and was very well compensated for it. She understands that you need to bring your best self to the workplace—because otherwise it's not easy to be the kind of leader you need to be. "If you can't make a hard decision and have difficult conversations, you won't gain respect," she explains. "And, if you don't deal with problems, what is your job?"

Belief in Yourself—The Core of Success

One other aspect of personality is key to a rapid rise to success: a belief that you are worthy of it. It's a phenomenon that psychologists call "high core self-evaluation," and it is made up of the following elements:

1. High self-esteem
2. Belief in your own skills
3. A feeling of being in control of your destiny[7]

Core self-evaluation focuses on the assessments you make about your worthiness, competence, and capabilities. Interview and survey responses by *Millionaire Mystique* women demonstrated that they were slightly more likely than average people to agree with statements like "I am satisfied with myself" and "when I try, I succeed," indicating high levels of core self-evaluation. They like themselves, have good self-esteem, and feel in control of their lives. "I was competent at what I did and was fortunate enough to have people who recognized that in me," one female partner in an architectural business said. "This gives you enormous self-confidence." Another female multimillionaire in healthcare told me, "I know I am highly qualified for my field and easily can be seen as an expert with the combination of education and years of experience I possess. I feel especially good about myself when I am publishing or speaking to national groups to share my expertise."

However, the successful women in my study were also more likely than the men to admit that they sometimes lack confidence. Overall, men reported consistently higher self-esteem, self-confidence, and feelings of control than women. In one respect, that's not very surprising. Cartoons and popular culture mock the well-padded, middle-aged man who looks in the mirror and sees a sexy hunk. It turns out that's not very far from the truth of what many guys believe about themselves. Women, on the other hand, have been conditioned to see all of our flaws in the mirror and none of our good qualities. Note: even our *Millionaire Mystique* women weren't always supremely confident but it didn't seem to hurt them. Women who struggle with self-confidence, paradoxically, sometimes seek to calm themselves by channeling this anxiety into ambition and hard work.

The male millionaires in our study also confirmed that they frequently encounter female executives who are lacking in self-confidence. In fact, virtually the only area in the *Millionaire Mystique* study where men outperformed women was in this area.

One female millionaire told me: "Even though I have achieved several degrees and wealthy status, I have days where I feel I have failed. I realize I am too sensitive to my environment and need to exert greater control over how I feel about myself. . . . Over time, I have become less dependent on what others think of me and have established a greater equilibrium."

If you don't always feel like taking the world by the tail and striding confidently into a room, my study shows that you are not alone. Later in the book, we will explore the impact of women also being in charge of handling the "second shift" at home, particularly in terms of how it affects their confidence. For now, realize that high core self-evaluation is a skill that can be learned and improved upon over time—and should be if you want to rise to the top.

A recent study called "How the Rich (and Happy) Get Richer (and Happier)" by Notre Dame management professor Timothy Judge (with Charlice Hurst) showed that higher core self-evaluations were associated with both higher initial levels of work success and steeper "work success trajectories."[8] In other words, people who think highly of themselves have higher job satisfaction, pay, and occupational status throughout their lives. Another study by Judge uncovered that people who had a high opinion of their abilities also reported "lower levels of stress and conflict, cope more effectively with setbacks and better capitalize on advantages and opportunities."[9]

Is there any better advertisement for developing those attitudes in yourself? Look around you at work and identify the people you most admire for their confidence and ability. You are looking at high core self-evaluation in action.

Our confidence or lack thereof is directly influenced by the parenting we experienced. To improve your confidence in your abilities, your feelings of control, and your self-esteem (and therefore maximize core self-evaluation), I suggest that you make a concerted, conscious effort to believe in yourself. The successful women around you may not say so, but they have probably struggled with self-doubt somewhere along the way, too. You can help yourself along by trying any or all of the following eight techniques, which have worked for clients of mine who wanted their finer qualities to shine through.

1. **Silence your inner chatterbox.** Just like instant messaging, constant negative talk in your ear can erode confidence and distract you from vital work. I suggest you get into direct contact with your annoying inner voice by inviting it for a chat. Find a quiet hour, take out a piece of paper, and have a "dialogue" with your inner critic. Give it a name, too, perhaps someone in your past who was hypercritical or a person from literature or popular culture. "Okay, Esmeralda, give me your best shot. What do you want to change about me?" Just be sure to write down *everything* your voice says to you. If it says to write a grocery list, do it: It is just trying to avoid telling you the truth. If you need to write down, "This is silly," do that, too, as many times as it takes to free your thoughts. You'll be amazed at what your inner critic is trying to tell you. Then answer back. Tell it everything that is positive about you. You'll be amazed at how much more supportive the voice will be after that, especially if you keep talking to it periodically.

2. **Debrief a stressful situation.** In order to move forward, it is often necessary to pause and reflect. Review a recent negative

incident you experienced at work. (Doing this exercise in your work journal is best.) Reflect on how you felt and what you did. Could you have responded in a better way? What were your strengths and weaknesses in the situation? It is not easy to accept your weaknesses, but you must be acutely aware of them or they will get in your way again and again. Acknowledgement of a weakness is the first step toward eliminating it. Trust me, your unconscious mind will start working on it right away if you approach it in this fashion.

3. **Have compassion . . . for yourself.** Are you too critical of yourself when things go wrong? If you didn't get that promotion or new customer for your business or job, do you beat yourself up for days? I suggest your best move in those situations is to hit *pause*. Think: "What would I compassionately say to a child in a similar situation?" Write your response down and say it to yourself, in a mirror perhaps. You could say to yourself: "You were courageous to try for that stretch goal. Let's figure out what you can do to get the job done next time." Then go out and give yourself your favorite treat—dinner out, an afternoon off, a massage, whatever—to reward yourself for trying.

4. **Stay grounded.** Be kind to yourself. Don't exaggerate what happens to you in any situation and get caught up in black-and-white thinking. *Never* and *always* statements should be banished from your vocabulary, particularly as they apply to you: "I always make mistakes." "I'll never persuade that client to sign with me." Besides being self-fulfilling prophesies, they are also self-defeating. How can you make positive change if you keep telling yourself that you will "never" change? With that in mind, don't blame yourself if you sometimes slip back into the always/never mindset. Just like when you banish desserts from your diet, you shouldn't beat yourself up if you have just one, every once in a while.

5. **Be graciously assertive.** *Millionaire Mystique* women ask for what they want, every time. It is a little intimidating, especially at first, to always speak up for yourself. But not asking can be

rough on your self-esteem, particularly when you feel you have earned whatever it is you desire. Asking can be particularly hard for women, who have been taught to be good girls. Or you may also find that you suffer from imposter syndrome, which tells you that someone will find out you're not good enough if you ask to be recognized. The key to being graciously assertive is to identify what is bothering you about any situation and decide how it could be resolved to your satisfaction. If you don't feel comfortable asking for that specific solution, role play with a friend until you can ask with humor and casualness. That way you can be gracious in your request, never stridently demanding. Also practice asking for big things by requesting little ones: "Boss, I'd like a couple of hours off on Friday to see my daughter play soccer." "I'd like to take the lead in that next presentation." If the answer is no, gather your facts and ask again later. Steely persistence with a smile also qualifies as gracious.

6. **Learn to feel "big."** Successful women capitalize on situations where they feel "big," that is, confident and in charge. Everyone has areas where they feel exceptionally confident and in control. Be aware of those areas by keeping a running list of situations that make you feel that way. You should also include on your list those situations where you felt nervous going in but scored a victory that sent your confidence soaring. What were you afraid of before the event? What allowed you to succeed? In addition, try to boost your observational skills in situations where you felt "little." For instance, someone with more technical skill compared to you might have ridiculed you in front of others. Find a skill you know well and offer to teach it to someone. You'll feel more confident the more you teach and mentor in your areas of competence. Humor also helps defuse the situation if you feel you are deliberately being made to feel little. Call them out on it. And if you interact with a person who continually erodes your self-esteem, you need to seriously consider ending that relationship. You'll be happy to discover how confident you feel when you put those toxic relationships behind you.

7. **Clarify your goals.** If you decide up front that you want to be a multimillionaire, many of your goals will be clear. It's unlikely that working for a nonprofit will get you there unless it can be a stepping stone to for-profit employers offering stock options. Think outside your personal experience, especially if you came from a middle-class or poor background. Read biographies of high-achieving businesspeople, observe the most successful in your company, and ask them about their career plans as they rose to the top. Then create a career plan. It is amazing to me how few people do this. Too many people, especially women, float from job to job and don't think about what they need to do to make progress. Do you need to know finance for the next job on your path to success? Sales? Leadership? How will you acquire those skills? With a clear career path in mind, you increase your sense of control, something all successful people have in spades.

8. **Build a web of connections.** You need people around you who understand what you are going through as you try to rise to the top. Ideally, you'll seek out people who are high in core self-evaluation, conscientiousness, extraversion, openness, and agreeableness—and low in neuroticism. They are most likely to make it to the top. But even more important is to choose people who like you and appreciate you. Your core group will be your cheerleaders and your source of inside information (feedback about you) throughout your work life. Establish early on that you are going to be honest with each other and mutually supportive of each others' goals. Then make sure you do something thoughtful for them occasionally. Don't be surprised if you are the first one they think of when an astonishing new opportunity comes along. (But don't expect it, either.)

All of us can improve our overall sense of worthiness, as well as our self-esteem, confidence in our skills, and feelings of control in our lives. Just be aware that you will not do it overnight. Improving your personality traits to give yourself a better shot at success takes a daily commitment to hard work. Just like rising to the top does.

Mystique Lessons for Aspiring Millionaires

Chapter 3: The Millionaire Personality

» All my *Millionaire Mystique* millionaires admitted having both positive and negative personality traits as well as occasional problems with self-esteem. You don't have to be perfect all the time.

» All personality types can be millionaires. Some—such as those who are not naturally conscientious—just need to work a lot harder at it.

» Be yourself, but enhance those traits that increase the chance for success: conscientiousness, agreeableness, extraversion, and openness. Minimize neuroticism.

» Believe that you are worthy of success, skilled in your field, and in control of your destiny. The self-esteem that results from believing in yourself will ease your rise to the top. You'll end up with higher pay, higher satisfaction, and higher status throughout your work life.

» Specific techniques for enhancing self-confidence include silencing your inner chatterbox, debriefing stressful situations, short-circuiting self-criticism, staying grounded, being graciously assertive, observing what makes you feel strong, clarifying your goals, and building a web of connections.

» Be aware of people and situations that erode your self-esteem. Eliminate them as much as possible from your daily life.

CHAPTER 4

The Millionaire Work Style

Work hard. Be authentic. Be generous. Be kind.
Don't make it personal.

—*Forty-eight-year-old dean of medicine and millionaire*

A s a young psychologist just beginning a job at a Fortun
company, I was acutely aware of how different the cor
executives looked from those I had worked with in the n
world. I eventually realized that super-successful women (a
are easy to recognize. It is just not always clear what quali
you to identify them so quickly. Yes, they are often ir
dressed in fashionably tailored high-end clothes. But
they care little about dress. (Think Steve Jobs and Bill G
high-achieving people often don't care for the trappin
like expensive clothes, fancy cars, ornate homes, and
choices. What stands out is a calm confidence an
style characteristics that set millionaires and multim
from others.

Almost all high achievers have a plan for thei
or for their business and are driven to achieve
professional goals. One female company presi
highly focused on achieving measureable and
ate a plan for myself and hold myself accoun
not have to be elaborate; sometimes the bes'
napkin. But the advice that works best for

planning document that serves your unique needs, from a simple bulleted action plan to an elaborate business plan complete with five-year financial projections. Unwritten plans aren't worth the paper they're not written on.

In the *Millionaire Mystique* study, I looked closely at effective work styles—the overall impression conveyed by a person in the workforce. This impression includes a combination of professional appearance, devotion to work, organizational skills, effort expended to exploit natural talents, and the ability to communicate well. The work styles I identified in *Millionaire Mystique* women showed them to be:

- Highly engaged in their work
- Willing to make an enormous effort while at work
- Skillful at social influence
- Able to communicate and work with people at all levels
- Committed to positive work attitudes and habits of mind

An outside observer would describe nearly all of them as passionate, articulate, focused, tenacious, organized, and relentless.

Success, to a very great degree, depends on these factors. And most of them are completely under your control. In other words, even if you do not naturally possess these qualities, you can develop a work style that helps propel you to the top.

Is every industry the same in terms of the work style it rewards? In general terms, yes. The work style elements we will talk about in this chapter can be used with good results in any field and in any setting, from corporate and nonprofit to small business. But there will be some variations, which you can pick up just by observing successful women in your industry. I suggest you become a careful observer of the women (and men) around you to determine their work style choices. If you notice that someone is successful despite rebelling against the norms of your industry, then she is worth observing even more closely, but note that she probably spent quite a bit of time earning the right to her individualism. What does she bring to the party that allows her to get away with such behavior?

How much you will need to change your work style (if at all) in order to become a high achiever largely depends on what *you* bring to the party. Your personality and your childhood determine how you approach work when you first start out, more than any other factors. And your talent determines, to a great extent, what initial opportunities you'll be offered. Throughout your work life, though, your behaviors and attitudes can be molded in different ways if you wish to develop an achievement-oriented work style.

When I was first starting out, I brought a natural tendency to connect with people, practical crisis intervention experience, a high level of the conscientiousness personality trait, and a highly developed work ethic. My first paid job in helping others was at the Y.E.S. crisis hotline in Minneapolis, where I stayed for nine years. I found I had a great aptitude in understanding crisis theory and possessed a natural talent for helping others. I also met "like-minded" students and professors who reinforced these values and skills in me; in essence they mentored me to become a crisis counselor and eventually a trainer of counselors. After a year, I met the program director, and I immediately knew on a very deep level I would get that job when he moved on. I felt a determination and I was compelled toward that position.

I eventually applied for the director of programs at Y.E.S., and due to my years of experience and dedication, I got the job. I worked many night shifts in an old house on the west bank of the university campus by myself. My parents were horrified that I had received a psychology degree at the University of Minnesota but chose to work in such a dilapidated setting. But, it was clear to me I had to pay my dues to enter into this field that I loved. While at Y.E.S., I completed a master's in counseling at the University of St. Thomas in Minneapolis and secured my Minnesota license as a psychologist. As a student in graduate school, I was a nonprofit leader amongst many business and human resources people who were far better dressed and poised than I. What I had going for me was my work ethic, natural talent, and experience in the field of psychology. And, I had chosen a field I was passionate about: I loved my classes, where I studied family systems, psychological theories, and clinical skills.

Later, when I joined Honeywell as an Employee Assistance Program department leader, I had to be much more focused on developing my managerial, administrative, and supervisory skills. I had chosen work that I loved, and I never expected a high-paying career, but once I got on that track, I did everything I could to emulate the work styles of successful people around me. And then for twenty-five years, I worked diligently to get to the top.

Work Effort and Work Engagement Are Key

Almost without exception, *Millionaire Mystique* women would be described by coworkers as incredibly hard workers whose work fascinates them. They are the people for whom the truism "love what you do and you'll never work a day in your life" was invented. They are highly engaged in their work. "Anyone can be successful if they work hard," one eighty-year-old owner of a construction company once told me. Her company is thriving.

Gallup Inc, the famous polling organization, defines "engaged" workers as people who are in jobs that "allow them to do what they do best" under managers that "allow them the latitude to use their strengths." A November 2013 Gallup poll showed that North American workers are the most highly engaged in their work of any in the world. Sadly, these workers finished first with only a 29 percent engagement rate. What that says to me is that there is a lot of room for engaged workers to shine on the job, as they will likely be surrounded by so many unengaged peers. (Workers in Australia finished second; Western Europe, fifth.)[1]

In my study, both women and men tended to score very high on three aspects of the "Utrecht Work Engagement Scale" developed by Boston University organizational behavior professor William Kahn: vigor, dedication, and absorption.[2] *Vigor* is a straightforward measurement of how much energy and effort you are willing to give to your work. *Dedication* is the emotional component, helping you assign priorities to important tasks. (People with vigor but no dedication will find themselves absorbed in busywork—or the Internet—way too often.)

Absorption refers to the capacity of really successful people be totally engaged in the important work in front of them. They do not get distracted by extraneous tasks; instead they impress people with their ability to concentrate on the important work at hand. "How does she get so much done in a day?" is a constant refrain from admirers around them. Love of their work allows them to understand where to concentrate their efforts and to be able to focus until the job is complete. And, when you work sixty hours per week, as I did at Y.E.S. for little pay, or juggle three jobs simultaneously (Y.E.S., mental health clinic, and Honeywell), the time will fly by and you will be so excited about your accomplishments, it doesn't feel like work.

Mihaly Csikszentmihalyi, former chair of the psychology department at the University of Chicago, calls this state "flow" and has studied its relationship to success. "Optimal experience depends on a subjective evaluation of what the possibilities for action are and of one's own capacities," he writes in his classic book, *Flow: The Psychology of Optimal Experience.*[3] More recently, his research has led him to believe that people who are motivated from within by the work itself ("intrinsically motivated") are the happiest and most successful. Intrinsically motivated people are also less likely to view work as a duty but rather as a challenge.[4] Overcoming those challenges is really what leads the *Millionaire Mystique* group to feelings of well-being about their lives.

High-achieving women and men simply have a higher level of *work engagement*: the extent to which they are involved with, committed to, and passionate about their work. In fact, study after study links work engagement to higher job performance, higher quality of work output, and greater overall company success.[5]

People with a high level of work engagement apply a great deal more effort to their work than the average person. They do not stay late in the office to impress the boss. They couldn't care less if the boss is impressed. And they don't put in long hours because they are inefficient. Rather, they stay late or come in early because they have a job to do and they want to do it to the best of their ability. They are the kind of people you'll find reading journal articles in their field while they work the treadmill at the crack of dawn, enjoying every minute of it.

Millionaire Mystique women, in fact, reported working an average of forty-seven hours per week. I actually believe it is much more—they just don't perceive that they are working when they are reading up on the latest development in the field, brainstorming ideas for new products or promotions, or networking with their colleagues. To them, all that is just fascinating. One female health care executive told me that she "worked 24/7 for years and years. Anyone can become successful. If they work hard, they can do it."

Do you need to show that level of work engagement if you want to rise to the executive suite? Yes, you do. As you make plans to succeed at work, consider these words from Robert Bohannon, former CEO of Viad Corporation, who told me what it took for him to get to the top:

> If you want to become a CEO, you need to ask yourself if you are willing to do the hard stuff. I traveled three weeks out of every month for three years. I knew those three years were a ticket puncher to eventually become a CEO. A lot of people don't have a realistic view of what it is going to take to get to the top. I moved fifteen times in seventeen years. So it is important to do a self-analysis. What drives me? Am I truly going to pay the price to get to the top? Or should I change my goal [and be financially successful, just not CEO].[6]

You will have a higher chance of success if you are realistic, as our millionaires were, about the tradeoffs on the way to the top. I'll talk more in Chapter 8 about balancing work and family. For now, please remember that our *Millionaire Mystique* women have shown me that it is possible to get to the top and be financially successful while raising healthy families. It just requires, as Bohannon points out, a bone-deep commitment to doing what it takes.

Develop a Platform for Success in Business

Whether you plan to rise in a corporate setting or as the owner of your own thriving business, ambitious women and men will want to follow the advice of the *Millionaire Mystique* study participants. Many of them advised that you develop a platform from which you can prove yourself worthy of advancement or prepare yourself to grow your business. Somehow, you must earn the attention of people who could pluck you from obscurity and ease your way to the top—or introduce you to people who could make your business soar. Doing this requires, ideally, that you position yourself in a job, a field, and a company that will encourage you to shine. (Most business owners start in the corporate world, too, making contacts that will serve them well later.) You should try to position yourself well, while also taking matters into your own hands and achieve significant advancement through your own efforts alone.

It should go without saying that the first step to a successful work style is to find work you love. If you do not like your current job, think about the times you managed to achieve flow and were working with no thought of time passing or deadlines—at work, at home, or when you were pursuing a hobby. What were you doing, precisely? Think beyond what job you had and your specialty. Break it down to the skills you were using at the time. Were you writing? Selling something? Speaking in public? Creating a beautiful website? Playing a sport or game? Helping someone? Once you've identified those situations where you achieved flow, try to determine a career path that will allow your talents to flow naturally. If you can't figure it out on your own, perhaps because you have no experience in work that uses talents like yours, consult a career counselor or take online career assessments to explore the promising fields you could pursue. There's no excuse not to move into a line of work you will love—even if you've been beating your head against the wall in your current field for years. You'll never be a stellar success in a field you entered because "it seemed a good idea at the time."

Archelle Georgiou, M.D., has had an absolutely stellar career, but it has not had a traditional upward trajectory.[7] She was an executive vice president and chief medical officer at UnitedHealthcare and now is senior advisor and chair of the Health Executives Roundtable for TripleTree, an investment banking firm in Minneapolis. She is also a commentator on Fox News, a health care consultant, and a millionaire. A whiz at math, today she believes that she became an internal medicine physician because being a math major was not acceptable in her Greek-immigrant family. Only five years into private practice, though, she got a job in health management at Cigna after a chance meeting in an elevator with a man who had just applied for the job. "I was in heaven when I found myself sitting in meetings examining health data," says Archelle. But her family was upset with the thought that she was going to "waste" her medical degree. "My mother-in-law actually said, 'She's going to sell insurance. She's going to be the Fuller Brush man!'"

Another job move found Archelle uprooting her family to move to Minneapolis—and taking a six-figure pay cut because her husband had to move his gastroenterology practice to come with her—in order to become national medical director for UnitedHealthcare. "It was not an upward trajectory, but we thought that if we pursued a good opportunity, the money would come." And it has. Because Archelle has always been open to possibilities, she decided to become a consultant for innovators when UnitedHealthcare made a significant leadership change a few years ago. And when Fox News came knocking while she was still working at UnitedHealthcare, wanting an on-air medical personality, what could she do but say "yes"?

Archelle offers some great advice about work styles to women and men who are considering following a nontraditional path to wealth, as she has:

- *Take every opportunity to be visible.* Archelle was asked to be photographed for her company's annual report once and jumped at the chance. "It gave me some visibility and earned me a phone call from a corporate executive wanting my help—if only I'd move to Minnesota. I told him I'd always wanted to learn how to ice fish."
- *Publicly share your strengths and weaknesses.* Archelle says she tends to be intimidating because she thinks so fast and used to roll her eyes when people couldn't keep up. "I'm aware of that now and keep it in check. But it really helps to warn people about that, to acknowledge any mistakes, and to allow myself to be vulnerable."

- *Make trust the foundation of your relationships.* As Archelle explains, "Without trust you cannot have meaningful, healthy conflict because you are afraid of losing the relationship. But without conflict, you will not get everyone's best ideas or their best work." In other words, a silent workplace is a dysfunctional one. There should always be a lot going on.

After you've found the job you love, you should aim to ground yourself in the positive work experiences the *Mystique* women insisted were necessary to advance in their companies or to support your own business endeavors. Here are the steps they recommend.

Develop Operational and Business Line Managerial Skills

Women are still too often assigned to support roles, such as human resources or accounting. If possible, especially if you own your own business or want to, every position you experience should make some bottom-line contribution to your company. Just over half of the *Millionaire Mystique* women saw operational or direct line experience—areas where the company makes its money, usually in product manufacturing, sales, or service delivery—as critical to their success. If you currently have a job that isn't revenue-generating, try to quantify the impact you have on the bottom line and figure out a way to make yourself vital to the company in other ways. Taking high-visibility assignments (or volunteering for them) and having a diverse range of work positions also prepares you for higher-level responsibility and greater compensation—or business ownership.

While I was working at Y.E.S., a psychologist came from Honeywell looking for someone to do a postgraduate internship in her employee assistance program. I had never met a woman who was so accomplished and beautiful. She was successful in the business world. She said she needed someone to help her with clients ten hours per week, and she would train and supervise the person. Probably because I had completed my graduate degree and had nine years of clinical experience, I was chosen for the job. Honeywell paid its interns a stipend, which I am sure was as much as I made at the nonprofit in one week.

I robbed my Mom's closet for appropriate clothes to wear, bought some makeup, and got a professional haircut. I had a definite style, good for paddling my canoe and hiking, but not suitable for a Fortune 100 company. I role-modeled my style after the beautiful woman, Jan Dolesji, who had hired me. Simple and elegant, she was an exemplary mentor. Jan taught me everything she knew about employee assistance service delivery and working in a corporation. One year later she told me she was going to move into organizational development at Honeywell and asked me if I would like to contract with Honeywell for fifteen hours per week at $75.00 per hour! Of course, I said yes. Now I was working two jobs, more than fifty hours a week, but I didn't mind. I was doing work that I was passionate about and learning to help people in a new way.

What ensued was the most intense and spiritually rewarding job I experienced in my work life. I spent the next nine years working with male and female clients for individual personal and work problems ranging from depression to alcohol and drug problems to work issues. I became an expert in the field of Employee Assistance Programs (EAP) and was put in charge of our division's employee wellness programs and medical services, with a big staff and budget. This was an important move for my career development because it was a program Honeywell valued and it also helped the company *save a lot of money* by integrating these services, increasing my visibility. All along the way, I had great mentors and was learning operational management skills I never would have dreamed I'd need as a counselor in a nonprofit counseling center.

Be a Master of Management Principles

You can hire better employees, either in your corporate job or business, if you take the advice of Ann Rhoades, author of *Built on Values: Creating an Enviable Culture That Outperforms the Competition*. She recommends studying what the best employees do at your company and then asking applicants to tell you stories about their past work experiences. That will show you clearly whether the prospective new hires hold similar values and will want to emulate your best employees.[8] You also need to be intimately familiar with good techniques for training, supervising, reporting, and strategic planning. An MBA can be helpful.

Learn Persuasive Communication

The women in the *Millionaire Mystique* study unequivocally state that the ability to express yourself with crystal clarity, whether you are writing or speaking, is absolutely essential to high-level work or business achievement. "A strong work ethic and good interpersonal skills were the keys to my early success," a fifty-three-year-old president of a firm in the hospitality industry told me. Her millions prove her point.

But if you can take it up a level—if you can *persuade* people to do what you want them to do—that special talent alone will accelerate your trip to the top. Most people are not born knowing how to convince others. Far from it. Our natural psychological instinct is to think of ourselves first and to phrase all of our requests as if we were still spoiled toddlers: "I want," "I need," "Will you do this for me?" (You may not think you are so blatant, but really listen to yourself and others talk sometime—you'll hear a lot of "me focused" talk every day.) We also tend to present ourselves as if we are inherently interesting to other people. That is, we introduce ourselves with biography: "I work at this prestigious company"; "I graduated from this school"; "My children are so talented." Truly persuasive people turn the whole conversational exchange process on its head, thinking instead of the possible needs and desires of the person in front of them. For instance, "This will help you get your job done" always gets people's attention. If you are not a naturally persuasive communicator, experiment with phrasing your presentations and requests in such a way that your listeners or readers are always your focus, rather than yourself.

Work for the Right Company or Start Your Own Business

Your platform for success is furthered by choosing work-enhancing opportunities that have the potential for rewarding you handsomely for your talent. You can be the most talented person around, the one colleagues pegged as "most likely to succeed," and never become successful in your chosen field. If your company is a mature one with little potential for future growth or is too small to ever generate significant revenues, it is unlikely you will become a millionaire. The math just doesn't work. That is not to say that you couldn't be perfectly happy and fulfilled at one of these companies—you just will not achieve your goal to be wealthy, if that is what you desire.

Many of the *Millionaire Mystique* participants recommended working at some time in publicly traded companies; they may be your best bet to achieve wealth because they offer stock options to executives. Tied to company performance (usually), options also reward high-level employees with compensation based on individual performance. The smarter you work, at these places, the more you earn. So, if you are considering a job offer from a public company, be sure to study its 10-K report to the SEC (or the equivalent stock market watchdog in other countries). You'll learn how the company compensates its top executives.

Starting your own business? Approach it as if you were going to take the company public someday. In other words, aim high. Write a business plan with projected revenue and expenses and discuss it with someone knowledgeable about start-up businesses. If you start to deviate from your business plan with no recourse to get the business back on track, reconsider your options.

Take Reasonable Risks

A friend of mine who was a manager at Honeywell, Joni Lapp, told me about a job ad she saw for someone to build a phone-based employee assistance program to provide services to companies around the country. I applied for this job at UnitedHealthcare and the CEO of Optum offered me my pick of the customer relations job or operations. An astute and harsh male business friend said, "First of all, you are leaving Honeywell and going to nothing. Nothing has been built, so you will be the director of nothing. But, if you are going to do it, take the operations job so you have the most secure and rewarding position." So I took the risk of leaping into the blue.

I left Honeywell and went to UnitedHealthcare to build something. I, along with Edward Bergmark, Phil Dell, and several other key staff, built the Optum program delivering 24/7 phone-based EAP counseling provided by masters-level counselors. We worked sixty to seventy hours per week developing marketing materials, writing contracts, and writing operational policies and procedures. I hired counselors, trained them, hired supervisors, created management consultation training programs, and flew across the country (at times, six-months pregnant) for sales presentations to Safeway Grocery Stores and Dial Corporation. Over nine years we grew from five employees to more than three hundred employees and created a face-to-face counseling provider network across the country. Today, fifteen years later, the Optum program has expanded to include pharmacy management, health information, and health management, providing service to over sixty-one million people.

Where You Can Shine: The Corporate Path

Once you're in a field you love, at a company with high potential, now is the time for you to draw attention to yourself so you'll be fast-tracked. Your work style must become focused on assignments that allow you to prove your worth to the company. The more you can propel your company toward its goals, the better. Cynthia McCauley, Ph.D., a psychologist and senior fellow at the Center for Creative Leadership in Greensboro, North Carolina, has studied how people become successful in corporations. She ascribes it to their willingness to take on "developmental work experiences" that allow them to develop their talents to the fullest. "To be effective in a wide variety of leadership roles and situations, individuals have to master new skills and develop proficiency in additional areas," she says in her book *Developmental Assignments: Creating Learning Experiences Without Changing Jobs.* "Instead of always relying on a limited set of natural capabilities, [potential leaders] have to become more well-rounded."[9]

McCauley says that opportunities to hone new skills and shine in the process will come at five distinct times in your work life:

1. At a job transition
2. When you are charged with creating change
3. When you are managing a high-stakes team
4. When managing boundaries (between inside and outside groups)
5. When dealing with diversity

I believe you should go looking for such opportunities and seize them, even if you have to do so voluntarily or outside of work time.

Fortunately, this advice works whether you are working within a corporation or are the owner of your own business. Here's what I advise.

- *Get in on the cutting edge of a new development in your industry, study it from every angle, and start writing and speaking about it.* Cyber crime and how to prevent it, for instance, is a promising area because it is affecting profitability in nearly every industry.
- *Start something new.* Anything. More than half of the *Millionaire Mystique* women created new positions for themselves at least once during their rise to the top. And a similar number also started their own businesses (as compared to just 10 percent of the general population). You may not even have to get permission on a new project from higher ups until you've worked the bugs out. Convince your employees to experiment with the new methodology and brainstorm approaches. If it's exciting enough, they'll help you every chance they get. The iPod and iPad were created with this kind of guerilla action at Apple.
- *Fix problems created by your predecessor.* You'll be a hero.
- *Motivate employees who lack experience or are resistant to change.* Everybody knows where the "problem children" are in the company: groups, locations, or departments that never perform well and sometimes threaten to drag the company down with them. If your persuasive skills are well-developed, volunteer to take charge of such a group and promise a turnaround in attitude. Then kill the problem with attention. Focus on enlisting the newbies and the resisters into a campaign to make their group the best in the company. You may have to fire a few, but

most will be eager to help you look good. They've been waiting for someone like you to show the way.

• *Take high-stakes positions, responsible for key decisions.* One female millionaire told us of her decision to start a new business line at her law firm. "I made my own opportunity and created new positions, which led to my becoming president of the firm's start-up affiliate." She could have failed, but she knew that sticking with the status quo would not allow her to use her entrepreneurial talents to the fullest in her big firm. She convinced her partners that it was the right thing to do and then she seized it.

• *Aim to take responsibility for multiple functions, products, or services.* A full 53 percent of the *Millionaire Mystique* women traced at least part of their success to taking on challenging positions and assignments. A female millionaire attributed her level of achievement to "cross-functional team leadership positions that involved important or even critical projects for the organization, projects with compressed time frames and challenging goals, and opportunities to attend senior level meetings as an observer or team participant." Too many executives believe that power comes from maximizing their control of a function or *area of a company*, often referred to as a *silo*. These silos effectively prevent the innovations that can develop when you allow functions to cross-pollinate. Ambitious people who gain experience in a variety of functions or product areas within a company are the best prepared to break down the silos they find and combat the fierce resistance they will encounter when they try to do so. You'll be handsomely rewarded if you can help multiple areas fly in formation.

• *Develop strong relationships with outside stakeholders.* If your company does significant business with the government or a particular industry, make yourself a star by volunteering for high-profile assignments in industry organizations where you can meet prospective contacts. You can raise your profile even further by making speeches or creating webinars on cutting-edge topics. Offer to put clients together when you can see that they can help each other. And if your company is unionized, get to know the union officials and active members. Even if you don't agree with union positions, being willing to reach out will have a beneficial effect on your company's labor relations.

Even if you are a business owner, but especially if you are a corporate up-and-comer, you need to find and seize as many developmental opportunities as you can as you rise in your work. For women, it is important to seek out challenging or risky experiences. Organizational researchers Eden King and Jennifer Knight reported in 2011 that women are much less likely than men to take on developmental work experiences that have a higher than average possibility of failure.[10] As a result, they don't gain as much from taking on these challenges or win as much credibility in their companies. Professors Eagly and Carli, authors of *Through the Labyrinth*, concur that female managers lack access to challenging and demanding assignments that result in recognition. "Meeting the challenges inherent in tough assignments and becoming recognized for having overcome these challenges are prerequisites to advancement to upper level management," they write, "but social capital is a prerequisite for winning the chance to take on such projects."[11]

You can't do it alone—and you can make a lot of good things happen by building relationships. So it is important for women with high ambition to build relationships first to attain the most challenging assignments they can find. *Millionaire Mystique* women are distinguished by their absolute commitment to their work. They may crack jokes about the stress but they almost never let any negativity leak out. You won't hear them complaining about work because they are too busy coming up with new ideas to get the job done. "Never let them see you sweat" is advice to always keep in mind if you want to convince people you can take anything in stride.

What Does "Successful" Look Like? Attitudes of the Working Rich

Wealthy women and men have a great deal in common with each other, and it's not just the amount of money they have. They also tend to possess a set of attitudes toward work and life that set them apart. These, too, can become the habits of mind of people on their way to the top.

They Are Optimistic

Everyone appreciates the person who can say, faced with failure, "We'll just find another way to get it done." The pessimist is too afraid of negative consequences to keep trying. The optimist determinedly accepts no other choice. The classic book *Think and Grow Rich*, by Napoleon Hill, proposes that people can think their way to wealth by adopting a positive attitude.[12] I think he's on to something: Bosses find it very refreshing to be surrounded by get-it-done people. But optimism is not the same thing as affirmations or happy talk. As psychologist Martin Seligman points out:

> [L]earned optimism is not "the power of positive thinking." The skills of optimism do not emerge from the pink-Sunday-school world of happy events. They do not consist of saying positive things to yourself. What *is* crucial is what you think when you fail, using the power of non-negative thinking. Changing the destructive things you say to yourself when you experience the setbacks that life deals to all of us is the central skill of optimism.[13]

So true.

They Are Passionate

You can persist at anything you are passionate about. If you are not passionate, coming back time and again from rejection is too hard. Being passionate helps you get a new idea through bureaucracy, get funding for your expansion plans, even in the face of budget cuts, and get approvals for whatever. You need to uncover what really pushes your buttons in order to discover your passion. What makes you go into a flow state? What makes you buttonhole innocent bystanders (or your family and friends) to talk them silly about what makes your blood race? If you find that your passion is never related to anything on the job, you are in the wrong job. Alternately, you may just need to figure out how to get more of what you are passionate about into your daily work life. I've always been in love with helping people, so my work has never been boring. People in high places notice passion and reward it—it is an extremely good differentiator of people who are destined for the top.

They Are Engaged and Enthusiastic

Even if they are not passionate about a particular task, successful people industriously and enthusiastically get the job done. There is an intensity about everything they take on that is not seen in the average person. People who are super successful seem to be always working or thinking about work and, as a result, get a prodigious amount accomplished. The best of them are also able to completely disengage from work when it is time to focus on family.

Focus is the important word here. They can focus because they have a deep understanding of *why* they are doing each task and how it will bring them closer to a worthwhile goal. Doing a boring project for a boss you want to impress helps you become engaged, but an engaged person will also be thinking of ways to accomplish the task in a better way. A lot of them are people who would do their work even if they weren't being paid. They have found ways to make serious money at something they are already excited about. They are the kind of people who always want to read up on their fields, go to conferences to learn something new, and teach people what they find so fascinating.

They Know Who Is Important

Sure, it's vital to develop connections with people at the top of your company and your industry. But *Millionaire Mystique* women realize that everyone they meet is important. They have both a long and broad view of the concept of connection, and make friends with everyone around them. When your staff is glad to see you in the morning because you are always smiling and ready with a genuine compliment, they are people who will work as hard as you need them to at crunch time. Individuals in lower-level positions might be highly placed someday, in a position to give you something you want. Even the administrative assistants, if treated well, will go out of their way to ensure that your important papers are always at your fingertips.

They Make People Feel Comfortable and at Ease

This skill of *Millionaire Mystique* women may be the hardest to pull off. The best analogy to it is the graciousness of a hostess in her own home or at a fancy reception. She lets nothing phase her even though the caterer has brought a cake that says "Congratulations, Joe" but the honoree's name is Samantha, and she's already an hour late and didn't call. Instead, she carries on as if nothing is amiss, making sure the guests never sense how frazzled she is inside, which would just detract from their enjoyment. The same is true if you feel your presentation is not quite right or is under-rehearsed. Nothing could be worse for your reputation than to let those "facts" become obvious to everyone. Only a few people will notice problems unless you call attention to them. They are just not paying all that much attention to you most of the time—their own shortcomings are far more interesting to them.

If you let nervousness show, others will pick up on it and feel uncomfortable in your presence. Instead your focus should always be on others rather than on yourself. Always go with the kind gesture to others when you can. I'll never forget the day that my daughter returned to her previous school after spending a few years at a different one. The administrator stood up when we came into her office and hugged us. Her small gesture made us feel good about returning and eased our anxiety. Yes, you do have time for this because you may be repaid when others cooperate with you rather than working against you. This is more likely to happen, though, if you can make the gesture sincere, without any hope of repayment down the road.

They Sense the Motivations and Hidden Agendas of Others

People are not good at hiding their intentions. But few people train themselves to be astute observers, either. In fact, our brains are wired to ignore most things in our sensual field. Paying attention to everything around you would be overwhelming. The upshot is that most of us take in relatively little of our surroundings, particularly the quirks of other people. But journalists, in particular, are trained to observe the telling detail that reveals the character of their subjects. And *Millionaire Mystique* women are, too.

Take a quick look around your own space. What objects reveal significant truths about your character and motivations? Which ones seem out of place? Examining the objects others possess—as well as unusual facial expressions and conversations—will give you strong insights into their hidden agendas if you take enough time to really observe what constitutes "normal" for that person. Then anything out-of-the-ordinary about them will become glaringly obvious.

They Choose/Manage Their Reactions

One of the worst things you can do to your reputation at work is to cry or yell, at least in public. You cannot rid yourself of emotions, of course, nor would you want to. Nobody wants to work for a cold automaton. But those with the *Millionaire Mystique* practice the art of deliberate reaction. They step back and, at least for a few seconds, think about the best way to respond to the provocation, whatever it was. Never go with your first reaction (or possibly even your second) to an upsetting situation. With practice, you can modulate your work style to whatever the situation requires, remaining cool under pressure no matter what.

Work Styles Assessment

How well-developed is your *Millionaire Mystique* work style? Take this work styles assessment and find out. Subtotal each section to make scoring easier.

	Never	Rarely	Sometimes	Often	Always
	1	2	3	4	5
Work Personality					
1. I am confident I get the success I deserve in life.	1	2	3	4	5
2. When I try I generally succeed.	1	2	3	4	5
3. Rate yourself on the following scale. Casual/laid back → Conscientious	1	2	3	4	5
4. Rate yourself on the following scale. Undependable → Reliable	1	2	3	4	5
5. I am comfortable and proud of the professional image I project at work.	1	2	3	4	5
Work Behaviors					
6. I prefer to do multiple tasks at once at work.	1	2	3	4	5
7. I enjoy the daily challenge of having my work routine change unexpectedly.	1	2	3	4	5
Work Engagement					
8. At work, I feel bursting with energy.	1	2	3	4	5
9. I am enthusiastic about my work.	1	2	3	4	5
10. At work, I feel strong and vigorous.	1	2	3	4	5
11. I am proud of the work I do.	1	2	3	4	5
12. I feel happy when I work intensely.	1	2	3	4	5
13. My job inspires me.	1	2	3	4	5

(continues)

Work Styles Assessment (*Cont.*)

	Never	Rarely	Sometimes	Often	Always
Communication					
14. It is easy for me to develop good rapport with most people.	1	2	3	4	5
15. At work, I know a lot of "important" people.	1	2	3	4	5
16. I have good intuition or savvy about how to present myself to others.	1	2	3	4	5
17. I am able to make most people feel comfortable and at ease around me.	1	2	3	4	5
18. I am particularly good at sensing the motivations and hidden agendas of others.	1	2	3	4	5
19. I am able to communicate easily and effectively with others.	1	2	3	4	5
20. I can choose to be assertive or gentle/passive according to what the situation warrants.	1	2	3	4	5
Conflict Resolution					
21. I am comfortable arguing a point to closure.	1	2	3	4	5
22. I can debate an issue with a coworker and then leave the conflict behind.	1	2	3	4	5
Total Score:					
	88–110	Superwoman success			
	66–87	Increase your focus			
	22–65	Serious work needed			

Mystique Lessons for Aspiring Millionaires

Chapter 4: The Millionaire Work Style

» Really successful people exude a calm confidence that you can acquire. It comes from being highly engaged in their work, willing to make an enormous effort, being skillful at social influence, able to communicate and work with people at all levels, and being committed to positive work attitudes and habits of mind.

» Most self-made millionaires would be described as passionate, articulate, focused, tenacious, organized, and relentless. These are personal characteristics that are completely within your control.

» Become a careful observer of highly successful people in your field. Decide which behaviors you should emulate.

» To rise to the top, you must demonstrate that you are fully engaged in your work, which means that you are committed and passionate. If you view your work as a duty, you are doomed to average achievement. Find work in a field that grabs you and won't let go.

» Whether you are a business owner or a corporate executive, acquire operational and management experience in your field. Know how "it" is made or the services are performed in every aspect of your business.

» Broaden your mind. Get experience in as many specialized areas as you can so that you will be prepared to handle any opportunity that comes along.

» Communicate expertly with everyone, at their level, from their point of view. You can't communicate effectively if "I" gets in the way too often.

» Work for a company with generous benefits, tied to performance, or start your own company and do the same.

» Act like a millionaire even before you become one: optimistic, passionate, enthusiastic, able to treat people well and motivate them, and able to manage your own reactions to both failure and success.

Are You a Social Influencer?

Ask for guidance, observe, and listen.

—Female principal of a communications company and millionaire

One of the most important skills in business and at work is the ability to persuade people. You want people to feel comfortable saying "yes" to you in a variety of contexts. Among other things, you need to motivate employees to peak performance, convince customers (internal and external) to accept your ideas, and build your credibility. Almost two-thirds of the *Millionaire Mystique* women pointed to "politically savvy communications techniques" as vital to the success they achieved.

People skilled at using social influence are able to read people and use this knowledge to achieve their own objectives. They use their insight into people to convey a calm self-confidence and adapt to any situation. This self-confidence in turn attracts others, by giving them a feeling of comfort. People high in social influence skills are also socially astute, always knowing what to say in any situation.[1]

Skilled social influencers are easy to identify—just watch one enter a room full of powerful people. She speaks to each person she encounters, shaking hands firmly and asking about their family or work situation. She shares funny anecdotes with them, and both men and women listen to her, although she doesn't dominate conversations. When she meets someone for the first time, she spends a little time establishing commonalities or shared interests. Then she promises to send them something helpful related to that interest. She makes note of what she promised on their business cards so she can follow-up within twenty-four hours and cement her name in their minds.

A powerful social influencer does not get embroiled in long conversations. Instead, she spends a few intense minutes with as many people as she can before graciously heading off to say hello to another person or group. If someone wants to break into her conversation, she seamlessly includes the new person. She does not make a beeline for the most powerful person in the room but gets there eventually, having made a roomful of new or renewed friends. And she continues to do this even after she has reached the top of her field because it is one of her values to connect well with others.

If you are not yet this woman, don't despair. Women who aspire to reach the top ranks of corporations or to own a significant business must develop their social influence skills to a high degree to compete in what is still a male-dominated business world. The three areas where social influence comes into play are those well-known staples of business books and are highly recommended by my *Millionaire Mystique* research:

- Communicating
- Networking
- Mentoring

The difference is that the *Millionaire Mystique* women practice these skills in an innovative way. To be in the presence of one of these women is to be inspired by their depth of understanding of the way business relationships work, and how they effortlessly strive to enhance their place in it.

The Money Shot: Enhanced Communication

In general, women tend to be more verbally adept than men, but they are less likely to use social influence techniques in the workplace, particularly when men are present. In fact, study after study demonstrates that in all-women groups, women are likely to speak more often, interrupt each other, and give opinions. But the presence of even one man can activate a woman's socialization to be quiet and listen, unless she counters this behavior deliberately.[2]

A 2013 study of Harvard University students showed that this tendency directly influenced women's grades in business school.[3] This study of class participation by 800 students of both genders showed that women were being downgraded in class participation because they did not jump in with an answer like the men did. Asked about it later in the process, many women reported that when they thought about it, they realized that their hesitancy to participate was linked to a largely unconscious impulse to be liked by the men. In addition, women acknowledged their socialization to defer to men in groups; in psychological terms, it was "learned passivity." Similarly, professors did not call on them as much because they felt the women were intimidated by the men. A software program that instantly showed the professors their gender biases in calling on women corrected this problem, and due to many changes Harvard instituted to raise awareness, "the grade gap vaporized."

The point of this study is that, if women (and men) can be conscious of the communication biases that we all bring to the table, it will become easier to overcome them. Gut check yourself on what happens to your communication style when you are interacting with women versus interacting with men. What are the differences? When are you most effective at persuading others to see things your way among both groups? You may be surprised at what you discover when you engage in this exercise over a few days or weeks.

Another way that men and women differ in communication style is what Georgetown University linguistics professor Deborah Tannen, Ph.D., calls "rapport talk versus report talk." Rapport talk establishes intimacy and connection; report talk conveys information."[4] While not all women or men behave this way, a woman interested in advancing her work prospects should be aware that this could be occurring in the background of any conversation she has at work. Ambitious women learn to "speak a second language" at work, communicating with men and women they wish to influence in the style the listeners prefer. With most men, she will:

- Report just the facts,
- Expect to give and receive direction without seeking consensus first,
- Interrupt with urgent ideas, and
- Make sure that people are aware of her credentials or status.

Women should also be aware that men tend to resist receiving information from women, especially those higher in the hierarchy. Moreover, women tend to be more circumspect about stating information they know, particularly around men, unless they consciously fight this tendency.

Women will also want to adjust their speaking style when they are communicating with other women, especially because many women prefer to hear a language of connection and intimacy. Most women are naturally inclined to seek agreement and consult others, attempting to preserve the sense of community in any setting. The emotional template many women approach life with is "Do you like me?" while men are thinking "Do you respect me?"

Unfortunately, this mindset may set women up to be perceived as indecisive and weak at work. But, in many situations, the sense of caring that a female leader conveys may be highly motivating to the employees she supervises, both male and female.

The ideal, of course, is to strike a balance. If a female manager has both men and women reporting to her, then she needs to master both rapport and report talk. If you are in this situation, don't stereotype men and women, but identify where they are on the rapport/report spectrum. Listen to the words they use. You are looking for phrases such as "Just give me the high points" versus "What does everyone else think about that?" It's essential to note that some males and some females display the opposite communication style that you might expect from their gender. The key is to make no assumptions based on sex but to *listen and identify their specific style.*

Another area of communication that is vital for women to master is the art of being assertive. Being assertive is not about being bossy. Rather, it is *calmly and clearly* knowing where you stand on an issue and *respectfully asking* for what you want. Obviously, your nonverbal behavior should match your verbal request. Assertiveness is neither passive nor aggressive. Assertive behavior with people you have already built trust with is almost never a problem.

Here are some good examples of passive versus assertive language and behavior from the workplace.

Passive	Assertive
"I wish I had a longer timeline for this project."	"The project is coming along well and I think you will be pleased with the quality of the results. I would like to extend the deadline by five days to ensure all of the necessary details have been resolved. Would October 15th be an acceptable deadline to you?"
"I wonder when I will get promoted."	"I noticed Bill, Phil, and Mike have all been promoted to vice presidents with stock options while I have twice as many employees, my budget is four times their budgets, and the scope of my responsibility is much greater. I am sure you have thought about when I might be promoted. Would you let me know what your plan is for me?"

I was surprised to find (although maybe I shouldn't have been) that more than half of the *Millionaire Mystique* women were extremely comfortable arguing a point to closure. And more than 60 percent of them had been told that they were argumentative by friends and family, by which we meant, willing to defend their opinions strongly and fight for what they think is best. This is in direct contrast to research (and life experience), which demonstrates repeatedly that women are socialized to ask questions, be pleasant, and focus on others. Obviously, these millionaires and multimillionaires have transcended society's messages about "good girls" to the point that they have developed a strong voice. Not only are these women comfortable being assertive, but they relish a good argument. They'll stand up for their employees' bonuses or their importance to the firm at layoff time. And they do not personalize the conflict. When the argument is over, they walk out of the room and on to the next issue at hand.

That is not to say that they are angry. But if they are, a word of caution: Men and women are perceived very differently when expressing anger. Victoria Brescoll of Yale University asked the question, "Can angry women get ahead?" in three separate experiments. In fictitious job interviews, men who expressed anger were rated by observers as more competent and deserving of higher-status positions while the women who did the same were judged harshly.[5]

Both women and men are more likely to succeed at calm, rational arguments if they have solid, persuasive facts at their fingertips. So make sure you prepare well for any situation in which you have to marshal information in order to be persuasive. (And be prepared to do so on short notice.) You might want to study techniques of formal argumentation and conflict resolution so that you can identify logical fallacies and call your opponents on them. Men will admire you for being able to name the techniques they are using to try to snow you. ("That's a straw man argument—here are the facts . . .")[6] Above all, never let them make you angry.

Make Friends in High Places

Every multimillionaire woman I know has a huge network of friends and spends a good deal of time cultivating them. But "networking" in the old-school, hand-a-stranger-a-business-card sense? They don't do it. Somehow that seems too obvious, too much like taking advantage of people. However, that doesn't mean they do not consciously create a web of relationships to help them power their work lives. They just don't call it networking: *Millionaire Mystique* women call it *friendship*. Nevertheless, almost two-thirds of them call these relationships an important aspect of their professional success. Most of them agreed with statements like "I spend a lot of time and effort at work networking with others"; "At work, I know a lot of important people and am well connected"; and "I am good at using my connections to make things happen at work."

Former ambassador to Finland, Barbara Barrett, was an executive of two Fortune 500 companies before she was thirty, a bank chairperson, and a pilot (among many other accomplishments). Barbara credits relationship building with most of the good things that happened in her work life.[7] She told me:

> Time after time . . . I had opportunities arise. For example, I went to a dinner party that at first glance just appeared to be another dinner party, but I met the first female prime minister of Canada, Kim Campbell, there. She was teaching at Harvard and it was improbable but she ended up recommending me to teach there, too. Take the opportunities that arise.

As a result of that dinner, Ambassador Barrett became a fellow at the Kennedy School of Government, teaching leadership.

Millionaire Mystique women scored higher than the average person on a Political Skills Inventory created by Gerald Ferris, professor of management and psychology at Florida State University's College of Business, which measures relationship-building talent.[8] Ferris has found, in fact, that "political skill gives individuals a calm sense of self-confidence that inspires trust and confidence in others and promotes credibility." Political skills—a concept that makes many people uncomfortable—really are nothing more than personal influence. People who are good at connecting with others, in other words, are more likely to get ahead. According to a study by Ronald S.

Burt, professor of sociology and strategy at the University of Chicago Booth School of Business,[9] compared to those with fewer ties, people with more connections within their companies and with people in other companies have actually been shown to:

- Have higher performance evaluations,
- Be more likely to be promoted, and
- Have higher compensation.

Sara Dial, who had been both an investment banker and the director of Arizona's Department of Commerce by age twenty-nine, has always had very high standards when it comes to building relationships for her work.[10] "Building solid relationships with people of differing experiences and political views is critical. I am not interested in light party conversations but more meaningful dialogue. These are relationships where we help each other, but it cannot be simply 'what's in it for me?'" says Sara. She points to a project called the Discovery Triangle in which she brought CEOs and mayors together to revitalize two urban areas and connect business and educational resources. She explains,

> I was able to do that because of my long-standing relationships with political and business people. It is essential to build alliances with those with opposing views. And, whatever happens, never burn any bridges because it eliminates future opportunities.

Relationship building can happen in the least expected ways and times—at social occasions or in informal interest groups, for instance—provided you don't think of it as a one-time or short-term thing. To accomplish this, I simply put myself into situations where I can meet people who may find it mutually beneficial to know me. I would never attempt to develop a relationship with anyone I don't feel an immediate connection to on some level. Otherwise, maintaining the relationship would just be too much work. Nor do I analyze each potential relationship to determine who would be objectively useful for me to know. Instead, I begin with someone who simply attracts my attention for some reason and then take it from there.

Candyce Williams, M.D., is a well-respected spinal cord injury specialist and millionaire who practices with the Arizona Center for Neurosurgery, a seventeen-person operation.[11] Candyce has one of the strongest circles of supportive friends among the *Millionaire Mystique* women. "As a physician, people trust me with their stories and I like connecting people," she says. "If profitable business connections occur, it is for others, not for me." But she has certainly depended on her circle as she moved around the country, first working in underserved areas in rural Illinois to fulfill a requirement of her medical school scholarship, then looking for a place where two married physicians of different races could comfortably raise a family. She advises women to have a trusted circle of friends who understand and empathize with you. She warns against surrounding yourself with people who tell you things "for your own good" without being fully committed to your success. "Be aware of who you are letting into your inner circle," she says. "They are so important to your well-being."

Developing your own inner circle can be as simple as providing an excuse to get together with like-minded people. But what I am proposing goes far beyond getting together with random friends for a regular chat. Of course, there is nothing wrong with hanging out with low-pressure friends, but *Millionaire Mystique* women and men tend to have a special group dedicated to a higher purpose.

When I was a manager at Honeywell, the employee assistance psychologists in different divisions decided to get together monthly for case consultations on difficult employee situations. We became a supportive network of friends. Your aim should be to build a business family of sorts, a family that you can always trust to tell you the truth. You have to be able to trust them not to divulge your secrets to anyone—and they need to trust you in the same way. Never tell a secret, no matter the temptation, and remember that your words and emails are never really private. If you develop a reputation for absolute integrity with confidential information, you will create a "halo" around your name and greatly enhance your reputation *and* your attractiveness to others as a network member and friend.

You can also expand your network of friendships by getting things done in a friendly and cooperative manner as a volunteer in your professional and industry associations. Always do what you promise and do it in a positive, upbeat way. If you attempt to impose your agenda on people in volunteer situations, you won't be doing your reputation any favors.

Of course, the easiest way to build a web of social influence is to give to others without any expectation of return. For each person you meet, figure out something you can send to this new acquaintance (a link, a contact?), and do it soon after you meet the first time. This will put you in people's minds, they will feel gratitude toward you, and they will be motivated to help you next time. And as a bonus, after such gestures you will be more likely to remember their names and at least one of their interests the next time you meet—a gesture that really cements them into your network. You will also be more likely to remember them the next time something relevant to them crosses your desk, giving you even more chances to nurture these relationships. This is called the "rule of reciprocity."[12] Your actions feel good and will probably be reciprocated by the people you try to help.

You will find that your reputation will snowball as you expand your circle. People will start approaching you with opportunities to speak, to write, and to lead. A strong circle of influence is also the best way for women to overcome the biggest obstacle they face on their way to the top: the desire to take time off for at least a little while when they have children. Your circle can be a way to maintain full contact with your industry even if you work from home—or don't work outside your home—for a while.

One other important consideration is that your circle of relationships should never be gender specific. Unfortunately, women can feel uncomfortable building networks with men, but building relationships with both genders is critical for success. Studies have shown that many women at work have a relationship style called "tend and befriend" in which they exchange more personal information than men do and offer support on personal issues.[13] Instead, you should work to develop friendly relationships with your colleagues that avoid getting too personal. Three-quarters of *Millionaire Mystique* women said that they network in this way. By setting such boundaries, you will likely make networking with men more comfortable.

If you are not an enthusiastic relationship builder overall, understand that networking offers you a chance to polish the self-confidence that most female millionaires possess. Ronald Ferris notes that good relationship builders "are astute observers of others . . . which allows them to comprehend social interactions and accurately interpret their behavior and that of others."[14] Not a bad set of skills for an ambitious person to develop. Executive coaches can be very helpful to polish social influence skills.

Mentors to the A-List

If my life and research have taught me anything, it is that success is within our control. But getting there is a lot easier if we have a mentor—a strong, guiding hand to show us the way and clear a path. Tapping several mentors is even better because no one knows it all, not even multimillionaires. *Millionaire Mystique* women were highly likely to have had at least one mentor; a full 66 percent of them credited a mentor for easing their way to the top. These successful women figured out how to motivate people to give them an advantage, and so can you.

The word *mentor* comes from Greek mythology and originally meant a relationship between a young man and an older one, who would demonstrate the ways of the world. Now it has broadened to include people more experienced in any skill you feel you are lacking. And it is now very acceptable for women to have male mentors and vice versa. Informal mentoring is also on the rise, where nobody ever really identifies the relationship in that way.

Your goal should be to find at least one mentor who is willing to show you the ropes in your field or company and who will take an ongoing interest in your upward trajectory. Your success may depend on it. Tammy Allen, professor of psychology at the University of South Florida, and her colleagues studied mentoring relationships in a wide variety of settings.[15] They concluded that:

- Career-related mentoring was associated with higher salaries, greater overall compensation, and more opportunities for promotion, compared to those not mentored.
- People who were mentored—rather than just befriended—were more satisfied with their careers.

Of course, that doesn't mean it is easy to find someone who will care about *your* success. Many people are too busy looking after their own career path. You can't just go up to someone and ask, "Will you be my mentor?" But the female millionaires and multimillionaires I talked to actually had a much higher level of mentoring than the average employee throughout their careers, even though many of them did not come out of formal mentoring programs. One said, "I found a mentor through observing or hearing about women in a professional setting that I wanted to be in, that is, several rungs up the ladder or in parts of the organization that I wanted to break into. The mentors that my workplace found for me have been less effective."

With that in mind, in my own experience a company with a culture that rewards "taking good care of your most talented people" does increase your chances of finding a beneficial mentor. For instance, when I was at Honeywell, supervisors were expected to take charge of their employees' training, development, and opportunities for advancement. My first supervisor there, Susan, taught me all facets of supervision from writing performance appraisals to reading financial reports. She always took an interest in the employee issues I was trying to resolve and advocated for my advancement with senior staff. I was lucky to get such a solid start on my upward trajectory.

But what should you do if your employer is not so enlightened, especially with female employees? Is it worth *the time that it takes* to develop someone into an effective mentor? I asked the question that way deliberately. Yes, you will probably need to mold your own mentor (or mentors) if your company doesn't do it for you. Thankfully, it is not hard to do—it simply takes time.

If you've had trouble finding good mentors, then it might be good advice to broaden your scope. There may be mentoring programs in your community, for instance. And have you ever thought of family members as mentors? If you have a trusting, respectful relationship with a family member who is experienced in the business world, it might not be a bad idea. A *Millionaire Mystique* woman who serves as the director of client services for a health insurance company found several mentors this way.

> I have had several mentors throughout my life. I found mentors in family, friends, employees, and coworkers. I have always bounced ideas off people and then taken what made the most sense to me from each and formed my own decision on how to proceed in each instance.

Just be careful that your boss doesn't feel threatened if you look outside your company or division for a mentor. Due to business privacy concerns or the possible appearance of lack of loyalty, you may want to be very discreet and not let it be known that you have a mentor outside the company.

The best mentor tends to be a person you like and admire already, someone with a similar work style who can teach you something (or more than one thing) you are currently lacking. Mentors should not make decisions for you, but they can certainly help to illuminate the path. Once you identify a potential mentor, ask questions and listen to the answers. Report back what you did with the advice they gave you. If the mentor seems irritated that you did not follow *all* of the advice, discuss it together and see if you will be able to continue to work together. Also, make sure that you don't become codependent. Do not run to your mentor for advice when you should be making your own plans and decisions.

You will also want to ensure that there is some element of reciprocity—something that you can give your mentor in return—even if it is just a bit of public credit for some of the good things that happen to you. As one female millionaire told me: "I found [mentors] by locating the brightest people I could who had integrity, and then doing my best to provide something of value to them."

Women should also be sure to seek out male mentors, ideally at the executive level. These men, if committed to your success, can become sponsors and ease your way to the top. But no matter the gender of your mentor, just having one, studies show, is likely to increase your income and professional success.[16]

Overwhelmingly, the *Millionaire Mystique* women recommended having at least one mentor, no matter where you find them. "Many times, having a mentor gave me the confidence to make difficult decisions," another female multimillionaire told me. "Other times they challenged my thinking to help steer me in a different direction based on their experience. I would not have been able to achieve what I have professionally or personally without the support of a mentor."

The best mentors are the ones who will become sponsors and open doors for you, so be sure you choose your mentors carefully. Listen for stories around your company of people who have helped others make a leap upward. Make yourself known to those people by completing excellent work and volunteering for things they are interested in. Take your time to cultivate a mutually beneficial relationship with people who can move mountains for you. You never know when you'll need to move one.

Social Influence Assessment

How well-developed are your *Millionaire Mystique* social influence skills? Take this assessment and find out.

	Never	Rarely	Sometimes	Often	Always
	1	2	3	4	5
Networking					
1. I spend a lot of time and effort building a positive network of coworkers and colleagues.	1	2	3	4	5
2. At work and in the community, I know a lot of important people and am well connected.	1	2	3	4	5
3. I am good at using my connections and networks to make things happen.	1	2	3	4	5
Mentors					
4. I have a mentor(s) at work or in my profession who guides me and provides advice.	1	2	3	4	5
5. I use my direct supervisor as a mentor as much as possible.	1	2	3	4	5
6. I try to help my mentor whenever possible.	1	2	3	4	5
Total Score:					
	24–30	Great social influence skills			
	18–23	Increase your focus			
	6–17	Serious work needed			

Mystique Lessons for Aspiring Millionaires

Chapter 5: Are You a Social Influencer?

» Business success requires the ability to persuade people to say yes to you much more often than they say no. Those who aspire to be millionaires need to become masterful social influencers who persuade people in subtle ways. If you learn to read people well, it will be easier to craft win-win situations.

» Realize that networking must be based on an actual desire to create strong relationships with people. It cannot be a one-time thing if it is to be effective.

» Focus intently on whoever is in front of you at any given time to establish and nurture strong relationships.

» Speak up and give your opinion in problem-solving situations. It demonstrates your passion to contribute to the success of the group, which helps single you out as a high achiever.

» Communicate with people in the style they relate to. With men, that is often "report talk." With women, "rapport talk" usually works best. But not always. Listen.

» Learn to be forceful and argue a point to closure—without rancor. Arguing does not have to mean fighting; you are simply finding a solution to a problem when you state your argument and the reasons why it is a good one. Then, win or lose, you'll feel good about trying your best.

» Consciously expand your circle of relationships to include people influential in your field. Find areas of common interest and ask questions you really would like their opinion about.

» Make and keep small promises at the beginning of a relationship to get it off to a strong start. This "rule of reciprocity" is especially important when you have offered to share something with them.

» Build professional relationships with men as well as women.

» Mold an informal mentor out of someone you already like, who shares a similar work style and can teach you something you currently lack but need to have in order to rise further.

CHAPTER 6

The Millionaire Way: Leading with Grace

In all my research, the greatest leaders looked
inward and were able to tell a good story with
authenticity and passion.

—Deepak Chopra

Sandra Day O'Connor, former U.S. Supreme Court justice, knows something about rising to the top of her field and becoming a leader of others. One day last year, when I asked her to share her insights, she told me:

> If you want to be a successful leader, you must perform in the most effective and competent manner in whatever area you have chosen for yourself. Make a name for yourself in whatever area you have undertaken. Be available and don't shy away from taking new jobs or tasks and be willing to do them. You can't have as a goal "to become a leader," but make a name for yourself by performing well and then by taking on bigger and bigger roles.[1]

Sandra Day O'Connor was the first female Supreme Court justice, retiring in 2006. But when she graduated third in her class from Stanford Law School in 1952, more than forty law firms refused to even interview a woman. She eventually found work as a deputy county attorney, after she offered to work for free and share a desk with a secretary. In that job, she stood out for her willingness to get the job done, whatever the job was. Still, it seems absolutely amazing that O'Connor was able to rise to the pinnacle of leadership with such obstacles in her way.[2]

Probably the most insightful part of our conversation was something unexpected that she said: "You can't have as a goal 'to become a leader.'" Truly effective leadership, in other words, grows out of a conscientious effort to achieve excellent performance in any role that you take on. Large, important projects (like rendering Supreme Court decisions) require the cooperative efforts of many people. Despite what many leaders—both corporate leaders and business owners—seem to believe, true leadership has nothing to do with amassing power or prestige. Authentic leaders are simply those who help others get the job done in a conscientious and agreeable manner.

Three Legs of the Leadership Stool

There are volumes of sophisticated research and books on leadership styles, but with all their theoretical nuances, I am not sure how much these books help you become a better leader. The focus in this chapter is what over 160 female and male millionaires and multimillionaires recommend in terms of a leadership style—what has worked for them *in practice* and what has not worked. The good news is that it's not complicated.

I have also confirmed the *Millionaire Mystique*'s recommendations with my own years of executive coaching practice, along with the experience I gained during the twenty years I spent managing and supervising others through downsizings, transitions, critical incidents, and employee problems. To reduce it to its simplest form, effective leadership comes down to:

1. The relationship you have with others, built with trust and communication,

2. Industry knowledge, operational expertise, and good, old-fashioned management skills, and
3. The relationship you have with yourself.

All of the people I have coached have an issue in one of these areas. Someone can teach you the first two sets of skills, but if you can sprinkle in number 3—a strong and comfortable sense of self—then you will be a great leader, someone who is authentic and caring. This means that to learn to lead others, you must learn to manage yourself first. One of our multimillionaires, a sixty-year-old female employee assistance director in health care, acknowledged that self-doubt may be the most powerful force with a potential to undermine leadership. To combat this, she explains, "I know I am good at what I do, so I try not to question myself." It can be a struggle to give yourself credit for being a good leader, but I advise all women with high aspirations to do so.

Leading with Grace

It can be awkward initially to be in a leadership position. The title and responsibility may feel like a sweater that doesn't quite fit. To lead with grace requires knowing who you are, which allows you to inspire people to help you move the organization toward its goals. Leading with grace means that you can project calmness and clarity even if you don't feel it.

How is that possible? Men and women who lead with grace seem to have two important attributes in common: *authenticity* and *compassion*. Perhaps the most authentic and compassionate leader we have on the world stage today is Pope Francis. Many church leaders seem genuinely shocked that the pope tends to say whatever he believes. "We were not watching someone trying to act like a pope. We were watching a person unafraid to be who he was," notes Chris Lowney, a former managing director of J.P. Morgan Chase and a former Jesuit seminarian, in his book *Pope Francis: Why He Leads the Way He Leads.* Lowney summarizes the pope's leadership style this way: "Be comfortable in your own skin. Know who you are, the good and the bad. And find the courage not just to be yourself, but the best version of yourself. These are the foundations of self-leadership, and all leadership starts with self-leadership because you can't lead the rest of us if you can't lead yourself."[3]

Authentic leadership, at its most basic, means not being "someone other" at work than you are at home. If you pretend to be one way at work and act another way at home, your behavior won't be natural and you'll come across as awkward and unsure, which will create distrust.

Take a few moments to think about the way you present yourself at work. Do you act like your genuine self? Are you confident in your ability to lead? If not, you may find that you are actually hiding your true (more playful? more engaging? more humble?) self from your subordinates. Before you start work, consider doing some deep breathing to calm yourself so that you start in a relaxed frame of mind, which helps you project your true self.

Authentic leaders are not afraid to show their vulnerability in front of employees. They are self-aware, which requires knowing and understanding themselves. They know that their vulnerability helps them to connect because people sense that they're genuine. One male *Millionaire Mystique* participant put it bluntly: "I think that the most important thing in leadership is authenticity. I have seen [a lack of authenticity] in men but more [often] in women—the desire to fit some preconceived notion of what a leader is and then coming off as 'less than.'"

Authentic leaders also have strong enough self-esteem to admit mistakes.

Because they are mission driven and focused on results, these leaders don't have a problem admitting that something is wrong when the results are less than expected. They put the organization ahead of their own self-interest. And, because authentic leaders focus on long-term shareholder value, they see the wisdom of training people to assume higher levels of responsibility in the company. This step doesn't threaten their egos because they know that bringing promising people along makes the company stronger in the long run.

Compassionate leaders tend to put employees first. They attempt to be as flexible as possible if their employees have had difficulties, like a death in the family or divorce. But that begs an important question: How can you be a compassionate leader and still hold employees accountable to job performance standards? For instance, if you have an employee who is experiencing grief or is in a crisis, what do you do if that is negatively impacting the person's work? How do you express support without sacrificing job standards or a deadline? How do you avoid being *too* empathetic or, perversely, too hard on the employee? Learning to balance authentic and compassionate actions with accountability is the key to leading with grace. Let's find out how.

The Secret of Graceful Leadership

Think about the leaders you have admired. They all seem to be more interested in the success of the team than in personal success. Maybe ambition was driving them originally, but they were able to put self-interest aside and make personal sacrifices to accomplish goals that were bigger than themselves. They were able to communicate a sense of their mission-driven excitement to everyone around them. And what was the result? Almost certainly, people worked harder for them and loyalty increased as everyone strove for common goals.

I developed a leadership program at the University of St. Thomas Business Center to help both women and men in Minneapolis-based companies learn how to be more effective leaders. My goal was to facilitate their awareness of their natural strengths and weaknesses and to show the advantages of being more "transformational" leaders. Transformational leadership is the most effective of the four broad categories of leadership styles:

Laissez-faire: "Oh, do whatever you think is best."

Transactional: "Do what I say because I give you money and benefits."

Authoritarian: "Do it my way or get fired!"
Transformational: "Let's achieve these great goals together."

Not surprisingly, the *Millionaire Mystique* women and men report using the transformational style of leadership more than twice as often as the average leader. Taking the harder path, transformational leaders figure out ways to motivate their employees to achieve performance beyond normal expectations by transforming the employees' work attitudes, beliefs, and values. To accomplish this, they:

• Communicate a vision,
• Empower employees with the necessary authority,
• Provide support,
• Lead by example,
• Celebrate new ideas, and
• Carefully train staff in the needed skills.

If the transformational leader is also naturally charismatic, all the better, but a more introverted leader who is passionate about a mission will inspire just as well.

One male business owner told me how absolutely important this style of leadership is to success: "There are very few businesses that can exist today and be successful and sustainable without using a transformational style of leadership." Our millionaires told us it takes an average of seven years to become comfortable as a transformational leader. Here are some tools to help you become a transformational leader a little faster.

Use Social Influence

Almost all *Millionaire Mystique* women and men (94 percent) agreed that leaders can and should use strong interpersonal communication skills to (1) understand the motives and communication tactics of others, and (2) to influence and persuade other people to act in ways that make it easier to achieve the organization's goals and objectives.

By this, they do not mean that leaders should manipulate people into doing their will, as the stereotypical back-slapping politician is believed to do. Instead, it is a matter of using the good manners you've learned to make the people you meet feel like the center of your world. Individuals skilled in social communication convey a sense of personal security and calm self-confidence that attracts others, and gives them a feeling of comfort. This particularly applies to listening to people with all of your attention.

In his book *Focus: The Hidden Driver of Excellence*, Daniel Goleman, the bestselling author of *Emotional Intelligence*, notes that "the common cold of leadership is poor listening."[4] Graceful, transformational leaders know that there is nothing more vital to team cohesion than a boss who listens. The problem with most leaders, says Goleman, is that so few of them hear you because their minds are racing to the next problem. As a leader, make the effort to pause, reflect, listen, and really hear. You'll be surprised at the difference it makes.

Practice Leadership by Consent

Robert Bohannon, former chairman and CEO of Viad Corporation and executive vice president of operations at General Electric Capital Corporation, shared with me an insight into leadership that I found very powerful. "To be a leader, you truly have to be a people person. [As other leaders have discovered,] people will follow you if they think you can take them to a place they can't get to without you."[5]

Nelson Mandela compared leadership to the techniques of a shepherd: "He stays behind the flock, letting the most nimble go out ahead, whereupon the others follow, not realizing that they are being directed from behind."[6] This view of leadership has been championed by Harvard professor Linda Hill for many years. Hill recommends that leaders understand both that leadership is a collective activity and that "displays of assertiveness" (e.g., yelling, ordering people around) are not usually effective leadership techniques.[7]

Hire More of the Best People

Want to shine brilliantly as a graceful leader? Simple. Always hire "A Players." The trick is to be able to recognize A Players who will fit into your company's culture. "You know what A Players look like," says human resources consultant Ann Rhoades, author of *Built on Values: Creating an Enviable Culture That Outperforms the Competition*. "They are those people who are committed, dedicated, and successful in their jobs. They do more than is required, live the company's values, and truly add value to the organization."[8]

Rhoades points out, though, that a person who is an A Player somewhere else might be a C player for you. Why? The main reason is that his or her values may not align with the values of your organization. To take a simple example, say your company's top value is speed of delivery. If your new hire excelled at a company where the strength of the relationship with the customer is the highest value, no matter how much time it takes to do that, then she probably won't be a very good fit for you. She excelled in implementing a value that is the opposite of what your company needs. You could hire her, but it is likely that neither one of you will be happy with her performance. To lead with grace when it comes to hiring, try to figure out what values your company or department *really* espouses—this may be very different from the mission statement on the wall. Then hire and reward accordingly.

The Skills of a Millionaire Leader

To better understand women and work success, we must also figure out how women act and lead when they are in positions of influence and what contributes to their success. The *Millionaire Mystique* study included both women and men with senior-level positions and experience in leading large organizations or their own businesses. As a result, we were able to get the perspectives of both genders on effective leadership by women. Given their success in this area, it was interesting to explore what specific attributes this group considered important to effective leadership. The following two questions were used to assess key attributes of leadership: "What personal characteristics are essential for successful leadership?" "What skills are essential for successful leadership?" I used open-ended questions in addition to a checklist of leadership skills that participants rated. Many of the categories were rated so high and were so similar in the rates of positive responses from all participants that I decided that the only correct assumption is that the great leader "has it firing on many levels all at the same time." Therefore, my co-researcher, Dr. Mark Attridge, and I grouped the recommended skills and characteristics into Three C's—communication, competence, and character.[9]

> *Communication:* 75 percent of our leaders stated that effective communication skills were most critical to their success. This included the sub-elements of listening, giving feedback to others, ensuring clarity of verbal expression, being persuasive, and having strong writing skills.
>
> *Character:* 70 percent of our business leaders and owners volunteered that integrity and honesty were critical to their success. These individuals were very clear that in order to engender trust from their peers, subordinates, and customers, good character as shown by humility and respect was essential.
>
> *Competence:* 62 percent of the survey respondents listed managerial competence—including industry knowledge; operational expertise; hiring, firing, and supervisory skills; and financial management—as critical to success.

There were many other categories that ranked almost as high as the top three C's. For example, 50 percent of our women and men cited as important: being self-confident, being dedicated and hard working, and having a strategic vision that is well-communicated. Forty percent of our millionaires also recommended having a team orientation, displaying emotional self-awareness, motivating others, and being a good decision maker.

As you can see from the results noted above, the path to being a successful and powerful leader comes from developing your knowledge of people and business acumen simultaneously. Developing these elements can also put you on the fast track to leadership. One of our millionaire leaders, a woman, put her advice succinctly: "I outperformed female and male peers to be recognized as someone who wanted a leadership role." As simple, and as complicated, as that.

Here are a few other recommendations about good leadership that were gleaned from the participants' comments.

1. **Cultivate a competitive spirit.** Even if you are not super competitive, you need the will to win to carry you to the top. Many women, if you observe them closely, have a quiet determination to win that is just as strong as most men's, although not as overt. You don't have to be boastful or loud, but you must have a constant commitment to excellence. Winners are the ones of either sex who are the most determined and the best prepared.

2. **Know when to break the rules.** When you've been in school a long time, as many *Millionaire Mystique* participants were, following the rules becomes ingrained. Look around you now, though. Who tends to get ahead? People who try new approaches that work. People who don't listen when they are told that "we don't do things that way here." People who think of a way around a problem when the road straight through is blocked. Sure, you'll have to fight for your right to break the unwritten rules, but it's worth it.

3. **Welcome conflict.** If you are not comfortable with conflict, it's going to hurt your chances of advancement. Practice assertiveness and conflict management techniques. Plenty of people are willing to argue politics these days, for instance. Just prepare yourself with some facts and see what happens. Talk to people outside your work circles about that topic or anything else controversial they want to discuss. Jamie Thorsen lamented that too few women learn the art of healthy debate from their fathers or mothers. "Women generally do not like to work in

an environment of conflict, and I think that is a reason they have not done better in the workplace. Men can have significant conflict, agree to disagree, and move on. Women tend not to be able to do that."[10]

The Personality of a Leader

Naively, many people believe you become a "leader" when someone gives you a supervisory title and a group of people to manage. Robert Cialdini, Ph.D., in his book *Influence: The Psychology of Persuasion*, notes that "titles are simultaneously the most difficult and the easiest symbols of authority to acquire. To earn a title takes years of work and achievement. Yet, it is possible for somebody who has put in none of this effort to adopt the mere label and receive a kind of automatic deference." He describes this as a "click whirr" automatic response to authority. Studies have shown that the use of a title changes the tenor of the interaction immediately: People become more respectful, accepting, and even attribute to the leader a couple of inches in height.[11]

The experience of *Millionaire Mystique* participants, though, argues that attaining the title is actually the least important aspect of leadership. All it does is make the people you manage wary: Who is this new boss and how is she going to affect my life? Some of them fear the worst. So, in order to get off on the right foot, it is important to go in with a smile on your face, care about their well-being, and be optimistic that everything your team does is going to achieve a high standard of excellence.

As we saw in Chapter 3, *Millionaire Mystique* women (and men) are higher than the average person on four of the Big Five personality characteristics: conscientiousness, extraversion, agreeableness, and openness to new experiences. They are also low in neuroticism. Of course, they bring those personality traits to leadership, as well. For that reason, I believe you will be a much stronger leader if you are able to develop these personality traits in yourself, even if they aren't present in you at a high level now. But watch out for the pitfalls inherent in these traits as well. Let's take a closer look at how four of the Big Five characteristics can make you a better leader.

Getting the Job Done: Conscientiousness

Millionaire Mystique women leaders are exceptionally high on the trait of conscientiousness. Aspiring leaders who put "getting the job done" first are going to be the most respected and the ones who get promoted fastest. I heartily agree with what one forty-three-year-old female department head in a Fortune 100 company told me:

> Conscientiousness facilitates trust and respect. In my experience, people will tolerate decisions or rules if they believe that they are applied consistently and reliably after a thorough examination of whether the rules or decisions are necessary. Miss any of those, and the result is mistrust and loss of respect.

Inspiring Others: Extraversion

Intriguingly, *Millionaire Mystique* women are only *a little* more extroverted than the average woman. Rather than being gregarious, these leaders seem to possess a well-developed ability to inspire people to great heights of performance. What inspiring leaders seem to have, says Daniel Goleman, author of *Focus*, is a high degree of integration between thought and emotion, and an ability to understand the thoughts and emotions of others. He explains:

> Leaders who inspire can articulate shared values that resonate with and motivate the group. These are the leaders people love to work with, who promote the vision that moves everyone. But to speak from the heart, to the heart, a leader must first know her values. That takes self-awareness. Inspiring leadership demands attuning to both an inner emotional reality and to that of those we seek to inspire.[12]

Best Interest of the Organization: Agreeableness

The agreeable leader is not one who says "yes" to everything, but one who has the best interests of the organization at heart. Leaders high in agreeableness value the team getting along with one another, are trusting, and trustworthy. As a leader, you will find that employees know when you are putting your own interests ahead of the organization or its people. In the worst cases, they'll gossip about you and not cooperate. *Millionaire Mystique* women are very high in the trait of agreeableness, much higher than the average person. Many noted the need to display dedication, commitment, and loyalty to the business and to their subordinates as key to successful leadership.

The Lure of the New: Openness

Millionaire Mystique women are higher than the norm in openness to new experiences, as well. As a leader or business owner, you'll get further than your peers if you are open to new ideas, creative, and insightful. Forming new and interesting relationships, taking on unusual work tasks, generating new ideas, and being resourceful are all characteristics of an individual high in openness. You are already higher than the norm in openness if reading the "to do" list I just mentioned gets your imaginative engine revving instead of making you tired.

Unfortunately, as we all know, creativity and new ideas aren't always welcomed by organizations. You may find this to be doubly so if you are relatively new to the corporate maze. Some of that resistance probably is, in fact, resistance to the fact that the idea is coming from *you*. However, even if you haven't established your credibility or reputation as an innovator whose ideas actually work, you may be able to get them implemented anyway. The key is to use a little back-door strategy. Look for opportunities to learn about your company in as much detail as you can by taking on responsibilities outside your department on a volunteer basis. Or, outside of work, get to know the people you want to convince, perhaps by showing an interest in their favorite cause if it interests you. If you can be seen as creative and open to challenges by those who can make decisions about your ideas, you are more likely to find a receptive audience the next time you try.

Banishing Neuroticism

A leader's understanding of his or her internal landscape is the gateway to success. As a leader, you will want to have a clear understanding of how your life has shaped you as an adult (e.g., hardworking parents, entrepreneurial parents, a Harvard education, abuse in the family). Most *Millionaire Mystique* men and women reported little of the psychological trait of neuroticism. Rather than being anxious or nervous at work or home, they project a calm exterior. If you are not there yet, identify your issues (e.g., insecurity, sadness, anger, passivity, fear of conflict, depression, anxiety, ADD) and get to work on them. Use meditation and write in your work journal to become more centered. If you have a history of abuse, which increases the likelihood of discomfort with anger and conflict, seek the support of a counselor to get through it.

Are Men and Women Different As Leaders?

Research has demonstrated over and over again that most people who hear the words *leader* or *manager* think of a male filling those positions.[13] This dynamic influences how women act as leaders and are reacted to by others. Fortunately, being a supervisor, manager, or director means that ultimately, if push comes to shove, you have more power to make decisions than those you supervise. Power is just the ability to influence the behavior of people around you. The conundrum for women is that using your power, however judiciously, is seen in society as unfeminine. But to deny your own power, which is what many new female managers do, just confuses everyone. Therefore leadership requires acceptance of your newfound power.

Admitting that you have more power than others gives you an opportunity to express it as you choose.

Since many women have been the object of the misuse of power—to control or dominate them, at work or home—it may be a bit harder for them to acknowledge and accept their own power to influence others. When I work with women leaders, I recommend facing the issue head on and saying, "Yes, I have more power than the individuals I supervise. What kind of leadership style fits with my values so that I can express this power in a respectful and effective way?"

One fifty-eight-year-old female executive who was part of the *Millionaire Mystique* study told me:

> Women need to feel comfortable with their power—both personal and positional—and use it appropriately. This is also an issue for some men. Power used well by men or women can accomplish great things.

As leaders, we just need to learn to use our power in ways that will enhance our effectiveness at work. And those ways are often very different for women than for men.

Fifty percent of the men in the *Millionaire Mystique* study told us that they believed that women lead differently, but this was not seen as a negative. One male millionaire in his fifties told me that "women should be true to who they are (and men should be as well). If they are nurturing, then [they should] use nurturing to motivate and influence staff." In fact, a full 94 percent of the *Millionaire Mystique* group, both men and women, recommend developing a transformational leadership style combined with a dash of the autocratic.

The great news for women leaders is that they naturally gravitate toward the transformational style of a good teacher or coach and can capitalize on that. Many of them are already doing so. Based on twenty-five years of leadership studies, psychology professors Alice Eagly and Linda Carli recommend that women combine assertive competence with supportive friendliness to achieve managerial goals. Collaboration and shared power engages employees' willingness to work.[14]

Our *Millionaire Mystique* participants—male and female—were all accomplished leaders, so I asked them what they thought was preventing more women from becoming high-ranking leaders. Here is what they told me were the most challenging factors.

1. *Women leaders must be more competent than men.* Yes, this is an unfortunate fact we must live with for a while longer. So, be sure you know your business from the ground up and be knowledgeable about your technical field. Have all the credentials you need, or more, because you will be judged more harshly. Psychologist Madeline Heilman, Ph.D., of New York University has identified a "male boss preference bias," particularly among males when women work in male-dominated fields.[15] For this reason, women leaders report that they must establish themselves as being superior in ability and performance relative to their peers to continue to be promoted—or even to survive.

2. *Women leaders must walk a fine line.* Women leaders need to be competent enough to be taken seriously yet also be friendly enough to avoid social backlash. The best female leaders have a balance between supportive friendliness and a business focus.

3. *Women leaders are expected to be better communicators.* One female millionaire told me, "Women need to be careful about their tone. Never too harsh and direct, never too soft or cute. There is a smaller window of acceptable communication for women than for men. This is not necessarily bad, but it is important to know for success."

4. *Leaders are assumed to be men.* When a woman is in a leadership role usually occupied by a man, it forces others to come to terms with their own stereotypes and prejudices. This requires getting to know and respect each other as people before moving on to a more relaxed relationship and getting the work done.

5. *Women leaders are penalized for success.* They will often be judged as less likeable merely *because* they hold leadership positions. Be aware of this and be sure to regularly reach out to peers with friendly gestures.

6. *Women leaders who express anger are criticized harshly.* Expression of anger is still seen as more of a male characteristic. This

point emphasizes the importance of a woman combining assertive behaviors with a supportive style.

7. *Women leaders are (mostly unconsciously) expected to display the characteristics and behaviors of male leaders.* Women who are not as analytical or who express compassion may find their leadership skills questioned. So be sure to demonstrate strong business skills at the same time you display a supportive work style.

One seventy-year-old male millionaire expanded on these thoughts: "In my opinion, leadership is just tougher for women. They, more so than men, must be professional and demanding of staff without appearing totally cold. And if they relax in a senior job, they are thought of and reacted to as soft." I am surprised at the level of residual sexism all of these beliefs reflect, but they are reality as experienced and observed in a wide variety of industries by our *Millionaire Mystique* leaders. In my experience, if you are armed with the facts, you may be better able to recognize and navigate the landmines when they threaten to undermine your leadership.

The Female Advantage: Bonnie Morcomb's Story

Most registered nurses don't become millionaires or corporate lead-
ers, although they provide invaluable services for society and for their patients. Bonnie Morcomb, R.N., M.P.A., didn't set out to do that either.[16] But when she found herself on the street as the result of a nurses' strike in Minneapolis one day, she decided to take her career in a different direction. A health care company hired her to start a division called "nurse triage," in which nurses would recommend what kind of treatment patients needed. "I started all by myself in the basement of a building and eventually built it into a twenty-four-hour nurse line with 500 employees giving phone and online support." As chief operating officer at a subsidiary of UnitedHealthcare, she led an operation that provided service to over fifteen million people in the United States. She now heads a similar, though smaller, division at Coventry Workers' Compensation Services in Minneapolis.

While reflecting on her career changes she told me, "There are some differences when you work for a smaller company—you've got to roll your sleeves up as a leader and wear many hats. And when you've grown the business into a large one, you depend on people who are experts in various fields. But one thing doesn't change and that is the need for a leader to build trust among employees, just like in the best families." She notes that women are especially good at this because building relationships is second nature to them. A simple example, she says, is how women and men tend to respond to emails. A man may respond with a quick "yes" to something he approves of. Women are more likely to respond with encouraging words to show that they've read and support the proposal. And they may have more suggestions, ideas, and encouragement to offer.

"When I worked with male bosses, I often didn't know what was going on in the rest of the organization, just with my team or department," Bonnie remembers. "I try to show employees how their work is impacted by developments in the larger company." Although some secrecy is desirable or required (with competitive information, say), Bonnie is transparent with employees to the highest degree possible, which helps them to trust that what she shares with them is both important and the truth.

"We women create a work family, I think, and this does two things," says Bonnie. "First, people feel that their voices are being heard, and second, people feel more satisfied because we all have a common goal." That goal is to make sure that the "family" prospers. Bonnie is a true transformational leader and demonstrates how female attributes can be parlayed into building a successful business.

Advanced Leadership:
Dealing Gracefully with Problem Employees

One of the many difficult and significant tasks of an executive is to handle performance problems. And our intensely competitive business environment makes graceful leadership much more complicated when negotiating the line between providing support for employees and holding them accountable. As an executive coach, I am asked to help leaders develop strategies for "compassionate accountability" when an employee's performance is suffering.

The first step in dealing with the situation is to be honest with yourself about how your employee's situation may be affecting *you*. If you just went through a stressful situation personally, you may be tempted to give your employee too much leeway. All of us as leaders have our own "trigger" issues that are based on our own past experiences, whether that is divorce, alcoholism, or death of a family member. Knowing your sensitivities helps mitigate their impact on your judgment.

Second, realize that enabling your employee to continue their disruptive behavior (whatever it is) does not provide pressure for your employee to improve their personal situation. After allowing the employee some time off, if necessary, holding a recently divorced employee accountable may be exactly the push he or she needs to join a support group. Overall, when you make sure that standards are upheld, you may actually help troubled employees by giving them an incentive to focus on job performance, rather than the overwhelming emotions of their situations.

With that in mind, you should always be prepared for a negative reaction. An employee under these circumstances may become defensive and angry when given negative work feedback, which often gets mixed in with their personal troubles, exaggerating the response. It is essential for you to stick to the facts and deliver the feedback with a compassionate tone and an acknowledgement of the employee's situation. Be firm, make a plan for improvement, and follow it up in writing. Make it a practice, too, to refer people to your company's employee assistance program or community resources if they can use the help.

Remember that these very sensitive discussions will be watched closely by others in the group. They don't want their peers to "get away with" poor performance. At the same time, nobody wants a person with personal problems to be punished. Your compassion should lead you to work out creative methods of getting the work done if employees are truly debilitated. Tough love, consistently applied, will take care of the rest.

Leading Gracefully Through Transitions

Acquisitions, downsizings, layoffs, and other corporate crises are almost routine these days. I know one person whose company changed ownership five times in the last five years. His desk has stayed in the very same spot in the same office building all along, but his company keeps getting acquired by bigger ones. Even in those situations where nobody loses their jobs, corporate transitions are still traumatic as employees try to figure out their place in the new configuration.

Managing the transition with the least possible disruption will gain you respect and possibly admiration, which may put you in line for bigger responsibilities. I advise that you approach such transitions in stages, as recommended by William Bridges, Ph.D., the acknowledged expert on transitions and author of *Managing Transitions: Making the Most of Change*. Start with the ending, Bridges says, then proceed to a neutral zone, followed by a new beginning.[17] Let's look at how that works.

> **The ending: Make it kinder.** First of all, Bridges recommends acknowledging at the appropriate times that the transition will be accompanied by discomfort, anxiety, reflection, lowered productivity, lowered motivation, lowered self-confidence, as well as resistance, but also, after a period of time, by creativity. Also realize that you personally will experience feelings of loss (and actual loss if you have to forgo a promotion). You'll also be fearful of the future, the same as your employees. This is like the first stage of grief. Do all you can to simultaneously help yourself and your employees through shock, bargaining, anger, and sadness so that you can move toward acceptance. A helpful tool is the use of rituals to symbolize endings and new beginnings, like a

luncheon to thank employees for their past work and acknowledge the ending.

The neutral zone: Communicate. Because the unknown creates anxiety, you can specifically tell people that there is what Bridges calls "a neutral zone" in your office where communication is encouraged, no matter what they have to say. Emphasize that everyone will be going through this together. At Optum, when we acquired another large company doing essentially the same work as my division, I knew that integrating the two would be difficult. I held town hall meetings where employees could ask whatever was on their minds and get a straight answer. However you do it—in person, in a blog, by email—make sure that everyone understands what is actually going to change, and paint a clear picture of the future. Use a coach or consultant to get an outside perspective if needed.

New beginnings: Do it carefully. Similar to Dr. Bridges, I recommend creating a transition-monitoring team to figure out where conflicts lie, where change is essential, and where the status quo can prevail. There is no need to make changes just for the sake of change. Let some of the old ways continue to ease the transition. But where things must change, communicate specifically what will be happening, because this is the most stressful time. Make sure everyone understands the reasoning behind new organizational structures. One forty-eight-year-old female multimillionaire, a Canadian chief administrative officer in the financial services industry, told me that, in her experience, conflicts are minimized "by being open and transparent. People can take hearing bad news more easily than hearing no news." She explained, "My style has always been to be upfront with people as that is how I prefer to be treated."

Put yourself in the shoes of the people you are leading, and communicate what you would like to hear about what's happening. Recommend to everyone that they take time-outs, reframe future expectations, and experiment with new behaviors. Some other suggestions from Dr. Bridges and other experts on how to manage transitions wisely include:

- Time the beginning carefully to minimize disruptions during busy seasons.
- Paint a picture of how the successful outcome will look and feel.
- Communicate a step-by-step transition plan.
- Give everyone a role to play in the transition. Delegate.
- Treat the past respectfully and celebrate past triumphs as you begin again.
- Convince people to "leave home" and try the changes with an open mind, just as if they were leaving for college again.
- Clarify cultural beliefs and values. Which ones will hold sway in the new organization?
- Reinforce desired new behaviors with rewards and be consistent.
- Ask employees to describe problems experienced in the transition. Promise to address them. Then do.

The aim of all of this is to rebuild trust in the organization and get everyone working in the same direction again. Don't forget to take care of yourself in this situation, too. My research shows, for instance, that bank managers after a robbery experience twice as many mental and physical problems, possibly due to the dual role of taking care of themselves and taking care of their employees.[18]

I believe leadership is made up of daily short-term actions, longer-term visionary practices, and critical moments of intervention. Your legacy as a leader will be determined by all of these factors, both in everyday actions and in how you handle crises. For instance, former New York City mayor Rudy Giuliani will be forever remembered as the mayor of 9/11. Within minutes of the towers toppling and at great risk to himself, he rushed toward Ground Zero, called television stations, and urged calm. He spoke with a trusted voice and outlined the painful steps to restore confidence and safety. A well-handled adverse situation, even if not so dire, will not only help your employees, but suspend your reputation at a higher level for years to come.

Women in the Leadership Pipeline

In December 2012, General Motors became the first auto company to name a female CEO.[19] Mary Barra, fifty-one, rose through the ranks of the company, beginning as an intern and experiencing almost every aspect of the company's operation on her way to the top. Along the way, she married, earned a degree in electrical engineering and an M.B.A. from Stanford, and had two children. She was most recently senior vice president in charge of global product development as well as responsible for GM's supply chain worldwide, searching for greater efficiencies and savings for the entire company. A few years earlier, when she was in charge of global human resources as the company emerged from bankruptcy, she junked the company's ten-page dress code. It was all a part of her effort to help reinvent the firm. "The key to unlocking innovation at GM is to trust the people to do the very best they can," she said at the time.

She is the very model of the graceful, transformational leader. When a reporter asked her in December 2012 to describe her leadership style, she immediately replied, "Collaborative." She said,

> I try to create an environment where people feel they can voice their concerns, and where we can get the best ideas on the table and make the right decision. But at the end of the day, when the decision has to be made, if we don't have complete unanimity, I have no qualms about making [the decision].[20]

Mary is not alone. Many more women CEOs have been named in the past twelve months to help their companies prosper. So, if women are naturally suited for graceful, transformational leadership and companies profit by having such leaders, why have so few women risen to the top of other Fortune 500 companies?

The answer to that question may have to do with who is actually hiring those top executives: the board of directors. In GM's case, says Jacque Sokolov, M.D., CEO of SBB Solutions, who now serves on multiple public and private corporation boards, Barra's ascent to the top could have a lot to do with the new composition of the GM board. Four female members have been appointed (or reappointed) to the board since GM's recession-fueled bankruptcy in 2009. "Board governance committees are nominating board members based on discrete complementary skills—management experience, content expertise, diversity, et cetera—to create a high-performing enterprise board," says Sokolov. "In addition, there are many more female 'intrapreneurs' in companies, who are now being rewarded for their in-house innovations."[21] GM's Barra was one of these. Yet she became only the twenty-third current CEO of a Fortune 500 company.

Jacque Sokolov highly recommends that more women try to become corporate board members as well. "It is somewhat of a catch-22 that people without board experience can't get on boards. When you look at how people are chosen in a typical board, you find a portion who have had a traditional path after rising through corporate ranks. Women have a hard time with this because the traditional corporate path is usually many decades long." But now entrepreneurs are getting their chance, too. He gives the example of Barbara Bowles, who serves with him on the Hospira board, a publicly traded $10 billion company. Bowles built her own investment company and so had special expertise in finance and the investment community, equivalent to board members at Black and Decker, which was one of her major public boards. "She used that experience [as a business owner] to become an excellent candidate and ultimately was elected to become the chairman of the audit committee of the Hospira board of directors," said Sokolov.

Because starting on the board of a company as big as Hospira is unusual, Sokolov recommends approaching smaller companies or nonprofits that could benefit from your expertise. (Other special areas of expertise that are desirable in potential board members include compensation, auditing, human resources, management experience, content expertise, finance, IT, and governance.) As the example of Mary Barra shows, if more women become corporate board members, more women will rise higher in leadership.

If even the last bastions of male domination (autos, electric utilities, railroads, and the like) are waking up to the value of women leaders and putting more women on boards, things may be changing. Now is the time to accelerate your upward trajectory by carefully and strategically taking on high-visibility projects that no one else wants. Who knows? It could catapult you into the C-suite.

One sixty-year-old male millionaire told me, "Women have historically had to overcome barriers and prejudices about their business acumen. They have not been part of the 'club' at the top. Changing this reality has been very gradual and there is a long road ahead. However, I believe a great deal of progress has been made during my career, and I anticipate it will continue."

Are you ready to lead?

Assessing Your Leadership Potential

According to leadership expert Kevin Kruse of Forbes.com, good leadership is "a process of social influence, which maximizes the efforts of others, towards the achievement of a goal."[22] Your personality characteristics and your work style will both have an impact on your natural ability to lead in a graceful, transformational way.

Almost everyone can learn to lead well, but you need to embrace your natural strengths and get a clear understanding of your weaknesses. After you take mental stock of your leadership potential, consider discussing it with your supervisor and your team for feedback. Your human resources department or an executive coach can take you through a formal leadership assessment process and help you improve weak areas.

Leadership Readiness Checklist

The following leadership checklist is for reflection and will illustrate where you need to focus to improve your leadership style.

1. Do I have an understanding of how my natural personality tendencies determine my leadership style? My most obvious personality traits are:

2. Do I have an authentic style that allows others to see who I am, and can I admit mistakes? When was the last time I admitted a vulnerability or mistake to others at work?

3. Do I actively try to know employees I supervise and demonstrate understanding and compassion? What is a recent example?

4. What is the feedback I have received on my verbal and written communication?

5. Do I know the difference between autocratic, transactional, laissez-faire, and transformational leadership styles? What are two examples of times when I have consciously used some of these styles in the recent past?

6. What organizational vision, goals, and outcomes have I recently communicated to employees? Would the employees in my area of responsibility be able to clearly explain them to others?

7. What formal leadership training programs have I completed and how many of the leaders in my department have had formal education in the area of leadership?

8. Do I know the specific steps to follow when there is an employee performance issue, and do the other leaders in my department also know? Give an example.

9. Which steps did I follow during a transition to help my department leave the past behind and move to a new beginning? Was there anything I could have done differently to have garnered more cooperation? How did my natural personality traits help or hinder in this situation?

10. What overt and covert obstacles are in my organization for women in leadership roles? What can I do to raise awareness and make changes in the company?

11. Am I taking the time to mentor other women in my company? In what ways?

Mystique Lessons for Aspiring Millionaires

Chapter 6: The Millionaire Way: Leading with Grace

» Realize that good leadership is not about power or prestige. It is about helping others get a job done.

» Create a "learning organization" where you and your employees are not afraid to admit mistakes and learn from them. Develop a culture of constantly trying to improve techniques and strategies.

» Be sure to handle adverse situations well; this not only helps many employees, but can enhance your leadership reputation. Don't avoid them simply because of the risk of failure. Seek them out if you believe you can succeed.

» Know yourself—your strengths and weaknesses. This is a must for leading with grace. Such self-knowledge gives you a calm assurance that inspires others to help you move your organization toward its goals.

» Don't be afraid to be authentic. Be honest about challenges and admit mistakes. Employees would rather follow someone who will ask for their support in difficult times than an authority figure who demands to be obeyed.

» Show compassion to employees with personal problems. Help them to find solutions that will not affect the productivity of the company and make appropriate referrals to your company's Employee Assistance Program so they can get support.

» Treat problem employees with "compassionate accountability." Be supportive, but expect that they will perform at their highest level within a reasonable amount of time.

» Develop a transformational leadership style. The most successful leaders motivate employees with a shared vision of the company's mission, listening to concerns, celebrating good ideas, providing necessary training, hiring people who share the company's values, and being role models for desired behaviors.

» Cultivate a competitive spirit. Know when to break the rules. Educate yourself on conflict resolution techniques.

» Become more conscientious, extroverted, agreeable, and open. Also work to become less neurotic.

» Remember that women *are* actually judged more harshly as leaders than men. Therefore, *Millionaire Mystique* participants recommend that aspiring leaders be superior in both industry/technical knowledge and relationship building in order to overcome "male boss preference syndrome."

» Aim to be asked to join a corporate board. If you have not been a CEO of a large company, develop expertise in business ownership, compensation, human resources, auditing, financials, or board governance. Read corporate annual reports and 10-Ks until you understand how boards contribute to the success of companies.

Choose to Be Resilient

Self-made success has given me the confidence that I can do anything.

—Fifty-nine-year-old vice president, real estate and banking, and millionaire

One of the most admired and successful business women I know is Angie Hallier, who is the owner of her own twenty-five-person all-female law firm, Hallier and Lawrence in Phoenix.[1] Yet her early life would not have led anyone to believe she would end up a multimillionaire. After escaping an abusive marriage, and with no possibility of child support, she took any job she could find. She always wanted a better life for her daughter and the things that money could buy, so she made the conscious decision to achieve significant financial success. "I was coming off a bad marriage and knew it was going to be 'on me' to provide for myself and my child," Angie says now. "I wanted a secure future for both of us and especially to be able to provide her with [a fine] education and adventures." Angie can now buy whatever she wants because she persevered through law school, received great internships, and started her own all-female law firm.

As an attorney, Angie practices family law, including a lot of divorces, so she's had a wealth of experience helping clients manage difficult situations. That doesn't mean that she hasn't had her share of challenges. But she has developed a resiliency in her personality that doesn't allow challenges to slow her down. She remembers going a little crazy over the difficult decision to choose which of her two good friends, who were also her colleagues, she should make into a "name" partner—the person who would get her name on the door. One was a very hard worker while the other's specialty area was not a very good fit for the organization. The decision should have been easy, but the friendship got in the way for a while. Angie wished she could have given both friends a partnership.

"In the end, I decided to think of my firm as a patient in the hospital," she says. "I needed to make the decision that would leave the patient the healthiest in the long run. That took out the emotional component, and I was able to do what was right for the firm—and right for my former colleague, too, as it turned out. She went on to be a top achiever in her specialty area at another firm."

Angie discovered, as she felt her way to a good decision in this case, that you can take control of what you choose to be stressed out about.

She continues, "You can't get bogged down in the small stuff because then you just get stuck and paralyzed. Women can learn to be great businesspeople if they let their left and right brains work at the same time. An integration of logic and emotion can lead you to the best decisions as long as you don't let one aspect dominate." Many women believe—sometimes unconsciously—that their self-worth flows from how well they tend to the needs of others, both at work and at home. But resilience in the face of difficulty flows from a belief in yourself that ultimately you'll be successful if you just keep trying.

The Persistence Factor

If there is any single personality trait that distinguishes wealthy, successful women from others, it is resilience. Like Angie, people who achieve at a high level just don't seem to recognize the concept of giving up. The women who rise to the top do so, in large measure, because they persist—even over a long time frame—until they get what they want. Yes, they experience stress, but their primary focus is the problem at hand. They are strong and resourceful, don't crack under pressure, and seem to possess a grace under fire that those around them admire. Where does this strategy come from? Is it something that only certain people are born with? And, just as important, how can you develop it in yourself and in your staff?

Millionaire Mystique women reported much higher resilience and flexibility than the average person. We asked them about how they would respond to statements such as "Changes in routine are interesting to me," and "I enjoy the challenge when I have more than one thing to do at a time." One female multimillionaire, who is the forty-four-year-old CEO of a media company, told me that her greatest strength was her "ability to *not* take no for an answer." She said:

> There is *always* someone telling you that you can't do something and few people encouraging you to continue on your path. Once I started to realize that it was not personal, I realized that I needed to fight for what I'm passionate about and not worry that 90 percent of the people I meet are going to tell me my ideas are off base. Now it motivates me to prove them wrong. I feel if you don't get that fire in your belly, you won't be successful. Because no one is going to go to bat for you.

In other words, these successful women are people who have learned to cope with stress and adversity in a positive manner. Resiliency is not an inborn trait, but a process of interacting with the world. The women in my study built on their Big 5 personality traits of *strong conscientiousness, extraversion, agreeableness, openness,* and *low neuroticism* to create a strong inner core that could withstand setbacks. And they seem to particularly draw on the trait of *openness* to create this ability to cope. The more of the world you are ready to experience, the more resilient you will be. The world knocks you down and you get up. Every time you have a bad experience, it is an opportunity to learn from the world.

People who are not open to learning from experience believe they are protecting themselves. Instead, the lesson they draw from experience is to take fewer risks. That is not the way to resilience. Taking the "safe route" only makes you more brittle and more likely to suffer harm from bad experiences.

"Biologically, resilience is the ability to modulate and constructively harness the stress response—a capacity essential to both physical and mental health," say Steven Southwick and Dennis Charney, authors of *Resilience: The Science of Mastering Life's Greatest Challenges*.[2] Because of this, the resilient person is more likely to bounce back to a normal level of functioning after a major stressor, such as the loss of a job, workplace reorganization, a death, or divorce. And even in more normal times, developing resilient behaviors will help you minimize stress and lead you to greater personal and work success.

Think about how wonderful it would be to be flexible and open about change on a daily basis, while maintaining certain non-negotiables. It would certainly help you feel less guilty about the balance of work and family. Let's say that you've finished your work for the day and will be heading out a little early for your daughter's dance recital. If your boss arrives with a project he wants you to start on immediately just as you are packing up, do you say, "Sure, I'll get right on that," or "Would it be okay to get it to you first thing tomorrow?" The resilient person, having already negotiated with the boss for the early departure, quickly evaluates the real urgency of the situation and responds accordingly, without panic or stress. Almost everything can wait a few hours, but the resilient person is also prepared with backup plans in case the boss is not exaggerating the severity of the situation.

I encourage you to be prepared ahead of time with a backup plan to get out the door. Of course, you don't want to miss the dance recital. Family first.

Plan ahead and not only inform your supervisor about leaving work early, but have one or two of your "A" players on call to get started on an unexpected project while you run out for an hour and a half. If something urgent at work comes up, delegate to one or two competent individuals to get started on the project and give any needed instructions before you run out the door. Inform two of your directors or managers ahead of time that this is an important event and you may need them to pitch in so they are not surprised by the request. Let them know what time you will return.

Stay calm and remember the perception you create will either enhance their "opportunity" or make it more difficult to accomplish the task.

A Sense of Control

Having a sense of control over what happens in your life is the key to establishing and maintaining a balanced life. Resilient people are willing to act to influence events. They are also confident when they do so because they know their strengths and weaknesses and have identified the talents they bring to the table. They accept responsibility for both their triumphs and their mistakes. And they see change not as frightening but as an opportunity for growth and excitement.

"I'm always looking for the 'next peak,'" says Angie Hallier, who plans to write a book for women giving a tutorial about how to have a "good divorce." (Angie's words) "I envision my success and make it happen. And I think that's been good for my daughter, who has learned a lot from observing me and remembers when we were broke and poor. I want her to understand that you can choose what to be stressed out about. She understands you just have to keep moving forward. She now lives in L.A. and was even recruited by Yahoo. No doubt about it: Her understandable pride in her daughter's achievements has made the hard road to the top seem worthwhile to her.

Think about the most successful women you know. They seem to have a quality that convinces you that they can take on any challenge. They might not succeed at everything they try, but they will take the risk, knowing that they can bounce back from job and life challenges. They trust their interpretation of situations, not wasting energy on self-doubt. In my study of *Millionaire Mystique* women, resilience came up over and over as an important factor in success. Most of the men and women who responded to my questions had experienced at least one major work or family "detour" or outright failures. Yet the vast majority of them responded as this fifty-four-year-old female health care president and CEO did: "I was fired from a loved job and did not know why—I had to come to terms with this issue and finally decide to shake it off, learning from it as to how I might be more responsible for my own actions and not just shift blame elsewhere, and to use it to help me understand others better."

It is that kind of focus on problem solving that really defines resiliency in wealthy, successful people. They are, in a very real sense, less dependent on the opinions of others and more willing to take action in a crisis. The *Millionaire Mystique* study found that resiliency is a strong characteristic of successful people and is something they can easily draw on when need be to maintain their self-esteem in the face of career or life struggles.

Women may find it more difficult to be resilient, though, because they are fighting against years and years of socialization. They hear society say, "You can only be a good wife, a good mother, a good daughter, a good worker if you put the needs of others first." Many women sometimes unconsciously believe that their self-worth flows from how well they take care of others, both at work and at home.

Moving up in the business world requires that you modulate these societal pressures by knowing exactly what you can control in your life—and what you cannot. One way to develop a great sense of control is to prevent other people from dictating your choices. But women, to a greater extent than men, simply for the good of their families, too often fall into decisions rather than making those decisions consciously. When you fail to take control and make conscious decisions, you may feel trapped, eventually damaging your work, relationships, or family.

My research has shown that wealthy, successful women tend to be able to step back and ask themselves why they are making the decisions they are making. They always question themselves as to what each decision means about their values and needs. "Any detour or failure has allowed me to regroup, rethink, and go forward," a wealthy female physician told me. "There is always a lesson learned in challenges and failures." The owner of an interior design and architectural firm pointed out the obvious, but helpful paradox: "Part of success is fear of failure." By acknowledging this, we better prepare ourselves when failure happens.

Adriana Holy, M.D., the millionaire owner of the twenty-employee Center for Advanced and Aesthetic Dermatology in Phoenix, has a whole philosophy that helps her remain in control and resilient when faced with difficulties big and small.[3] Her advice, in a nutshell:

- *Always profit from your mistakes.* "My [previous] office manager made a very costly decision and I had to work much harder to make up for it. As a result, I expanded my business, earned much more, and essentially took my business to a new level."
- *Have a really positive attitude.* "Carry that to your employees," Adriana says. Your customers will experience your business in a whole new way.
- *Stay calm by creating a weekly schedule.* Adriana recommends including time for body, soul, and mind. Include exercise at least three times a week and time to get in tune spiritually, however you do that. Also schedule time to be alone, especially if you have introverted tendencies. Being consistently "on" at work drains you terrifically and makes you less able to be creative.
- *Don't run on automatic.* If you are a busy person, this is always a temptation. Adriana explains, "[I am] always seeking out innovative ways of making my business and my practice better."

Learn to Welcome Conflict: Fighting the Good Fight

One Minneapolis female executive said that she learned how to handle conflict when she was moved into a leadership role above many men who wanted the job. "Many of them wanted a 'piece of my pie,'" she told me. Those men clearly felt they could better lead the part of the company she was managing, and she was surprised at the lengths some of them would go to undermine her decisions and credibility, trying to make her look bad. A friend, who was a CEO in his own right, taught her to hold steady and give it right back to them.

In other words, it's important for you to fight "fair" but not allow people to walk on you. Since you may have your financials or decisions questioned, you need to know your facts at all times and have the most current information at your fingertips. Be prepared for anything and think strategically about what might be used against you. This is not fighting dirty; it is self-preservation at the highest levels of business. Think of it as a chess game: an intense, master-level chess game.

Being a good fighter is, perhaps surprisingly, a key to becoming resilient. I have already mentioned that being willing to argue a point to closure is an effective work skill for successful women. In fact, more than 50 percent of the *Millionaire Mystique* women said they feel comfortable doing so. Yet this is absolutely not the case with women in general. Women are typically not willing to engage in this type of conflict resolution, preferring to be seen as "nice," modest, and caring.

Of course, women who are assertive can meet negative responses. Deborah Tannen's classic work, *Talking from 9 to 5*, is a seminal book on the gender differences in workplace communication and a must-read for women embarking on their career paths. Her research has shown that "at work women often take it personally when someone disagrees with them or openly argues." But her research has shown that once you work up the courage to engage your colleagues in "logical animated arguments" and see them through to resolution, it often increases the level of trust between you and your colleagues.[4]

This is exactly what we found with the successful women in my study. Too few women, unfortunately, are willing to "risk it" by getting involved in intense or territorial debates, especially with men. Fighting wisely is the key if you want to prosper—at work and at home.

How can you do that? First, you may have to work hard to overcome your conditioning. Girls are taught to "tolerate" conflict, rather than digging in and learning to fight well. Many girls are taught to feel good when relationships are free of conflict and don't truly understand that strong conflict-resolution skills can lead to better relationships with coworkers. Unfortunately for them, neither corporate America nor business ownership rewards people who avoid conflict, nor does it help women get their needs met at home. You must get comfortable with disagreement and respond according to your work style—use your full quiver of tools:

- Don't lose your sense of humor.
- Know the facts and the data cold.
- Use your relationship with the person involved to figure out what she or he wants.
- Know what *you* want.

By building good relationships in advance, something women are typically *very* good at, you can have a frank debate about the merits of your case while caring about the person you are having a conflict with.

This combination of nice, yet steely, behavior is what many resilient women practice to perfection to get what they want in a conflict situation. By failing to roll over and give in "to preserve the relationship," they keep the focus on the actual matter in dispute. Your challenge is to keep your emotions out of the debate, at least on the surface. When I worked at Honeywell as an employee assistance psychologist, I spent ten years working with the union stewards in tense situations and was often challenged to emotional debates. Because I was able to keep my emotions in check, in spite of provocation, we were usually able to focus on our common goals—whether that meant getting help for someone with chemical dependency or domestic abuse or almost anything in between. This required not personalizing the situation—keeping my "self" out of it. The union stewards came to respect my ability to help them and the 3,000-plus union employees at our Honeywell division.

Each of us has a unique tolerance for conflict and a level of skill for conflict resolution. Women who have grown up in warm but argumentative families are more "naturally" able to cope with the need to argue their points than other women. But, if you have grown up in an abusive family, you may avoid conflict at work. However, you can learn to overcome this hurdle. More than 80 percent of the wealthy, successful women in my study had experienced an "adverse event" in childhood, including 20 percent who had alcoholic parents and a similar percentage who witnessed or experienced domestic violence. Yet many were able to get past the idea that argumentation is the kind of yelling, emotional drama they have experienced in their childhood homes.

If you struggle with standing your ground, try to view conflict as a way to move forward along an agreed-upon path. To be more resilient in the face of challenge, you have to get used to arguing your point to closure using every fact and logical argument at your disposal. And do your best to keep emotion out of the equation—at least while you are arguing. Be prepared for anything by knowing your job and industry well, and think strategically beforehand about what might be thrown at you so you won't be caught unprepared.

It's also essential to be able to identify and ask for what you want. Girls are often taught to get along, to be nice, to share. That often means that they are overly flexible when others make demands on them, and that they fail to be assertive about requesting things from others. My boss at UnitedHealthcare, Dr. Edward Bergmark, former CEO of Optum, taught me a valuable lesson when he made sure I understood that success in the business world hinges on *not* being *overly* flexible when it comes to conflict resolution. Insisting on what you want, he told me, is the only way to make sure you achieve it.

"You can't be wishy-washy," he reiterated to me recently. "Successful people see where they want to go and set a plan to get there. If that doesn't work, they are adaptable and come up with a new plan, which is not the same as being flexible. The key, really, is a stubborn inflexibility. 'I'm going to get around or through that wall even though I now have a big bruise on my head.'" Flexibility, he told me, implies that you're willing to give up, and if that is a part of your mindset, then you won't take the significant risks that are always necessary for a big win. "Yes, you could fail, but that's okay if you can become stronger from your failure." He added, "There are a lot of people who take risks but never seem to learn from failure."[5] Bergmark instead recommends a clear-eyed, hard-headed approach, just the opposite of weak-kneed flexibility.

Resilient people are also pros at managing the pessimism and discomfort that can arise during conflicts. You cope by consciously identifying what's happening in the moment and staying optimistic about reaching a solution. Eastern philosophy calls that consciousness of the moment *mindfulness*. Being present in the moment requires you to step back and observe your surroundings without reacting. Hard to do? Without a doubt. It takes self-control and practice to slow down in a moment of conflict rather than overreacting.

Speaking of negotiation, whole bookshelves could be crammed with the books that have been written about the subject of resolving conflicts in a win-win way. All that advice comes down to two basic insights.

1. You can get more of what you want by *giving the other side more of what they want.*
2. You need to know what you want.[6]

Resilient people are rarely intimidated by conflicts or negotiations because they see them for what they are—two people trying to make sure their own interests are served. By treating conflict as a negotiation between conflicting interests, you're more likely to win, especially if you keep your emotions in check.

Rely on Your Cognitive Abilities versus Your Emotionality

Do you have to suppress your emotions to rise to the top of the heap? Many women think so because they've been negatively reinforced for showing emotions. In my coaching practice, I have discovered that the process of appropriately dealing with emotions (and becoming resilient in the process) is more of a channeling than a suppression. Successful people notice when they are getting emotionally aroused, so they are then able to slow down and consciously adjust their reactions. The *Millionaire Mystique* men and women aren't robots, but they do have an ability to step back, observe themselves as emotions arise, and tolerate their distress. Because of that, they can usually wait (even if just a few minutes) for the intense emotions to subside *before* they take action. Feeling the emotion but not letting it control your behavior is the key to resiliency.

It can be a difficult balancing act to become more aware of your emotions without inappropriately expressing them. Writing in your private work journal, that you keep securely at home, about your emotional reactions to people and situations at work is a safe way to express your emotions and brainstorm possible solutions. As well, you can almost always find a way to postpone dealing with a situation (but not avoid the situation) until you are able to calm yourself. For instance, if you get a call from a reporter asking for a quote about a facility closing in town or a major service problem, tell them that you'll have to call back in a few minutes. Then take some deep breaths and release them slowly to be sure you are completely composed before you call the reporter back. If the stressor you face is less acute and more long-term, make a well-thought-out, written plan to deal with it. For example, if you find your supervisor's style offensive, first identify what's triggering your hot button reaction, then create a written plan for respectfully dealing with your supervisor and moving on with specific tasks and deadlines. Having a written plan can help you deal with emotions over the course of resolving the difficulty because it forces you to think through in advance several possible outcomes and develop choices you can make. Feeling in control always makes you calmer.

Again, it's important to stress that this doesn't mean you should cut yourself off entirely from your emotions at work. Too many times, I have felt like I was expected to deny my emotions, and you have probably felt this way, too. Men and women who attempt to do this almost always fail. Worse, those "denied" emotions may burst out when you are under stress and damage your credibility. Integrating daily emotions into decision making is a much better way to strengthen your resiliency.

What Do Values Have to Do with Resiliency?

Having clear values makes you stronger because you are more aware of what appropriate choices are for you. You are more resilient when you know what you believe. When I ran the employee assistance department at Honeywell, I had my most rewarding and spiritual experiences as an employee and found myself to be very resilient and easily able to cope with a lot of situations that came up. My personality and values were in alignment in this position because I was fairly autonomous and had opportunities to help my clients (Honeywell employees) in a very deep and meaningful way. This happened because the company allowed me free rein to help employees cope with depression, family crises, workplace violence, and other traumas. This work reflected my values of helping people and empowering them to change.

As my experience shows, the more "value alignment" you can create between your personality, your values, and your emotions, the more successful and content you will be, and therefore the more resilient. A job that is a good fit for your personality and allows you to do work that you believe in strengthens your resiliency, too. *Value alignment* specifically refers to the connection between the work you are doing and its personal importance to you. If you feel distressed in a work situation, you should examine which of your basic values is being violated—and by what aspect of the work. To state an obvious example, any organization that would ask employees to violate customer or client confidentiality would clearly be asking most to violate their professional ethics. Having to cope with this kind of stressor regularly would make you much less resilient to other stressors. Often, distress at work means that your values are in conflict with your situation. Try writing a narrative in your work journal about what is happening and how it makes you feel. Once you feel you've completely described the situation and your emotional reaction, identify which values underlie the positive and negative aspects of the narrative: honesty versus dishonesty, respect versus disrespect, helping versus hurting, and so forth. You'll find that this exercise, as simple as it sounds, can help you achieve clarity and therefore increase resilience in personal situations as well.

Four Core Principles of Resilience

Along with their successes, 74 percent of the female millionaires and multimillionaires in my study reported work detours and 51 percent experienced outright failures (very similar to the *Millionaire Mystique* men). But the perseverance and intensity with which high achievers approach their work seems to blunt the negative impact of their obstacles and failures. The classic "pick yourself up, brush yourself off attitude," in other words, helps them navigate through life. They don't dwell on negatives or "rehash" to any great extent, but look for resources and try alternative solutions. They learn what they can and move on.

What is unusual about highly successful people—male or female—as compared to average achievers, is that they often display a singular purpose and commitment to their work and a mental attitude that others can cultivate. Have you ever met someone whose department was being eliminated or downsized and faced this without apparent fear? A resilient leader or manager is likely to be more concerned about your reaction to that news than she is about her own fate. She focuses on calming employee anxieties, the best outplacement options, and what to do next, rather than on her own fears for the future.

Are these warriors created by nature or nurture? As mentioned, a vast majority of the women in my studies had "adverse" events in their childhood backgrounds that may have positively affected their level of hardiness. Regardless of the impact of the trauma in your background, you can strengthen your mental, physical, and emotional skill sets to help you overcome the unexpected and dramatic ups and downs that are inevitable in any life or work. It is essential to meet your own needs, express your own feelings, and learn to say "no" without guilt.

Dr. Salvatore Maddi, professor of psychology and social behavior at the University of California, Irvine has studied resiliency extensively and discovered that there are four basic ways that you can become more resilient and able to cope with anything life throws at you.[7] These include:

- Increasing personal control,
- Enhancing connectedness to others,
- Discovering a sense of meaning and purpose, and
- Developing a sense of hope and positive expectations.

Based on my experience as an executive coach and therapist, I believe that these factors also apply in the workplace. A small number of "supercharged" women seem to have been born with these traits. Others must consciously develop them. Let's look more closely at each behavior and see how you can utilize them in your work life.

Increasing Personal Control

You are in charge of what happens to you. When you are asked to do too much, have inadequate control over employee or financial resources, or are given an unrealistic deadline for a project, your resilience can definitely suffer. To strengthen that resilience, start with small things that will give you more of a sense of personal control. For instance, if you have a project with a challenging deadline, figure out internal deadlines and then create a project plan and a work plan to meet them. Make sure everyone knows what the timelines are, including who is responsible for what, and put them in writing. As you and your team meet smaller goals, acknowledge each achievement.

If you lack sufficient resources to accomplish a project, meet with your boss and peers to jointly decide on priorities. In too many companies, people run around (figuratively) shouting "Outcomes, outcomes!" as if any outcome will do, when the focus should be on thoughtfully planning what outcomes are possible given resource constraints.

Personally, I like to take it one step further by setting goals that cover all aspects of my life from work to relationships. (Remember, I fall very high on the personality trait of conscientiousness, as the majority of *Millionaire Mystique* women do.) I promise that if you take the time to formulate a comprehensive life plan, and think about your values, you will see how all aspects of your life fit together, and you will be able to make the adjustments necessary when difficult choices come along.

Take the time to reflect on your values and the accomplishments that would really be rewarding for you over the next five to ten years. Next, think through what steps would be involved to make sure those accomplishments actually happen. What barriers are in the way? For example, in addition to my professional goal of researching and writing this book, I wanted to make sure all three of my children were prepared for college and were able to successfully navigate their teenage years, with my help. This required putting both personal and professional goals into my plan and establishing both short- and long-term timelines.

Even if you don't go all out with a really elaborate life plan like I do, you can profit from annual or semiannual goal setting. Putting goals and dreams down on paper is actually the first step to accomplishing them. Even if you just write them down and place the paper in a drawer, you'll find when you look at them later that you've achieved some of them, undoubtedly because you've given your subconscious mind "permission" to start accomplishing your goals just by writing them down.

Really successful women, though, tend to be more systematic about goal setting and accomplishment. They break large goals and dreams into manageable supporting goals, make timelines to accomplish them, and set to work getting the job done on time. They also make a list of the obstacles that stand in the way of their goals (including negative self-talk), review alternative choices, and make plans to overcome obstacles. This sounds like a very simplistic approach, but it is critical for high achievement. It is even more critical in times of work and life transition. If you are ambitious, don't skip this step. And if you find that your ambitions aren't clear enough to write down, then recognize that they're probably not clear enough to achieve. Be sure to fine-tune them as needed.

Enhancing Connectedness to Others

Peer confidantes help you establish strong and trusting relationships at work. I recommend that you seek out at least one high-quality relationship at work with someone you can depend on. It also helps to have someone to laugh with about the craziness and to share your triumphs. If you find the right relationship, these qualities are often present in the same person. Such friends are rarer than we'd hope as we navigate the corporate maze, but they are essential, especially in times of stress. If it isn't possible to find a friend at your company, look to your professional associations for someone to share mutual support. With that in mind, if you find that your work environment is simply hostile, find a way to leave. Constant and intense conflict will bring people together to commiserate (no atheists in foxholes), but eventually the toxic environment will drive everyone apart.

Research by UCLA psychology professor Shelly Taylor, Ph.D., has shown that if women reach out to other women at work, it actually decreases their bodies' physical response to stress. She was the first to call these actions "tend and befriend," which we discussed earlier, and she showed that befriending people at work increases the release of oxytocin, which reduces the body's inclination to fight or take flight in the face of stressful situations.[8] In this way, women can be more resilient at work from a simply biological point of view. In contrast, men under stress tend to withdraw and thus find it much harder to break an escalating cycle of stress reactions. Thirty-five percent of the *Millionaire Mystique* women solidly agree that the "tend and befriend" style is helpful at work. Both men and women can benefit from feeling connected and supported by a social network, whether family or friends, to reduce the negative impact of stress.

Discovering a Sense of Meaning and Purpose

People with a "calling" or an overarching purpose in life have been found to be the most resilient to stress. Engaging in challenging activities that enhance your sense of meaningful participation in life can greatly reduce stress because you can channel it into productive activity. Outside of work, women say that exercise, kids, spiritual beliefs, and charity work are among the things that give them a kind of overall contentment that allows the ordinary strains of everyday life and work to flow off to a great degree.

The very lucky—or those who plan well—find deep meaning on the job. When we built UnitedHealthcare's twenty-four-hour employee assistance subsidiary, Optum, it was very demanding, but I was surrounded by people whose values I shared and respected. We were able to build a business to help people cope with life and work-place problems, as well as truly traumatic events like bank robberies, suicide threats, and even the Oklahoma City bombing. I went home every night exhausted, but not too stressed because I had excellent program managers, a cohesive, talented group of counselors, and I felt as if my life had meaning; we helped many people throughout the United States.

Of course, very few people have the opportunity to build a division from scratch or regularly make an impact in life-and-death situations. But you don't have to be involved in something that dramatic to discover meaning at work. By knowing your personal strengths and what makes you happy, you can choose work that fits your values, providing you with great satisfaction. Just read CEO interviews: the most successful men and women always seem to say that they made an effort to find work that really satisfied them and it made all the difference.

Developing a Sense of Hope and Great Expectations

Positive expectations are what allow people to operate on an even keel when everything around them is going to hell. Resilient people, sometimes unconsciously, find new perspectives, trust their own perceptions, and try to find positive outcomes. They appear to others to be naturally hopeful. They find the silver lining in any situation, sometimes to the extent that it inspires disbelief and admiration in those around them: "How can you believe that something positive is going to come out of this mess?" others say. But something positive can always be found, even if it is just a learning experience that allows you to hone skills, increase your knowledge, or make contacts for the next job.

Sara Dial is my ideal when it comes to a resilient person who has always looked for the positive in any situation.[9] She'll tell you that she just plows ahead and does whatever job she is asked to do, but she has impressed many people with her big-idea focus and creativity in a variety of situations, all from a very young age. A graduate of Stanford, with a degree in international relations, she was named the director of the state Department of Commerce in Arizona at age twenty-nine. She eventually left the agency when she had a child and started a highly successful economic development consultancy. She was even asked to return as a consultant to Commerce to change it into a public/private partnership under Governor Jan Brewer.

"I learned to cope from looking at my mom, who was a hospital CEO. She lost jobs, got jobs, and modeled for me that change is just part of life," says Sara. "When change comes to me, I don't melt down. Clients come and go, kids get sick, but I'm always prepared for things to change. I can transition quickly from role to role as mom, wife, and businessperson. I guess I attribute it to being spiritual—that gives me a lot of calmness in my heart. I just ask myself what are the *five* most important things I have to do right now and I do them."

When Sara left Commerce to start her own consulting firm, specializing in government relations and economic development, she was able to attract a stellar client list, including Google, Facebook, Fisher Investments, and Comcast. She says, "Some people, especially women, were critical when I stepped down from Commerce. At some level, that made me want to prove that I could have a successful career after slowing down to have my children. One of my biggest strengths is that I'm a good planner as well as a risk taker. Becoming a mom just made me much more aware of all my actions and decisions." Through good planning, she didn't leave her job until her business was established; she had her first client on "day one" and has been at it for seventeen years, making a very good living in the process.

And in the future? Sara is optimistic: "I'm opening myself up to new opportunities. Now that my kids are older, opportunities just seem to come along and I try to always be open to them."

To combat stress and boost resilience, look for positive outcomes and concentrate on achieving them. This approach lets you ignore much of the day-to-day anxiety of any situation because you are focusing on a part of the big picture, where you can exert control and have a positive impact.

You can also help subordinates become more resilient by helping them concentrate on the possibilities for positive outcomes in challenging work situations, an action that can give you and your team hope. When your employees can't see the possibilities, ask them to brainstorm about ways to resolve the problem in a positive way. Resilient people learn to always reconstruct stressful situations, look for new possibilities and ways to influence others, and find positive outcomes whenever an avenue closes off.

How Resilient Are You, Really?

At this point, you may be wondering just where you fall on the resiliency scale and whether you have what it takes to be a wealthy, successful woman. My answer to that is that almost every woman has what it takes. But some will find it easier because they are already more resilient than average; they were "born ready" to accept challenges and had strong adult role models. Others will need to work hard to develop their resiliency with the techniques I present in the next two chapters. This self-evaluation tool will help you see the changes you need to make.

Resiliency Risk Assessment

Assessing your resilience begins with taking a realistic account of where you are in relationship to yourself, others, and the world around you. Answer the following questions to determine whether you are at risk for resilience or have a resilience reserve.

Resiliency Reserve	Moderate		Resiliency Risk
1. I am aware of, and limit my exposure to, the people and situations that currently erode my self-esteem.			
Definitely yes	**Mostly yes**	**Mostly no**	**Definitely no**
4	3	2	1
2. I nurture and am committed to a network of caring and supportive friends and family.			
Definitely yes	**Mostly yes**	**Mostly no**	**Definitely no**
4	3	2	1
3. I have individuals at work I can confide in and trust.			
Definitely yes	**Mostly yes**	**Mostly no**	**Definitely no**
4	3	2	1
4. I can experience difficult situations and observe my emotions without overreacting.			
Definitely yes	**Mostly yes**	**Mostly no**	**Definitely no**
4	3	2	1
5. I take care of my health through eating a nutritious diet and engaging in regular physical exercise.			
Definitely yes	**Mostly yes**	**Mostly no**	**Definitely no**
4	3	2	1
6. I regulate my use of prescription medications, alcohol, and excessive eating.			
Definitely yes	**Mostly yes**	**Mostly no**	**Definitely no**
4	3	2	1
7. I allow myself to see the humor in life.			
Definitely yes	**Mostly yes**	**Mostly no**	**Definitely no**
4	3	2	1

(continues)

8. I have integrity and my life is a reflection of my values.			
Definitely yes	**Mostly yes**	**Mostly no**	**Definitely no**
4	3	2	1

9. I believe I have control and the ability to act and create a life of my choice.			
Definitely yes	**Mostly yes**	**Mostly no**	**Definitely no**
4	3	2	1

10. When facing obstacles or failures, I accept responsibility for my actions as a first step to moving beyond the problem.			
Definitely yes	**Mostly yes**	**Mostly no**	**Definitely no**
4	3	2	1

11. I am excited by challenges that lead me to grow personally and professionally.			
Definitely yes	**Mostly yes**	**Mostly no**	**Definitely no**
4	3	2	1

12. I am optimistic and feel hopeful about my future.			
Definitely yes	**Mostly yes**	**Mostly no**	**Definitely no**
4	3	2	1

13. I am aware of and seek activities that nourish and renew me even during times of stress and transition.			
Definitely yes	**Mostly yes**	**Mostly no**	**Definitely no**
4	3	2	1

The interpretation of this assessment is simple. The more questions you answered yes to puts you further along on the path of building resilience. The closer you are to a score of 52 translates into a higher reserve of resilience. A score of less than 26 is an indication to implement significant changes to improve your overall life satisfaction and resilience.

Scoring:		
Resilience Reserve	Moderate	Resiliency Risk
52	39–26	13
(Super woman)	(Super charged)	(Super stressed)

While each of these items may not seem important individually, the positive steps added together clearly strengthen you. And, alternatively, each positive step *not* taken decreases your strength and hardiness. Utilize the low scores of 1s and 2s to develop a plan of action for yourself. For example, if you answered *definitely no* to number 13 (*I am aware of and seek activities that nourish and renew me even during times of stress and transition*), perhaps due to work and the time needed for the children, then you should take extra steps to schedule a bike ride, a walk, or another refreshing activity daily, if possible. Hire a sitter or ask your spouse to help in order to get that alone time to recharge.

Write down three action steps to increase your resilience this month.

(For example, *I will be mindful of what energizes and nourishes me and record it in my work journal; I will ride my bike three times per week; I will volunteer at the animal shelter twice a month.*)

1. _____
   _____

2. _____
   _____

3. _____
   _____

Is Your Resiliency at Serious Risk?

Some childhood adversity, if overcome at an early age, may put you on a trajectory toward success, but too many adverse events may make it difficult for you to optimistically problem solve and succeed. Please reflect on and answer the following sensitive questions.

1. I have experienced more than two adverse childhood events, such as an alcoholic parent, emotional/physical abuse, or death of a family member.
   Yes _____ No _____

(continues)

2. I would label my childhood as often chaotic.
Yes _____   No _____

3. I have been diagnosed with mental health issues, such as depression, anxiety, ADD, or a personality disorder.
Yes _____   No _____

4. I have been diagnosed with significant medical issues.
Yes _____   No _____

5. If diagnosed with a physical or mental health issue, I sometimes don't follow through with treatment for my diagnosis, including therapy or medication.
Yes _____   No _____

If you answered yes to more than two questions above, your background may have compromised your natural tendency toward resilience. As noted, having a couple of childhood problems is the national norm and may increase your strength in handling difficulties as an adult. However, too much physical, mental, or family adversity may result in less resilience as an adult. **Excessive childhood adversity requires a very structured plan that you actively work on daily to increase your resilience during adulthood. The use of an employee assistance counselor may be very helpful.**

Mystique Lessons for Aspiring Millionaires

Chapter 7: Choose to Be Resilient

» Take control of what you choose to be stressed out about. Don't get bogged down in the small stuff. Focus on the most important problem and solve it. Then go on to the next one.

» Don't take "no" for an answer. Use "no" as a motivation to prove people wrong and change minds.

» Learn to say "no" without guilt, appropriately express your feelings, and meet your own needs to maximize your resiliency.

» Be open to challenging experiences and learn from the hard knocks you'll get when you take risks.

» Do not depend on the opinions of others. *Millionaire Mystique* women are less dependent on others' opinions; even when fired, they do their best not to blame others but learn from the experience to know what to do better next time.

» Increase your sense of control by refusing to let others define you or dictate your actions. Step back from any big decision and analyze why you are making it—and for whose benefit.

» Practice fighting for your ideas with all the facts at the top of your mind so that you win the arguments.

» Get comfortable with conflict and welcome it as a chance for healthy debate. Stand your ground and don't go along just to be nice. Go for a combination of behavior that comes across as nice but firm.

» In negotiations, increase your results by being cooperative. Try offering the other side something they want. Of course, you'll have to find out what they want first, which requires having a conversation instead of a competition.

» Consciously deal with emotionality in the workplace by being aware of it, tolerate your own distress, realize that your internal dialogue can work against you and problem solve alternative actions.

» Remember that values count. Write in your work journal about any work situations in which you were uncomfortable to determine which of your values were being compromised.

» Increase your resilience by creating and sticking to a life plan, surrounding yourself with a network of people who will support your plan, and finding a calling that speaks to your soul.

» Look for the silver lining in any situation. It will attract other positive people to your cause.

CHAPTER 8

Great Kids, Great Work Life:
The New American Dream?

When I am with my family, I am 100 percent
focused on my family.

*—Female general manager of a health care
business and millionaire*

At the dawn of the women's movement, all we wanted was the
vote. Then America went to war in the 1940s, and women got
a strong appetite for going out to work and earning their own money.
When the boys came home from World War II, women were encouraged to return to the home, to raise kids, and to be happy about
it—and some were, but not all. By the time Betty Friedan came along,
women knew that the "Feminine Mystique," which promised that all
women could be totally fulfilled by home and family, was a myth.

And yet, as women have increasingly taken on leadership roles
in companies or built their own businesses, achieving wealth in
their own right, the challenge of raising happy, healthy kids while
we compete at work never goes away. Many days, especially when
the clients are unhappy and the boss is being unreasonable, we long
to chuck it all and quit. Wouldn't it be easier to just stay home and
take care of our homes, our partners, our kids? Yes, of course it would
be easier . . . until the day we wake up and realize that we are letting

our potential slip by and that we might only achieve a fraction of our life's goals and dreams.

For some of us, these detours seem to be out of our control—at least, for a while. For instance, years ago, due to circumstances I couldn't control (my husband's new job out of state), one day I found myself sitting on my living room floor in a new town where I knew no one, putting together a crib surrounded by three children under the age of two. I had been on a corporate fast track, earning a six-figure salary, and had just earned my Ph.D. I thought, "What am I doing?" I loved being a mom, but I missed my job, my work, my colleagues, and my friends, and I had moved away from family at a time when I needed them most. Even though I had a Ph.D. and high-level work experience, I had hit a career detour due to the responsibility of three babies very close in age. And I was so overwhelmed, I couldn't imagine how I might ever recover my career.

The good news is that many *Millionaire Mystique* women also suffered from some kind of career detour but learned how to thrive again. An astonishing 74 percent of the female millionaires and multimillionaires told me that they had career path detours due to children or other family concerns. In general, such detours can cause women to have fewer years of continuous employment and fewer good job opportunities. Many women's income streams never quite recover from the blow, and they forgo higher financial earnings over their lifetimes. Yet that obviously didn't happen to the women in the *Millionaire Mystique* study. Seventy-two percent of them became millionaires and multimillionaires while raising a family. They became millionaires and multimillionaires despite the detours, even though a full 72 percent of them had children and 84 percent were married.

There are a number of strategies that successful women have used to bounce back from career detours that temporarily throw their paths to the top off course. The most common, among the *Millionaire Mystique* women at least, was starting a business. The president of an executive search firm who has become a multimillionaire told me: "I worked for a large corporation and achieved tremendous success [by the time I wanted to start a family]. After my first child was born, I continued to work and travel until she entered school. [Then] the travel was no longer an option for me, but I did not want to take a drastic step back in my career. [Unfortunately,] my company was inflexible. Out of necessity, I created my own company . . . and now I dictate when I travel and who my clients are. I make more money and have a wonderful work-life balance. I would never have been able to achieve this had I not started my own firm."

Another of our multimillionaires, the owner of an interior design firm, parlayed her family needs and those of her friends into a successful business. "I was the mother of two children and needed a flexible work schedule to fulfill my children's needs. I hired other talented women who had the same family needs as I did. Our business became a very [family-]friendly environment for mothers—and these same women became successful producers." I'll give some tips, later in this chapter, about how to launch a successful business.

Of course, not everyone wants to—or can—overcome a detour by starting a business. Money may be tight or your skills may not adapt well to business ownership. Fortunately, there are still some things you can do to make sure a detour does not turn into a permanent sidelining of your talents:

1. Maintain your licenses and certifications, if you have any. This allows you to re-enter your profession much more easily.
2. Take courses that will help you focus on this phase of your life and what your "new goals" should be. Consider this a chance to get prepared to follow your dreams after your detour. Think big.
3. Stay current with developments in your field by taking continuing education classes and faithfully reading industry journals, blogs, and tweets. Attend industry conferences.
4. Start your own blog in an area of interest, particularly professional. If you take it seriously, interview people who are experts in the field, and regularly provide insider insights, you will soon develop a good reputation throughout your industry and a valuable level of recognition.

5. Consider pursuing part-time or freelance work that utilizes your skills but in a new industry or field so that your resume shows growth during your detour.

6. Practice the resiliency techniques discussed in Chapter 7 and become mentally tough.

The Balancing Act

How have successful women been able to cope with the problems of integrating family and meaningful work that women have faced for at least a generation? In the *Millionaire Mystique* study, I questioned more than one hundred female millionaires and multimillionaires to collect advice for women who are planning to have kids, continue practicing their profession, and become super successful. Their responses suggested that knowing your priorities, defining success for yourself, making deliberate choices, and planning how you will cope with them is the best way to stay on track to achieve great things in your work life. Nowadays, there are creative ways to stay in the game, but you must have a well-thought-out plan that will allow you to remain engaged in your field no matter what your childrearing duties become. Many times, this will require releasing a long-held image of yourself and your work. You may move from a corporate senior leadership position to practicing a professional skill. For instance, although I have left the corporate world, I am now a well-paid executive coach, which is a lucrative and flexible way to apply my skills to help clients while still earning significant money and having a more balanced home life.

The executives I studied recommend that you approach the combination of work and home consciously and meticulously, just as you would any work project where excellence is expected.

1. **Define what "balance" means to you.** Know your truth. Balance will probably not mean the same thing to you as it means to your friends at work. Does it mean keeping all the balls in the air at work and home? Does it mean cutting back hours or

asking for a flexible schedule so you can be with your kids at important times in their lives? If you're working long hours and hating it, does it mean preparing for a career change? Does it mean hiring the best possible help so you know everything is being taken care of? Does it mean making an equal parenting partner of your spouse? Some combination? All of the above? To the extent possible, identify your family and professional goals based on your values. This exercise will help you figure out what steps you need to take to make balancing easier. You might find, for instance, that you need more longevity and seniority at work before you start a family because then it will be easier to negotiate a flexible work schedule. Rise high enough in your company (or start your own) and you can have a direct influence over whether its culture changes to become more family-oriented. It's worth doing. Most of the *Millionaire Mystique* women said that life satisfaction comes from personal, rewarding relationships and making deliberate choices about career goals.

As we each age and move through various levels of development—whether that be completing college, starting a committed relationship, achieving a graduate degree, having children, or taking care of elderly parents—our definition of balance changes. It greatly eases your transitions if you don't hang on to the past too tightly—I encourage you to appreciate your past successes, let yourself grieve your losses, learn to tolerate the "in between" or limbo phase, but then focus on developing/creating your new life.

A recently completed study at Harvard University interviewed 4,000 executive leaders worldwide to study all aspects of their lives. Essentially, half of the women and men reported that—professionally and personally—balance for them had to do with rewarding relationships. Personal success also meant happiness/enjoyment for almost 20 percent and work/life balance and a life of meaning for almost 15 percent. About one-quarter of the women stated "making a difference" and having passion for their work was important to professional success.

The lead researcher on the study, Harvard Business School professor Boris Groysberg, described that the participants had a sophisticated and nuanced approach to balance: "They've discovered through shared experience that prospering in the senior ranks is a matter of carefully combining work and home so as not to lose themselves, their loved ones, or their foothold on success. Those who do this most effectively involve their families in work decisions and activities. They also vigilantly manage their own human capital, endeavoring to give both work and home their due—over a period of years, not weeks or days."[1]

My executive coaching practice has revealed that balance is not only determined by the overall ratio of personal and work balance, but there are various categories within each area that contribute to balance. In other words, *professionally* having rewarding relationships and a life of meaning and happiness/enjoyment contribute to having an *overall* balance in one's life. And, this also applies in the direction of personal satisfaction. Making a difference, gaining respect from others, and having passion for your work lends itself to the overall balance between work and family. *They complement each other.* It leads me to believe that both personal and professional balance are necessary for overall life satisfaction.

2. **Get a good support system in place now.** Whether you have moved to a new place where you know few people, or you've reached other unexpected obstacles, kick your networking with other women into high gear to create a strong circle of support. One woman I know started a networking group in her specialty just so she could get to know high-powered women in her new city. According to Elizabeth Bing and Libby Coleman, authors of *Laughter and Tears: The Emotional Life of New Mothers*, if you plan to have children, your goal should be to create "concentric circles of support" made up of your immediate family, your intimate friends, and, eventually, professional caregivers. "You benefit from having [an intimate circle] who can give you support and advice as well as practical help with child care."[2] To give to others, you must get nurturing love yourself!

While emotional and psychological support is essential, you must also hire good help. Not one of the *Millionaire Mystique* women was able to achieve what she did without some sort of help at home. They recommend having a strong network of paid help to do the more mundane household chores so you can be free to handle the more important childcare duties. The challenge is to find people who come up to your standards, people you can trust with your home and kids. Remember, for every person you hire, it is not going to be a one-to-one substitution of their time for yours. Rather, it is likely to be a one-to-three-quarters substitution once you account for training, paperwork, and the inevitable crises that sometimes keep them at home. As Bing and Coleman remind parents, "Don't be surprised to discover that every potential helper is also a potential problem." I have minimized problems myself by hiring on a trial basis and being very upfront about the arrangement. As a result, I've had some great helpers over the years who eased my mind more than they will know.

3. **Choose the right partner and/or negotiate with the one you have.** Men are beginning to spend more time on family tasks, according to a 2010 Pew Research Center study.[3] Unfortunately, women still spend more than twice as much time working in the home as men do, with more time devoted to "physical care," such as tending to kids' needs. "We are socialized as women to take care of the home," says Tamar Kremer-Sadlik, who teaches anthropology at UCLA. "We are still supposed to be the perfect mother and have a beautiful house."[4] So it should be obvious that one of the most important decisions you can make for your *work life* success is which partner you choose. You want a partner who expresses interest and commitment to sharing the "second shift" of household and childcare duties. Thankfully, more younger men consider this a part of being married than their fathers did. "My husband has been a fully engaged parent, doing his fair share every day," says one appreciative *Millionaire Mystique* woman, a fifty-three-year-old president and CEO in the hospitality industry. Another, a fifty-two-year-old president of a media

and entertainment business, emphasizes how key your partner can be to your success. "One of the most important decisions a woman makes is who her partner is in raising a family. I have an exceptional partner who helps me balance my work-family life." In other words, make sure you share both love and family values with your partner.

If you are already in a committed relationship and have kids you can still negotiate a better balance with your partner, focusing on what the family's current needs are and each partner's work schedule. Sometimes you'll need to take more responsibility and sometimes your partner will. Talk about it specifically. "How do you see us handling nighttime feedings after I go back to work? What will we do if one of the children is ill—could you take time off of work?" If you don't get supportive answers to these questions—if you can't expect to get the help you need from your partner—that should be reflected in your plan to achieve balance in your life. Will you be using some of your compensation to hire a really good nanny? Or will your extended family step in to help? Reliably?

In fact, having a supportive partner, household help, and extended family are the factors that *Millionaire Mystique* women (and men) most often identify as being crucial to their ability to achieve at high levels. The study showed that the *Millionaire Mystique* women actually perform somewhat less household work than the average woman (75 percent of the tasks), which shows that some of them have been able to negotiate this successfully. But they do *significantly* more than the *Millionaire Mystique* men, many of whom are in traditional relationships and only take responsibility for an average of 5 percent of these tasks versus about 50 percent for the women. Makes you admire the *Millionaire Mystique* women even more, doesn't it?

"There is no balance, really, if you want to be successful," one managing director told me. "I had the good fortune of being able to depend on my mother to be there when I couldn't."

Another one said, "I was fortunate enough to have a spouse who was willing to assist me in parenting. We were able to share in that role so that one parent was always available in the evenings."

One male *Mystique* participant, a company president, concurs. "My wife and I viewed all aspects of family life as a partnership and shared responsibility for all such demands."

But do these attitudes and arrangements mean that the actual distribution and performance of tasks at home is equal? No, not in most cases.

Psychologists Alice Eagly and Linda Carli studied the division of labor among men and women and found that, even among wealthy couples and people who hire household help, women still do more of the work around the house. For every hour that American men put in at home, women contribute 1.7 hours. When it comes to sharing childcare duties, the men do even less: 2.1 hours for women for every hour that men work. "If men's nature can't explain why they occupy most of the leadership positions, perhaps the division of labor in the home can," they say, with only a touch of humor.[5]

One Solution: Find a Flexible Company

Today's women want to have it all: wealth, a high-powered career, and a happy family. So what approach should you take? Raising a child will occupy at least eighteen years of your life. However, if you step down from any management or leadership position you have attained, *it will cost you*. In fact, you could forgo hundreds of thousands of dollars in potential salary and suffer even greater opportunity costs in lost benefits and promotions. For example, let's say you are making $150,000. If you stop working outside the home for eighteen years, you'll experience a potential loss of $2,700,000. (This does not take into account promotions or raises; the financial hit could be even worse.)

The bottom line is that you should plan to continue working. And while part-time work may be an option for the short term, if you want to become a millionaire, I do not recommend it. Over the long term, opting out of full-time work or business ownership simply does not work because it can put you seriously out of the career track loop, limiting your earning potential.

A much better solution is to choose one of the companies that now make it easier for women (and men) to raise their families without either stepping off the fast track or going insane. "Ask employees what benefit they most value. Flexibility is at the top of their wish lists," says Cindy Krischer Goodman of *The Miami Herald*. "Flexibility has evolved to mean leeway in where and when the work gets done." Corporate flexibility was, in fact, the number one trend Goodman identified as changing the way we work. She also shared the good news that 80 percent of working parents report "at least a little flexibility" in their current job.[6]

Of course, "a little" may not be enough in your situation. For instance, you may need more extended options than just knowing you can take an hour off in an emergency to take your child to the doctor. I recommend that you use your circles of influence, mentors, and other work-based contacts to find the most family-friendly firms in your area. Some of these firms even allow work from home, capitalizing on innovations like the tablet and mobile hot spot. Technology now allows you to work anywhere at any time, but be cautious about customers' and your employer's expectations for you to always give an immediate response, which could interrupt family time. (In fact, you may want to look beyond your area; many of the *Millionaire Mystique* women actually moved to find their ideal work situation.)

What should you be looking for? Above all, listen with your "third ear" for women in your field who seem comfortable about their home and work life balance. Maybe they are still busy, still caught up in the never-ending activity of raising kids, but there is a confidence in their attitude that you never find in women who have to struggle every day to balance work and family. Talk to them about how their companies adapt to their needs and accommodate their family responsibilities.

Specifically, you should be offering your talents to companies that have specific policies on flexible hours and working conditions that match your needs. Flexibility can include compressed work weeks, telecommuting options, and access to onsite food and fitness. One of the female millionaires told me, "I have always wanted both work and family life and was able to maneuver my career so that

I always had flexible hours to do what I needed to do." Maybe she was lucky, but I believe she fought for a nonnegotiable she absolutely needed in her life and achieved it.

Be upfront about flexibility if you are recruited or are asked for a second interview. This is important stuff that you should not be shy about inquiring into (just not in the first interview). Any hesitation on the company's part to talk to you about it, after the early stages of the interview process, is a huge red flag.

ParentingWeekly.com also recommends seeking out companies with childcare assistance, paid paternity leave, health insurance for dependents, and cafeteria-style benefit plans that allow you to set more of your salary aside, tax free, to benefit your family.[7] But above all, good attitudes toward families should be reflected in what senior leaders say . . . and do. Requiring managers to travel five days a week or risk being left behind when promotions are handed out is not the policy or actions of a family-friendly company, no matter what the annual report may say.

You are in the best position to negotiate flexible demands on your physical presence at work if you have made yourself valuable enough to the company. The key is to figure out, specifically, what will make your life most manageable at various stages in your family's growth and ask for them. (Here's where your planning comes in.) For instance, I worked for twenty years and, once I established myself in my field and Optum had been running well for eight years, I started having children at age forty. Although I wouldn't recommend waiting that long to everyone, I was able to get some accommodation from my employer because of my value to the company. Reasonable demands, backed by a logical case, will likely succeed. If not, find a new company. Simple as that.

A new movement also seems to be developing to modernize the way society is set up to better accommodate work-life balance. Yet there is still a long ways to go. Can anyone tell me, for instance, why schools persist in letting kids off in the middle of the afternoon and for three months in the summer? Since 64 percent of mothers with kids under eighteen are breadwinners or co-breadwinners, families continually have to contend with after-school arrangements that may fall through or simply aren't enriching for their kids. And summers off? Most kids don't do farm work anymore, which is why that tradition started in the first place.

A recent report called "A Woman's Nation Changes Everything," sponsored by Maria Shriver and the Center for American Progress, discovered that, no matter what their political leanings, both men and women want the government to be more active in solving the problem of home-life balance.[8] They found that 64 percent of conservatives (and 80 percent of liberals) want businesses to be required to give workers more flexibility in the workplace. "If there is one clear message emerging from this survey," say authors John Halpin and Ruy Teixeira, "it is that the lives of Americans have changed significantly in recent years, yet the parameters of their jobs have yet to change to meet new demands. Political and business leaders who fail to take steps to address the needs of modern families risk losing good workers."

Another Option: Build Your Own Flexible Life

For some ambitious women, it's just not possible to combine raising a family with corporate life. But playing the corporate game is not the only way to get to the top; in fact, it may not even be the fastest way. For maximum flexibility, you may need to start a business so you can be your own boss. This step may actually be the key that unlocks many opportunities for you. For instance, many more corporate boards, especially the boards of smaller and high-tech companies, are finding board members and executives among the ranks of female business owners. "When you look at the composition of corporate boards, you'll see that many of the outside directors are people with entrepreneurial experience," says Jacque Sokolov, chairman and chief executive officer of SSB Solutions, who serves on a variety of corporate boards. Many top-tier executive women, in fact, spent at least part of their working life as leaders in their own businesses, which can offer greater flexibility than traditional careers in corporations.[9]

That is not to say that the *Millionaire Mystique* women entrepreneurs just chucked it all one day and decided to start their own businesses. Many had planned their transition to business ownership for years with the goal of using their businesses to become financially independent. If you want to follow their lead, then plan to grow your business by harnessing the skills of others to provide a saleable set of products or services. Another good route to equity and flexibility is to start a promising company with a group of people, backed by venture capital money. Many a good business plan, like those for Google and Facebook, has been recognized early with infusions of capital for its owners, who are then off and running.

As you consider your options, it's important to note that one-person consulting companies typically do not put you on the road to millionairedom, primarily because you are limited as to the number of hours in the day that you can sell. I offer my services as an executive coach at $300 an hour, but it is still not nearly as lucrative as if I had a full complement of support people helping me sell and deliver my services.

What businesses should you avoid? You will likely find only heartache if you try to succeed based on a franchise, retail outlet, or restaurant. The profit margins are too small on these businesses (after rent and fees) compared to sales. Volume is the key in retail, and only a tiny percentage of start-up retailers ever attain "escape velocity," where they are returning even a modest profit to their founders. Going-out-of-business sales are all too common these days, and you are most likely to see them at a retail store. Online e-tailing is almost as risky, although at least you don't have rent and inventory to cover. However, you are still at the mercy of fickle consumers who may beat a path to your door . . . or not. And you might not ever figure out why.

The real money-making engines can be found in:

- Small manufacturing, like Sandicast (described in Chapter 1)
- Internet service businesses, like the next Groupon, GrubHub, or Facebook and
- Professional services, like health-care management and the law.

All of these options allow the entrepreneur to capitalize on personal talents while leveraging the work of others to provide a healthier income stream. The eventual sale of the business for a healthy profit should be your long-term goal.

The ideal time to consider entrepreneurship is when you are choosing what to do with your life. But many successful entrepreneurs started their businesses well after a first career, often when they had children and found that their employers were less than accommodating to their needs.

For instance, Adriana Holy, M.D. and current CEO of the Center for Advanced and Aesthetic Dermatology, formed her company and made the decision to leave a large physician group after she had her son. "I was the second highest producer in the practice, and they encouraged me to cut back my hours when I became a mother,"[10] Adriana remembers. "What that really meant was working 90 percent of my regular hours for 60 percent of the money." To make sure she was receiving all that she was earning, she started her own business fifteen years ago, and she has had to hire many nurse practitioners, physician's assistants, and other personnel as service delivery extenders as the business has grown.

Adriana planned almost from the beginning to enter a field that would allow her both flexibility and a high income. She explains, "From the age of five, I wanted to be a 'lady doctor.' I studied at Harvard and went to med school at Northwestern. The sexy, high-status specialties like neurosurgery attracted me at first." Then she dated a guy who asked her if she wanted the lifestyle that went along with that—always busy, never enough time for family. She decided to aim for the field of dermatology because it offered more of a chance to have a normal life, yet maintained the potential for a high income.

Today, Adriana's work as an entrepreneur with an ever-growing client list keeps her on call, but provides enough flexibility to handle the "second shift" at home. "Because my husband was so busy with his medical practice, everything about the house fell to me," Adriana says. With help, she still manages to do it all.

Adriana advises women who want to be successful entrepreneurs to practice "first things first." Put your kids' activities first by making them a priority when scheduling business duties to maximize your focus when you *are* running your business. For Adriana, that meant hiring a house manager and giving up the cooking, which she loves, to concentrate on things that "require a mother's effort."

She also advises hiring nannies and other household help on a trial basis. She explains, "I've come to learn that anyone can present themselves [deceptively] in an interview. The only way you can learn their real attitudes is to observe them in the work environment."

The *Millionaire Mystique* women agree with the need to hire help as you work to build a flexible life. One female executive managing director told me, "I have always traded money for time. I do not use time off to do chores around the house but pay others to do the work."

Develop the Traits of a Good Juggler

Do certain personality types find it easier to transition from committed working woman to committed working woman/parent? I believe that everyone has a chance to negotiate this minefield successfully. However, certain personality traits make the transition easier. These are vital traits to develop, even if it involves taking extra steps to do so.

The most important trait you can bring is a high degree of conscientiousness. High achievers who remain so after having children find that they become very focused and organized, both at work and at home. They write timelines, have to-do lists, and schedule everything, even time for exercise and personal recharging. So far, this doesn't sound much different from the lives of busy executives without growing children, but while the difference for parents is subtle, it's also essential. Because you need to be relaxed and focused on your children—and, ideally, not regimented by a rigid schedule at home—you have to be conscientious about confining your work to the time allowed. Preparing for a presentation could take two hours or ten hours depending on how focused you are on your goals. You have to learn to make it two.

Along these lines, Teresa Taylor, former COO of Qwest and author of *The Balance Myth: Rethinking Work-Life Success*, advises parents to be "present" for their kids at all times when you are with them, and focused on whatever work tasks are highest priority when you are not. For instance, Taylor says that if parents are forced to choose between a soccer game and a business meeting, the *commitment to the choice*—either choice—is what reduces stress. She explains, "You say: 'This is what I chose, so I'm going to do it 100 percent and not feel guilty and not try to do both.' If you try to do both, you do them both halfway. You can't give your best to both places."[11]

One multimillionaire told us what she did to make sure her focus was in the right place: "Children were the priority from five to eight in the evening. Everyone is required to be at the table at six fifteen; everyone senses that they are important to those around them."

Another multimillionaire woman, the owner of an interior design firm, said,

> Because I was in business for myself, I could plan my working hours around my children's needs. I attended school functions and hauled my kids around wherever they needed to go. I still got my work done because I was ambitious and very self-directed. I . . . worked some Saturdays when my husband could watch the children. It helps to have a good marriage, that is for sure. I also provided this same flexibility to the women who worked for me. We often had children [come in] after school hours, working in the sample rooms so their mothers could supervise them while working. In short, we all just did what we had to do. Those who wanted a successful career achieved it, even while being a good mother.

The key to success, no matter how you accomplish it, is to not waste time on unproductive things when you are at work. Focus and be mindful of what's in front of you at all times, whether it's work or kids. Figure out what's urgent and do that first, but don't be fooled by tasks that seem urgent but are really unimportant in the overall scheme of things. And don't let your boss completely dictate priorities—negotiate. Of course, the needs of higher-ups should weigh into your work schedule, but those needs should be subject to negotiation if you don't think those directives from on high are the best use of your time.

Just be sure to get clarification about the relative value of your duties in your boss's eyes. You may not be privy to everything that goes into upper management assignments. Do them well and willingly and you might get on the track for better things. It's all a matter of defining with your supervisor the relative importance of the things you are being asked to accomplish in the time you have.

You probably already know when you are most productive during the day (and it may not be morning). Schedule your most challenging tasks for those hours. Shut your office door, turn off your email and Facebook, and let the phone go to voicemail. Let everyone know that you will not be available for meetings during your golden hours. And then don't be available. "A woman needs to create a 'stop doing' list," reasonably advises the CEO of a hospitality company.

Take a few minutes, also, to make sure that you actually need to have an in-person meeting rather than a conference call or quick chat in the hallway. The parents among your peers (and most of them are parents) will understand. The last thing any of you want to do is have to take work home because you were called into an unnecessary meeting at work.

The hours you spend with your kids is the time when you want to be "unplugged"—that is, focused solely on them and their needs, confident that you have done exactly what you needed to do that day. A home scheduling system is essential for working parents, but you should be conscious of the pressure that it can put on kids. Try to make your scheduling as "organic" as possible so your family doesn't feel like they are marching to mommy's clock or that any deviation for unplanned fun will give her a screaming meltdown. At home, the schedule needs to have a lot of flexibility and extra time built in. Maybe it will take your daughter longer than an hour to get ready for her dance recital. Or your son may unexpectedly want to talk *now*. It's okay to let the schedule slip a little bit—as long as you've built in a lot of extra time to allow for contingencies. *Millionaire Mystique* women are highly scheduled at work, but the wise ones allow for slippage in the schedule. If they are not obsessed with their schedules, they can be relaxed and responsive when they are with their families.

"Sometimes I get tired of being so scheduled," says Adriana Holy, the doctor who started a dermatology center. "But I use my schedule to keep calm. I schedule exercise for myself three times a week, too, and for my husband, six times! It really helps to create a positive attitude and I pass that along to my employees."

The parents in the *Millionaire Mystique* group offered more great advice on how to stay focused at work and at home, based on their long years of experience. One female millionaire, a Canadian health care education dean, recommended, "Commit to spend money on excellent childcare in the early years. It is worth it. Know when to draw the line so that boundaries are respected for family time. I have had to be clear in my own mind what I would and would not do in order to be happy as a mother. For example, international travel is kept to a minimum."

Similarly, one male president of a company, who also participated in the survey, notes that men who schedule well also have more satisfying lives. "I travel a lot for work and that makes balance very, very difficult," he said. "When I'm at home, I focus intensively on family. I quit playing golf and schedule workouts at six a.m. when everyone else is sleeping."

Here's a brief summary of the strategies that the *Millionaire Mystique* women utilized to help them balance their work and home life:

- Define what success looks like for you at home and at work.
- Choose a supportive and helpful spouse/partner to actively share home responsibilities with.
- Create a flexible schedule by owning your own business or choose a company with family-friendly policies.
- Create a competent network of part-time and full-time helpers you can rely on—family, babysitters, nannies, housekeepers.
- Be highly organized with a schedule of your own and the kids' activities: exercise, doctor visits, etc.
- Prioritize, learn to say no, and have a "stop doing" list to preserve your energy.
- Practice mindfulness: Be 100 percent wherever you are—work or home—with no interruptions.

Of course, as Candyce Williams, M.D., told me, "There is not one truth for every woman. What works for one woman would not necessarily work for all women and what you need at a certain time of life is different as the kids get older and stages change." [12]

By now you'll have realized that all of this requires a pretty high degree of negotiation, at least at first, with your spouse or partner, boss, and employees to make sure you have the space you need to be as productive as possible. The more extroverted and open (creative) you are, the more likely you will be able to succeed in these negotiations. Communicate well with your supervisor so that he or she knows what you are working on, what your goals are, and what your schedule is. Maximum flexibility should be your aim. This is more likely in companies that value family life, but is also a possible outcome of an ongoing negotiation with your boss. This is the place to cash in on your previous achievements, because the more valuable your contribution, the more leverage you have. (Remember, I started my family after twenty years of management experience and eight years in my position.)

As we have discussed, negotiation with your partner will almost always be required as well. Many of the *Millionaire Mystique* women, in fact, mentioned a flexible spouse as a vital contributing factor to their ability to continue to be professionally successful while raising children. Almost all of them had managed to share at least some of the responsibilities with their spouses. By contrast, the vast majority of men in the *Millionaire Mystique* study admitted that they had more traditional marriages and sex roles where their wives took care of home and children, leaving them free to focus almost exclusively on work. The downside was that the men worked, on average, five hours more per week than the women did (fifty-two hours versus forty-seven for the women).

Here also is another place where high core self-evaluation is valuable. A woman's personal outlook is everything when it comes to coping with the demands of family and work. Women who know their own worth and are optimistic that they will be able to take everything in stride are more likely to actually get it all done. Think about it. If you can look on the bright side of everything, your enthusiasm will be contagious. And if you, as a manager or an executive, can lead by example, you'll help make your company more family-friendly all by yourself.

A generational shift is also coming as more men and women begin to recognize that while killer hours and slavish devotion to their employer may be a good way to get the highest rewards for their talents, it is probably not the best way to achieve their own personal definition of success if that includes a happy family. Television executives Claire Shipman and Katty Kay predict as much in the book *Womenomics: Work Less, Achieve More, Live Better*:

> So what do you get when you have a workforce full of talented women who finally understand that what they want is to work differently, a substantial percentage of men who are starting to see they'd like the same thing, a much-in-demand younger generation that won't be tied down, a looming talent shortage, and, most important, a staggering increase in the value of women in the marketplace? An explosive chain reaction. And what's so remarkable about the process is that the change isn't just coming in a slow wave, as savvy businesses start to open up their minds and company policies. It's also coming in forceful ripples, as *individual women everywhere*—newly empowered and doggedly determined— negotiate for [what they need]. Every individual success and every act of confrontation chips away at the antiquated structure and adds to the momentum.[13]

For most families, full-time parenthood is no longer a viable option. I was lucky to be able to work part-time and primarily focus on my kids while they were growing up, but to do that I had to step off the fast track and wander around a bit before I started earning lawyer-like compensation as an executive coach. Women who go into this with eyes open, conscious of the possible consequences of their choices and willing to fight for those choices, will not be deterred or slowed down by workplace barriers, as earlier generations sometimes were. In fact, they will use those barriers as stepping stones.

Balance Assessment

This self-reflective assessment is intended to help you see where you may be imposing extra stress on yourself through the way you handle family obligations. Please take the time to think about this and answer honestly.

1. Do I take care of myself physically and emotionally?
   Yes _____ No _____

2. Am I willing to let my husband/partner and others help me raise our children?
   Yes _____ No _____

3. How is this approach similar or different from how my mother raised me? What kind of values or belief conflicts does this bring up in me?

4. Am I prepared for possible disapproval from my own family and others regarding my choices? What will I say as a standard response to questions?

5. Have I identified what kind of help I need?
   Part-time? Full-time?
   Household _____ Childcare _____ Cooking _____
   Shopping _____ Lawn maintenance _____ Pets _____
   Other _____

6. What experience and credentials would my ideal household employees have?

(continues)

7. How might the responsibilities I give to a part-time college student differ from the responsibilities of a full-time nanny?

8. How much will my budget allow me to pay?

9. Household and childcare help needs constant communication and work direction. How will I provide this?

10. How long and what times of the week will I reserve for "just family" time?

Mystique Lessons for Aspiring Millionaires

Chapter 8: Great Kids, Great Work Life: The New American Dream?

» Remember that most *Millionaire Mystique* women who wanted children were able to combine work and family, but almost all of them had setbacks along the way. By taking steps to overcome their obstacles, they still became millionaires.

» Prepare to creatively outsource domestic responsibilities if you plan to achieve millionairedom.

» Know your own personal preferences and family values to define what balance means to you and then get the right support system in place to achieve that.

» Choose a spouse or partner who actively shares in the household and childcare responsibilities. If this is not occurring, renegotiate as needed.

» Work for or start a company with flexible schedules and family policies. Or try to change your unenlightened company. Show them that flexible policies lead to more productive employees of both genders.

» Be conscious about spending time both at work and with family, but be "present" for both, when they are in front of you. Split attention benefits no one and is likely to stress you and your children.

» Schedule your hardest tasks, whatever they are, for when you are most productive. Experiment if you don't know which time this is. You may find yourself flying through work in the late afternoon when everyone else is dragging.

» Be disciplined with your schedule but don't be so rigid that it makes you tense. Having a realistic, detailed schedule to follow is actually more relaxing than rushing through things haphazardly. Encourage your partner and children to help you build your home schedule every week so you'll all have time for each other.

» Schedule in activities for yourself, including exercise and seeing friends. Take care of yourself physically and emotionally every day.

» Change your routine and the support system you have created to reflect the needs of the children as they move through different stages of life (e.g., childcare needs are very different for a three-year-old than for a thirteen-year-old).

» Be kind and generous with yourself. Credit yourself for trying to accomplish a great deal, including a demanding career and a happy home life.

CHAPTER 9

The Unspoken Obstacles
for Aspiring Millionaires

> My strategy has always been to immediately
> demonstrate my knowledge rather than sit back and
> allow for any questioning of my capabilities.
>
> —*Female millionaire and vice president of*
> *operations in manufacturing*

Tom Peters, author of the pioneering business success book *In Search of Excellence*, recently expressed his utter bafflement at the continuing dearth of women at the top levels of major companies to Nilofer Merchant of *Time Magazine* when Mary Barra was named CEO of General Motors:

> Why don't companies "get it" [after all this time]? Women
> are invariably their primary customers. I've run out of logi-
> cal answers, so I'm left with only emotional responses such
> as "blind," "nuts," and "impervious to the obvious." The
> research clearly demonstrates that, overall, women's pref-
> erences for goods and services and the manner of the pur-
> chasing process differ significantly from that of men. What
> better, and, frankly, easier way to address this mammoth
> opportunity than to aim for/insist upon women's represen-
> tation, from junior engineer to board member, that more or
> less mirrors purchasing power?[1]

Good question, Dr. Peters.

Who would have thought that, so long after *The Feminine Mystique* was published, we'd still be witnessing criticisms of former Secretary of State Hillary Clinton that are based on her appearance rather than on her ideas? In 2012, for instance, the media went ballistic when Clinton showed up in India as secretary of state without makeup. *Elle* magazine then criticized her for wearing her hair in a scrunchy.[2] What about her policies and actions? And who would have believed that Janet Yellen, the first female head of the U.S. Federal Reserve Bank, would be subjected to stereotypes like the repeated accusation while she was a candidate for the job that she somehow lacked the "gravitas" to lead that organization? This was called out by Paul Krugman of the *New York Times*:

> Well, suppose we were talking about a man with Yellen's credentials: distinguished academic work, leader of the Council of Economic Advisers, six years as president of the San Francisco Fed, a record of working effectively with colleagues at the Board of Governors. Would anyone suggest that a man with those credentials was somehow unqualified for office? Sorry, but it's hard to escape the conclusion that gravitas, in this context, mainly means possessing a Y chromosome.[3]

Perhaps we shouldn't be surprised that factors unrelated to merit continue to stand in the way of women on their way to the top. Most men and women have experienced some type of prejudice and discrimination, whether it is due to gender, race, or disabilities, or even the schools they've attended. And it is a given that certain groups experience more discrimination than others, making success a more elusive goal. We asked the *Millionaire Mystique* women this revealing question: "In your career, have you personally experienced prejudice or discrimination just because of who you are?" Five out of every ten women reported having experienced gender prejudice and discrimination *that affected their work lives.* And an astonishing 98 percent said there were specific obstacles for women in work and financial success.

Those roadblocks included outsized responsibility for child and family care, stereotypes and sexism, exclusion from mens' networks, pay inequality, lack of mentors, and expectations that women will always act like men. The majority of both genders agreed that women face these challenges twice as often as men.

Many of these obstacles involve either blatant or latent *prejudices*—learned negative attitudes, thoughts, and feelings that people have about others of different ages, genders, races, sexual orientation, religions, and so forth. These prejudices are then used as justification to treat others differently simply because they are a member of a certain group. The act of denying a promotion or an interview to someone due to their natural attributes is discrimination. And it's not just women who experience it. Six percent of the *Millionaire Mystique* men reported that they had also experienced prejudice or discrimination due to their gender.

Yet if you were to survey your coworkers or friends on the issues of workplace prejudice and discrimination, many people would say that it no longer exists. As a group, we would like to think that we have moved beyond the need to judge others by their age, gender, religious affiliation, sexual orientation, or the color of their skin. In fact, when it comes to gender, sexism is still an active problem in the lives of women, whether they are aware of it or not. A businesswoman is seen by many people as qualitatively different from a businessman, even before their individual talents are evaluated. "I was told that I was too attractive to be successful," said a fifty-year-old president of a health-care consulting company and multimillionaire. And a female partner in a real estate firm told me, "I found some clients just didn't want to work with a woman."

Scientific studies have, in fact, repeatedly found that female contributions to projects are rated higher when observers can attribute them to a man.[4] As noted earlier, even the term *leadership* is thought of as male.[5] And some research shows that people of all ages and genders prefer to work for a male boss, making it even more difficult for women to succeed in leadership roles typically held by males.[6]

My purpose in including a chapter on prejudices and discrimination is not to discourage you. Rather, I want to put us all (men and women) on notice that the fight for true equality must continue until "female" or "Asian" or "African-American" are no longer news-worthy qualifiers that journalists must include in stories about our successes. After all, when was the last time you read about a "male" CEO being named at a company? "I dream of the day when her name and ideas make news, not the fact that she is a woman," says Nilofer Merchant of *Time* about General Motors CEO Barra.[7]

Fortunately, these negative attitudes are changing as more women excel at leadership, but it's possible that they may never go away completely. In the following sections, I offer some insights and tools you can use to minimize their impact on your rise to the top. After all, our *Millionaire Mystique* women didn't let the obstacles they faced stop them.

Subtle and Unspoken

Today, prejudice and discrimination are not as blatant as they once were. Years ago, it was pretty clear when someone was holding a prejudice against you. For instance, one woman told me about an experience that occurred early in her career: "As the first woman loan officer, I encountered resistance from some customers (par-ticularly women) who thought I was a secretary and would ask to speak to the 'real' loan officer." I had many similar experiences with clients who expressed visible disappointment to have been assigned to a young female therapist as their family counselor.

To make things worse, subtle, covert, and so-called *benevolent* sexism leads women to question their own abilities. This actually results in poorer work performance than occurs when they encoun-ter more obvious forms of sexism.[8] The benevolent sexist may be an older gentleman with preconceived notions of what women want and need, but it is just as likely to be an older queen bee who believes she is superior to other women. Benevolent sexists tend to take it easy on female employees, but they will be the first to pass them over for a promotion because they are not "tough enough."

So what causes people to lean toward stereotypes in the first place? All of this is more understandable if we think of it in evolutionary terms, specifically the fight or flight response for self-preservation. People are still hardwired to react quickly to new stimuli based on limited information: "Is it a tiger?" Their primitive reaction to meeting us may be to see only our overt qualities like sex or race. This can cloud subsequent meetings and set an unconscious pattern going forward in a relationship. For instance, in the workplace, quite unconsciously, a tape may roll in their heads at every subsequent meeting with us that tells them that there is something about us that makes them uncomfortable or uneasy. This is not something most of them are conscious of. They may react without being thoughtful, even though they may not consciously consider themselves to be prejudiced.

In other words, all of us have an inborn desire to initially treat people more as stereotypes than as individuals, in order to more quickly classify them as friend or foe. Daniel Kahneman, emeritus professor at Princeton University and author of *Thinking, Fast and Slow*,[9] spent more than twenty years researching our tendency to react before thinking. Kahneman uncovered that we have two ways of thinking: *automatic* and *deliberate*. To take one example of automatic thinking, let's consider a male executive who works sixty hours a week under high stress during a merger. He then receives a very tight deadline to promote one individual at the expense of others, so he defaults to the male candidate for the position because that candidate is most like him. In times of stress, we default to what we're comfortable with, what seems safe and secure, because it requires less energy and thought. In such situations, deliberative thinking doesn't come into play because, in a crisis, our minds can deal with only small amounts of information. The corporate executive has a cognitive bias toward loss aversion, which causes him to fear losses more than he values gains. He may not even consider added information such as a female candidate's greater education, longer work experience, and stellar leadership skills. Instead, he makes a quick decision based on self-preservation. If he makes the wrong personnel move during a merger, his own job is likely to be at risk. Despite these automatic reactions, people today are aware (if they think about it deliberately) that sexism and other prejudices jeopardize the well-being and overall success of organizations. And it has personal consequences as well. Whether the prejudice or discrimination that you encounter is subtle or covert (or evenly delivered), and whether it involves ageism, racism, or sexism (which is most often reported by women), you can feel it. The key is to acknowledge its existence in your work and social environments, because this awareness can help you manage its impact on your work life. Believing that it isn't important, that it is a thing of the past, or that it's somehow your fault is not the answer. Rather, allowing yourself to see the prejudices opens you up to learning to overcome them.

The Elephant in the Room: Ethnic Prejudice

People would like to believe that racism is not as prevalent as it used to be, especially in the workplace. Unfortunately, it is. Many women face the dual issue of racism and sexism, which further complicates the pathway to success. Your own individual experience will determine whether racism or sexism (or ageism or any other prejudice) is the most important roadblock to your own success. We no longer face "whites-only" facilities or job ads classified as "male only." But such things were common in the United States until the 1960s and still echo in our lives. Candyce Williams, M.D., director of spinal cord injury rehabilitation at St. Joseph's Hospital and Medical Center in Phoenix, is an African-American member of a biracial household.[10] She recalls that her mother, Nellie, was told she couldn't sit in the "whites only" section of a doctor's waiting room in Louisiana. "Yes, I can," her mom replied. No one said another word.

The values taught to Candyce by both of her parents were the importance of family, hard work, and education. She knew she was loved and felt a fierce protectiveness from her parents, and she observed firsthand her parents' determination to help make a better world for her. There was never a question about whether she would attend college. Both of Candyce's parents attained master's degrees in the 1940s, at a time when only 10 percent of the entire U.S. population received graduate degrees. This encouraged her to follow a career path dictated by her intellect—an undergraduate degree on full scholarship at Vassar, medical school at Duke, which she paid for with a National Service Corps Scholarship. That required her to provide medical care at several rural clinics in Illinois. She was, to put it mildly, not what the doctor ordered for some of her patients. She also experienced troubles getting a job in the same town as her white husband—in the 1990s! And yet she does not perceive that she experienced very much racism or sexism personally, perhaps because of her attitude and her accomplishments.

Candyce grew up with racism as a part of her everyday life. "My entire life I have known racism." She experienced racist comments at school, in restaurants, and by just walking down the street. "It was especially bad when I went to an integrated school at age ten." With healthy disregard, she lumps the prejudiced individuals she has met into the category of "asses" and sees their ignorance as a personality flaw. "I identify a person for what they are, label (the bias) for what it is, and set clear limits. I keep racists, misogynists and sexists out of my inner circle." It appears that Candyce makes a determination about an individual and, if they are racist or sexist, chooses not to give the interactions with them any thought or energy. She clearly has more important things to focus on, such as helping patients achieve their best possible outcomes even when confined to a wheelchair.

Today, prejudice and discrimination have gone underground, which actually has made it much more difficult to root out and eliminate. You may notice it in the form of joking wordplay, inadequate eye contact, or avoidance behavior.

Did He Really Say That in Front of Everyone?

Unless you work at a truly egalitarian company, you've probably already experienced thoughtless, sexist remarks from your coworkers or those in the professional organizations you belong to. Or not so thoughtless. If you observe carefully, you'll notice that the men or queen bees who feel that their status is threatened tend to engage in the highest degree of "playful" sexism. They are using it as a way to gain power.

Sexism is common and prevalent, perhaps more so in male-dominated fields, perhaps less overt in female-focused workplaces. And it becomes more common as women rise in leadership. One female millionaire told me:

> I worked in an industry that was an old boys' network and was treated like a little girl. It did not interfere with my success because they all thought I was harmless and went after each other as competition. It meant that I could quietly succeed on my own.

You need to have some tools ready in case you are confronted with blatant discrimination of any kind. Your most powerful tool is a strong internal compass to know where you are headed. A female millionaire told me about an incident that happened in her male-dominated industry:

> One manager came down very hard on me during a management change, and when I balked he laughed and said, "I was just trying to make you cry. I needed to know how tough you were." I called him out on it and he lost my respect. Interestingly, he was fired long ago and now I'm in senior management. So who really won?

Here are some other steps you can take.

- Do not allow the behavior to go on without trying to stop it. Calmly and firmly ask the individual to stop, even if you are in front of a work group or superiors.
- Acknowledge that there is a problem. Don't worry about appearing rude.

- Try an indirect approach: Refrain from laughing at sexist or racist jokes.
- Utilize your own humor to deflect comments. As Aristotle said, "The secret to humor is surprise." They'll be surprised when you return the volley.
- Never retaliate with prejudiced remarks of your own: "Men are all . . ." No, they're not.
- Don't let fear of retribution stop you from keeping the dialogue open. Never let prejudice go underground where it can fester.
- Seek out mentors who have navigated the issues and obstacles that face you.

Enlist the help of your boss, if necessary, to directly confront the offender. Think twice, though, about filing a lawsuit. Equal Opportunity or wrongful dismissal lawsuits are sometimes necessary if you can prove that you were fired because of discrimination and could collect back pay and damages. Unfortunately, these cases are very difficult to win. To combat discrimination that affects you personally, a more direct approach may have a better outcome. I suggest that you consider developing a personal strategy for thriving in a still-sexist society as most of our female millionaires and multimillionaires did.

Another option is simply to leave. One of our participants told me that she recently found out that her counterpart in another department, a man, was both earning more than her and benefitting from a bigger budget. "He was hired after me and didn't have the level of skills I had. As a result, he burned through his budget, hiring consultants left and right. One of my peers told me, 'this guy has one skill—he knows how to hire consultants.'" She decided to start a job search and ended up moving to Southern California, an area where two of her children were living. "I needed to be able to navigate my own course and not be defined by someone else's parameters," she said. She offered the following advice to readers: "If you have the financial resources personally, you do not have to acquiesce [to situations like this]."

Playing with Prejudices: Archelle Georgiou

Archelle Georgiou has done a lot of things to achieve financial success—doctor of internal medicine (Johns Hopkins graduate), chief medical officer of a multibillion dollar health-care company, Fox News health-care commentator, and, most recently, consultant to companies wanting to market innovative products.[11] She explains that she deals in facts, is direct, and is numbers-focused, but that she also loves to laugh and be sociable. Through it all, she's fought the perception that she is "too strong, too intimidating." She identifies the focus on that perception as one of the most important gender issues facing women in leadership. "If I was a man, no one would think twice about it, yet I got feedback from my mentors that I needed to make sure that people felt free to speak up."

Archelle has found that, although she's actually become stronger over the years, both superiors and subordinates appreciate her more because she has taken steps to ensure that her style is less confrontational. "One client told me that I come in with 'a velvet hammer,'" she laughs. In the past, she admits, she often reached conclusions too quickly, without seeking consensus. "My attitude was: If they don't get it, that's their problem." But she consciously moderated her style anyway so she couldn't be seen as "too pushy or too masculine." Her communication style now has both feminine and masculine elements and she tries to treat everyone equally . . . "I actively avoid using the pronoun 'I' in favor of 'team' and 'company,' and I often say 'Help me understand this result. People now trust that I will listen before making a decision."

Getting Past It: Overcoming Prejudices and Fighting Discrimination

Unlike Archelle Georgiou, too many women internalize their setbacks and failures. They blame themselves and lose confidence in their abilities, whereas men tend to blame outside forces and retain a high opinion of themselves. A friend of mine, Robert Bohannon, who spent most of his career in the highest reaches of companies like General Electric and Viad Corporation, is convinced that people often participate in limiting themselves. He strongly states, "The only person that can define me is me. Never let anyone else define you. There are barriers, but people are breaking them every day. You want to be one of those people."[12]

I agree. Women can and do rise to the top. But if it were easy, you'd be a multimillionaire already and wouldn't need to read this book, right? As noted, sexist behavior is common, and denial and avoidance do not work. The goal is to insulate and strengthen yourself against sexism from the first moment you recognize it. Let's look at some additional steps you can take to make discrimination a non-issue for you personally.

1. **Realize that you can't do much about people's automatic reactions.** People literally cannot help their instant reactions to you. If they are wired to be prejudiced, their initial reaction will still put one strike against you even if they don't want to feel that way. The best way to cope with such reactions is to be friendly and undeniably competent. Said one female millionaire: "I took steps to become friends with men who were in positions of power so that they were happy with our friendship. [I assumed and was right] that other men would see that and follow." Another suggested something that sounds like it comes from a 1950s dating manual, but is almost certain to work: "In working with others, especially men, who were known to be difficult, I would ask questions about their jobs, let them talk, and ask them if my organization was helping them meet their goals. I would also ask for their ideas for solving a problem I was having. Men love giving advice!"

2. **Don't take "no" for an answer.** Few people and organizations can resist a persistent person who doesn't threaten them directly. There are two basic reasons for this. First, most people are too busy (or lazy) to put up a vicious fight for territory they don't find valuable, and will give up eventually. Second, and most importantly, the resisters come to admire (however grudgingly) the

person who is willing to fight for what she wants. This female millionaire has the right idea: "I am *extremely persistent* and smart. I can usually find another route to what I want if one is blocked. If I were a man and this smart, I would easily have been head-hunted all the time with many more opportunities for promotion. As it is, it takes a lot for me to give up. I am very resourceful." Notice what she said—there are many routes to your goal. If you really want it, you just need to find one that is not so heavily guarded.

3. **Claim your seat.** Sheryl Sandberg says in *Lean In* that women should be assertive in claiming what would be rightfully theirs if they were men. But, she says, forward-looking men who want their companies to prosper must also step up to the plate. Her advice? Women: Don't sit in the background. Claim a seat at the table. Men: Welcome them.[13]

4. **Capitalize on and celebrate your appearance.** Several *Millionaire Mystique* women mentioned that physical attractiveness had been a problem for them. (Well, a problem for the men around them, actually.) One was told directly that she was too attractive to be promoted; another felt that men were judging her as "stupid and unable to contribute" because of her appearance. Another said, "Overcoming my physical appearance has been the most difficult factor in my life." Attractiveness—or just being female—can bring unwanted attention and comments. This is even true for women who are not conventionally attractive. It's just a misuse of power, a way to make women feel less powerful. I've experienced this, as well, and I can testify that it is your job performance ultimately that helps people see beyond your exterior. But there are other things you can do, too. Good humor is an effective tool to defuse any charged situations. And while one female millionaire suggested dressing in "severe" clothing, I think Archelle Georgiou, the Fox News health commentator, actually has the best idea: "Too many women try to hide their attractiveness. I've discovered that I could use my attractiveness—appropriately, that is—to my advantage to get attention, then I could sell my ideas."[14]

5. **Don't take it personally.** I have counseled hundreds of people over the decades and have found that all of us tend to personalize our crises. When a woman is starting out in her work life, she may not realize that obstacles and failures happen to everyone. No one can expect a career path strewn with roses and a steady series of triumphs. Nearly all of our *Millionaire Mystique* men and women described significant and harsh setbacks during their working lives. A lot of them had experienced severe prejudice and discrimination that closed off some avenues of advancement. Some had lost high-paying jobs, while others had seen businesses fail. The person on a high trajectory at work simply does not take failure personally, but rebuilds what was lost. What differs for each of us is the depth of loss of core self-evaluation (positive belief in ourselves) and how long it persists. In other words, the super-successful woman has developed a higher "set point" for her feelings of self-worth than average people have. Your goal should be to increase your personal set point over time and put the blame in the right place when you are hit hard by discriminatory behavior.

6. **Work hard, negotiate harder.** If there is one thread that goes through all of the comments of our *Millionaire Mystique* participants, male and female, it is that super-successful women work incredibly hard. One attributed her success to "having passion and the tenacity to make things happen." But when you are faced with blatant discrimination, what's the best course of action? Archelle offers an example of the right way to do it: "I was offered a promotion, but the title and salary weren't commensurate with the role. I accepted it anyway . . . and decided that I simply had to *prove myself.* Two years later, I was clearly adding value to the company. When they asked me to sign an employment agreement, I took the opportunity to negotiate—HARD—and won."

With that in mind, as noted earlier, in some cases the best option may simply be to walk away if you are not being rewarded for your work. Walking away can be especially hard after you've put in a lot of time proving yourself, but you should recognize that your time has not been wasted. Rather, you have also added value to yourself, which will be recognized by another employer or can be used to start your own business. Sometimes there is no other choice. "I left a company that seemed to recognize men more than women and started my own business," said one study participant. "Inequity in pay and promotional challenges awakened me to new opportunities elsewhere," said another. I confidently expect that one day in the near future, corporate America will realize that they cannot afford to let their best talent leak away.

One Last Bump in the Road: Reducing "Stereotype Threat"

Dr. Claude Steele, a social psychologist who is currently the dean of the School of Education at Stanford University, is known for studying how stereotypes about any group, overt and covert, can affect the performance of people who fall into the stereotyped group, whatever it happens to be. This issue is known as "stereotype threat," and it also has strong workplace implications.[15]

We know what the general stereotypes in our society are for women and men—women are not good at math, men are ignorant about emotions, women are too emotional to lead—it goes on and on. According to Dr. Steele, we internalize these stereotypes and, when we come face-to-face with a situation where we need to perform, they become active and may distract us from performing at our highest level. A specific example of stereotype threat is a female applying for a management position in a male-dominated company. This woman, even during the hiring process, wouldn't see many women working there. It may activate unconscious assumptions or anxieties that she is not qualified for the job. This could easily cause her to underperform in the interview and not get the job.

Factors that can reduce performance even further often exist when a task is especially difficult or you feel your ability is being measured. So how can you minimize the effect of prejudices and the resulting performance anxieties of those involved? First, use positive self-talk to reduce this reaction in yourself. Remind yourself, for instance, of all the women you know who are doing well professionally. Then try the recommendations of professors Steve Stroessner from Barnard and Catherine Good at Baruch College, on the website reducingstereotypethreat.org, to manage any stereotype threat you or your subordinates encounter[16]:

- Reframe the task. Make sure that people understand that anyone who is properly trained can do the task.
- Provide individual encouragement and awareness of your employees' specific talents (e.g., "You've done great financial projections for us before").
- Provide performance standards and reassurances of your confidence that the person can perform the task.
- Point to role models (female, minority, as appropriate) who have successfully performed at this level—this step can actually improve performance.
- Point out that performance anxiety can have an external cause, including stressors like starting a new job or taking on a new task, unrelated to the skills needed to perform well.
- Encourage your people to view their skills as evolving and certain to become stronger over time.

With proper preparation and encouragement, employees can overcome their anxieties caused by their expectations that people will view them differently because they don't fit into the company standard, whatever that is. And as our workplaces become more diverse, the issue of stereotype threat will hopefully diminish because overall expectations will change. For instance, at IKEA, which is based in Sweden, 47 percent of its 17,000 managers worldwide are female. "We develop all of our coworkers [male and female], and [ensure] that diverse coworkers will get the same opportunities for development," says CEO Peter Agnefjall. "Having enough diverse and competent successors for the future will secure the future success of IKEA." It must be working: Worldwide sales for IKEA increased by 9.5 percent in 2012, while prices were cut by 8 percent. Eleven new stores opened in nine countries, and twenty-five more stores will soon be opening in India. The company's goals are to double sales by 2020 and have 50 percent female leadership globally at all levels. That's the kind of representation that puts prejudice to bed because then people are just people judged on their merits alone.[17]

Wake Up, Corporate America

All of us who achieve leadership roles have a responsibility to identify and reduce prejudice and discrimination and to minimize obstacles in the pathway for women who want to be successful. As leaders, we have an obligation to find ways to nudge our employers into creating more equitable work environments. Otherwise, we'll continue to lose half of our most talented people, women who will find ways to escape. They'll quit, start their own businesses, and leave us with the old guard protecting its status quo, innovation be damned.

Unfortunately, according to researchers Alice Eagly and Linda Carli, even in female-dominated fields, men advance more rapidly than women. The terms most often used to describe good leaders have masculine connotations as well: *decisive, analytical,* and *charismatic.*[18] Fortunately, as more women earn the titles and responsibilities at the top, our definition of a leader will almost certainly change.

One way we can make corporations friendlier to women is by practicing transformational leadership ourselves, as recommended by our female and male millionaires and multimillionaires. This leadership style levels the playing field by emphasizing traditionally female personality characteristics, including:

- Providing praise and recognition to employees,
- Basing goals on the values of the organization,
- Being transparent,
- Communicating to motivate employees, and
- Providing professional development.

Leading in this way can demonstrate that women are just as talented as men when it comes to managing an organization. And in a more egalitarian organization, no one is treated differently.

Another way to support women, say Drs. Eden King and Jennifer Knight in *How Women Can Make It Work: The Science of Success*, is to make the workplace a prejudice-free zone. Top management must display and articulate a real commitment to ending discrimination of all kinds, a commitment that shows up in mission statements and training. There should also be a zero-tolerance sexual harassment policy. Companies, say King and Knight, should develop a network of reporting mechanisms that guarantee that claims can be made "without fear of retaliation."[19] Training, including for new hires, and regular organizational assessments of both prejudice and discrimination should happen often enough to gauge success or failure.

Let's Own It—All of Us

So, if prejudice and discrimination have such obvious institutional underpinnings, why do we often question ourselves when we become aware of something not quite right about our interactions with others? Why don't we place the blame where it belongs—on the people who are judging us automatically, by stereotypes? Simple. Because we've "come so far," it has become something of a faux pas to bring up any lingering prejudice or discrimination we notice. It flies in the face of the well-established and researched fact that women gain self-definition and self-esteem through relationships. Bringing up examples of subtle sexism at the company lunch table rarely strengthens relationships or builds harmony with anyone. Bringing it up to the power holders in an organization could even impact your next promotion or threaten your job. Nevertheless, I believe that it must be called out and identified. Otherwise, sexism and other forms of discrimination will continue to be toxic to working women.

Sheryl Sandberg, CEO of Facebook and widely admired author of *Lean In: Women, Work, and the Will to Lead*, notes:

We were taught to fit in, but . . . I was starting to think this might not be the right approach. I said out loud that there are differences between men and women both in their behavior and the way their behavior is perceived by others. I admitted that I could see these dynamics playing out in the workforce, and that, in order to fix the problems, we needed to be able to talk about gender without people thinking we were crying for help, asking for special treatment, or about to sue. . . . Shutting down discussion is self-defeating and impedes progress. We need to talk and listen and debate and refute and instruct and learn and evolve.[20]

Are you ready to recognize and deal with discrimination in your workplace? If you aren't, you not only will hurt yourself, but you may also limit the younger women in your organization who are starting to look up to you as a role model.

Mystique Lessons for Aspiring Millionaires

Chapter 9: The Unspoken Obstacles for Aspiring Millionaires

» Be aware that prejudice and discrimination still exist, even though they are now likely to be subtle and unspoken or play-fully delivered. Either way, bringing prejudice and discrimination out into the light can help weaken their power to hurt your career. Don't laugh at demeaning jokes or deflect them with the same kind of humor.

» Acknowledge the potential prejudices of others. Remain strong and assertive. Exceed everyone's expectations through your performance. Just refuse to let prejudice and discrimination get in your way.

» Don't take "no" for an answer, especially if it is based on people's automatic reaction to you as a woman.

» As Sheryl Sandberg tells us, don't reinforce prejudice by acting in ways that diminish you, like sitting in the back of the room. Take a seat at the table, right up front.

» Capitalize on your appearance and celebrate it. Wear bright colors if that is what you are comfortable with, and be a presence in the room. Draw attention to yourself and then to your abilities.

» Don't take it personally. Prejudice and discrimination are *not* your fault. Find the right time and negotiate hard for what you deserve.

» Help your employees be strong in the face of prejudice they may experience in the workplace or the marketplace. Hire more nontraditional employees to bring new perspectives to the party. Make sure all your employees are treated equally.

» Talk about prejudice and discrimination openly and encourage everyone you work with to do the same. Call it out whenever you see it. That's the only way to make it stop. Silence just makes it stronger.

CHAPTER 10

For Your Greater Good: Earning Satisfaction

I always feel like if there is something you can do to help someone, you should do it. Because honestly, I care.

—*Pat Petznick, founder of Fresh Start Women's Foundation and multimillionaire*

I've identified two final qualities that high-achieving women have in common: One, they manage their money wisely and two, they love to give back.

If you think about it, these are two sides of the same coin, so to speak. Most women, and particularly the *Millionaire Mystique* women, don't see money as an end in itself. They are more likely to see it as a way to help their families prosper, to give their children a good start in life, and to fund a secure retirement. Most wealthy, self-made women don't spend a lot of money on themselves. Spend $100,000 on a diamond and sapphire necklace? (Easy to do, if you have the money.) Oh, please. Women who grew up in challenging circumstances, like most of the *Millionaire Mystique* group, just wouldn't buy something like that. They'd prefer to invest their money for the future or donate it to a good cause.

Successful women would much rather give back to the community by donating their money, starting charitable foundations, raising money, and volunteering time. I am personally very involved in an organization called the Fresh Start Women's Foundation in Phoenix that helps unemployed women and displaced homemakers find their way back to gainful employment, financial stability, and higher self-esteem. Fresh Start has spent twenty years empowering women to transform their lives. I find it both satisfying and invigorating to take some time out of my busy schedule to help others.

I'd like to spend a little time discussing both money management and giving back because they are crucial for women who actually want to *feel* like they have achieved success. Looking at big numbers on a paycheck may be satisfying for a little while, but even that can grow old if you don't have a clear idea of how to maximize your money to achieve the greatest good.

The *Mystique* of Money

Leah Hoffman was determined to maximize her financial success from an early age. She and a partner started their own independent financial management business, The Hoffman and Hock Group, when she was just twenty-nine years old.[1] Leah's experience is similar to many millionaires and multimillionaires in that she did not grow up in a family of wealth. So why did she go into financial services to find her success?

For starters, she had always been good in math, had experience as a bank teller, and had attained a business degree in college. Leah began in the insurance side of the financial industry (Equitable Insurance) and observed friends and family members grapple with financial decisions and how to responsibly handle their finances. She believes that growing up without much money gave her the inner strength and initiative to want to be financially successful. Learning to manage your own finances well, she believes, is a first step that will "give you choice, freedom, and greater life satisfaction."

So, when she was offered an opportunity by the oldest independent investment firm in the country to buy them out, Leah grabbed the opportunity. She took out a small loan and she and her partners used much of their savings to make the buyout happen. The previous owner was confident Leah would handle his clients well during the transition and protect the integrity of what he had built. In 1996 her firm became the first independent firm in the country to transition to a fee-based financial planning practice (as opposed to a commission-based company). She also became a registered investment advisor and acquired a more sophisticated client base. She and her partners made the specific decision to cater to female clients, who had been underserved by the investment community. She incorporated in 1989 and sold the business in 2007. At the time of the sale, to R.W. Baird, she had $500 million in assets under management on behalf of her clients, and she ended up with a payday in the multiple millions.

The female millionaires and multimillionaires, like Leah, who answered our detailed *Millionaire Mystique* survey were remarkably consistent about the factors that contributed to their high net worth. One wealthy female business owner told me, "I learned years ago from a very good financial advisor who taught me that 'no one cares more about your money than you.' You have to be knowledgeable about investing and finances; don't leave it up to someone else."

If there is a formula for growing rich, the *Millionaire Mystique* women have found it. Let's take a closer look at Leah's ideas.

1. **Get stock options or profit sharing.** Don't be afraid to ask for what you want. People respect those who know their worth. Negotiate for better everything every time you get a new job. "If someone asks about your salary expectations, don't be timid," a fifty-two-year-old president of a Colorado health care consulting firm advised, based on her own experience. "If you think you're worth it, say so." Vitally important: Negotiate for stock options once you get to that level of management. "My compensation package put nearly 50 percent of my upside pay at risk for

performance," another female multimillionaire, the fifty-three-year-old president and CEO of a Virginia hospitality company, said. "As a result, my earnings have increased dramatically." And every employee should look for companies with generous 401(k) plans, including a contribution match. Start a profit-sharing plan if you own your own company, and contribute the maximum amount to it or establish a pension plan. Buy the building your business is in. Constantly track financial performance against budget projections.

2. **Avoid debt.** One *Millionaire Mystique* woman advises "having a good rapport with the local bank in town." This is a good idea if you own a business because a flexible line of credit will allow you to expand to meet opportunities. But many of the wealthy women specifically advised avoiding loans and other debt. One fifty-eight-year-old Tennessee human resources consultant and millionaire noted that she pays off her credit card bills every month, no matter what, preventing rates of 18 percent or more from gouging out her savings. Great idea.

3. **Keep your life simple.** Many of the women in the *Millionaire Mystique* study mentioned "living under our means" or "not spending money I don't have." In fact, most of them save a significant part of their earnings, with retirement and college funds for children as top priorities. They also take steps to help make sure their college-age kids are economically independent after graduation.

4. **Understand the power of cash.** If you pay cash for things, you'll tend to save more for the future and spend less. You'll know in your gut that even if you can afford to spend $1,000 on a purse, it doesn't make a lot of sense to spend that much on something that will wear out or go out of style. The same goes for small cash expenses. It's unbelievable how much an expensive cup of coffee adds up to if you stop every day and add a breakfast snack to your bill. I recommend formal budgeting to help you understand your expenses and get them under control. The best first step is to account for every cash expense. Sound like too

much trouble if you are making a significant income? Not at all, if you want to keep what you have earned.

5. **Invest in the value of time.** *Millionaire Mystique* women allocate their time and their money with an eye toward building wealth. Leah advises starting as early as possible to invest as much as possible. One millionaire bought her first house at age twenty; another started saving for retirement at twenty-two. A quick and dirty way to estimate how long it will take to double your money is the so-called Rule of 72. Just divide the interest rate or growth rate into 72 to get the number of years required to double your money. That's why it's not a good idea to keep a lot of money in CDs or cash these days. At 1 percent interest, $100 doubles to $200 in 72/1 = 72 years. Much better are investments that promise steady growth over time, like the stock market (an average 3 percent annual return over the long term) or some type of multifamily or commercial real estate.

6. **Diversify, wisely.** Women who build up wealth understand the value of investing in a wide variety of instruments. Most of them own stock, bonds, and real estate or real estate investment trusts; a surprising number invest in businesses, either their own companies or as venture capitalists investing in the innovative ideas of others. Once they attain sufficient net worth, investors can also take part in the initial public offerings of firms going public and large bond offerings. Investing your income should be as high a priority as your job is—because it has an even larger impact on your net worth. Use caution, though; one multimillionaire advised strongly against "getting involved in business with friends or family."

7. **Consult a team of advisors.** My female millionaires advised building a trusted team of financial advisors: investment advisor, accountant, attorney, and banker. Don't be afraid to change your team if you feel uncomfortable with any of the advice you get. Wise investors do not depend completely on investment advisors, but make the effort to educate themselves on investment techniques like Warren Buffett's famous value investing.

Otherwise, especially if they don't grow up around money, both women and men can be stampeded into selling into a market downturn and buying at the top of a market. Good investors have already recovered—and more—from the Great Recession (2009–2012). That's because they hung on to their portfolios when everyone else was selling their investments and, thereby, locking in their losses. The key, say most female millionaires, is to get good advice but make informed decisions on your own. One study participant explained, "I tried to keep a 'beginner's mind' so that I wouldn't bring expectations and assumptions that would cause me to miss things or to be disappointed if things did not follow my map."

8. **Don't fall into the "love syndrome."** Unfortunately, says Leah, too many women executives cede all personal financial decisions to others. Perhaps unconsciously, many women come to believe that they are not qualified to handle finances or that it's a man's job. "Once they get home from work, they focus on children and home and avoid financial decisions. I call that 'the love syndrome,' when relationships get in the way of sound financial management." Some women may too easily give away money to help people. Others may be tempted to leave finances to their spouses. They may also sign prenuptial agreements without deciding whether they are going to have children and without consulting an attorney, a poor decision that is often based on a belief that such a consultation would not be romantic and a fear that it might jeopardize the relationship. Instead, it's essential to realize that divorce is very common these days, and that women can become impoverished if they have joint accounts that spouses can legally empty or if they sign joint tax returns they don't understand. Just because you don't understand a form doesn't mean you aren't on the hook for back taxes if your spouse or ex refuses to pay. I advise women to maintain separate accounts for their income and investments, with joint accounts for joint expenses only. And please don't sign a prenuptial agreement if you are going to have children

because, most often, these agreements do not allow flexibility if your circumstances change.

The Power of the (Closed) Purse

Once you have money, you also need to be careful how you spend it if you're going to maintain your financial position. If you purchase a large home, make sure you have enough income to furnish and maintain the property. Nothing demonstrates too big of an investment in a home than not being able to maintain it.

The authors of *Millionaire Women Next Door*, Thomas Stanley, Ph.D., and William Danks, Ph.D., note the following distinction between average consumers and millionaire women:

> For most people, "enjoying the money" means spending a lot of it on oneself. It translates into bigger, more expensive homes, luxury automobiles, expensive clothing, and other possessions. But not for most self-made wealthy women. . . . Most are happy. They are content because they have fulfilled their need to be self-reliant and have become self-made affluent. They have discovered that happiness can be achieved—and, actually, greatly enhanced—without their becoming hyperconsumers.[2]

For some people, earning a significant amount of money creates a psychological urge to spend. They adopt an attitude that says, "I worked hard, I earned it, so I should be able to spend it." *Millionaire Mystique* women talk, instead, about making a plan for "wealth creation" that involves more investing and less spending. Almost all of them told me that they pursued a sound, clear-eyed approach to money their entire work lives. You, too, are in charge of whether you become wealthy or just pile up material goods to impress other people. "I love 'things,'" a forty-six-year-old CFO in the architecture business and millionaire told me, "but I am willing to save money rather than spend it on frivolous things."

Giving Back to Attain Richness

In our research, we discovered that most *Millionaire Mystique* women in the study no longer needed to work to pay the bills—they had accumulated enough to feel comfortable. Just over half of them still worked because they found it rewarding. But a significant chunk of them were devoting most or all of their time to causes in their communities or the world. One of them is Pat Petznick, the woman who discussed her challenging childhood in Chapter 2. She sold her business twenty years ago in order to establish Fresh Start to help other women and has no regrets. Pat told me,

> At some point, you realize that you have choices. I could have played a lot of golf and had a lot of lunches, but that would not be fulfilling. I knew I had a talent for opening doors and I wanted to do that because I knew I could help women.[3]

Pat and her sister Beverly began giving makeovers and motivation to women in need in her upscale salon twenty years ago. After passing through a "dark time" after her dad died and she experienced health problems, she began to realize that she would always be able to get help because of her wealth. "But what if I hadn't been well off?" she asks. Fresh Start evolved into an organization serving 5,000 women per year and raising millions to build and fund a women's center and ongoing programs. Pat's skills at opening doors and building relationships got Banner Health to donate land for the Center for $1.00 per year for ninety years. She obtained the help of talented architects from HKS for design at no cost, and she arranged for a company to donate the services of a female engineer for two years to expedite the building process.

Pat credits her grandmother, Audie Foster Dryer Jones, for inspiring her to give back. Audie lost a husband very early in life and raised two little boys alone, in poverty, one of them Pat's father. "Anyone at any socioeconomic level will feel welcome and get help changing their lives at Fresh Start," says Pat. "It makes you feel good to know how many lives you are changing." You can't help but feel that Pat's life has not only helped so many women, but has also changed her own by giving it an overarching purpose and meaning.

William O'Brien, CEO of J Bio Anti-Aging and former U.S. Marine, pointed out that giving back is important for good leaders and for people who want to rise to the top:

> Leaders should always do what they know is right. People know what is best for the greater good of everyone. Leaders have become very self-focused in the past decade and we need to return to working for the common good of your organization and your country.[4]

As a woman with ambitions, you may think it's impossible to find the time to offer your services to people outside your family. Granted, being altruistic and giving to people outside your family is quite difficult at certain times of your life, particularly when little kids are involved. Yet if you can find a way to manage it, then you'll see that the rewards are endless. Let me give you some more motivation.

You'll live longer! A British researcher, Dr. Caroline Jenkinson, and her colleagues examined more than forty studies of volunteering and concluded that those who help others on a regular basis may be less likely to die early.[5] Three-quarters of our *Millionaire Mystique* participants said they are in very good to excellent health.

You'll feel better! Dr. Jenkinson and her colleagues also discovered that volunteers may have reduced rates of depression and an increased sense of life satisfaction and well-being. "Doing good helps them feel good," observes Maia Szalavitz of Time.com, who took note of the study.[6]

You'll be in a better mood! Dr. Sonja Lyubomirsky, professor of psychology at the University of California, Riverside, found that "people with a tendency toward depression can help themselves by helping others or otherwise introducing positivity into their day-to-day lives."[7]

You'll be more satisfied with your life! If you can find a cause—or a company—that is doing things personally meaningful for you, you'll be more fulfilled than the average person. Activism, psychology researchers Malte Klar and Tim Kasser proved, is associated with greater life satisfaction, personal growth, and social connection. It's quite simple: Doing things for other people, in the company of like-minded souls, just makes you happier.[8] Perhaps it's not surprising, then, that *Millionaire Mystique* men and women report higher life satisfaction than most people.

Do you have time to make your life longer and better? Scientists believe that you can maximize your benefit from volunteering at about ten hours a month. Spending more time than that may force you to sacrifice time from other areas and may lead to burnout instead of fulfillment. Never take on more of a commitment than you can easily manage, even though this will require the courage to say "no" to many compelling causes. Pick the one that's right for you so you don't make promises you won't be interested in keeping.

Do you want to do more of what you do at work? Should you be a treasurer if you work with numbers all day? Maybe, if numbers are your passion. Or maybe you've always wanted to be an event planner. Plenty of fundraising galas are looking for a maven. (I have been the co-chair of the Fresh Start Women's Resource Center Programs and Services Committee for six years—a perfect fit for a psychologist!) Carefully consider the duties you are taking on, as well. Do they fit your personality and your work style?

Giving back clearly benefits the person giving. For those aggressively pursuing their careers, it can also be a necessary relief valve that helps to cut the pressure and raise your level of personal satisfaction. It doesn't really matter what "other-focused" activity you engage in. Stress relief can come from both charitable work or simply sharing knowledge or resources with colleagues.

Giving back can actually be *healing*, though, if you choose to devote your time to help people in the areas where you experienced obstacles in your own life. If you have experienced poverty, alcoholism, discrimination, abuse, or other serious troubles, find ways to help people going through the same experiences. Being an activist in an area where you have had problems yourself indirectly helps you heal. At Fresh Start, many volunteers experienced the wounds of abuse some time in their lives, for instance, and see volunteering there as a chance to put old pain to rest.

Mystique Lessons for Aspiring Millionaires

Chapter 10: For Your Greater Good: Earning Satisfaction

» Note that wealthy people don't get that way by spending money on "things." They are much more likely to save, invest, and support charitable work. They spend very little on themselves, relative to what they could afford.

» Avoid the trap of buying what you don't really need—radically adjust expectations to fit your current budget if your life has changed.

» Multiply your money. Figure out ways to maximize profit sharing or stock options, avoid debt, live below your means, pay cash, invest as much as you can as early as you can, and diversify.

» Don't fall into the "love syndrome." Your financial future and your spouse's are going to be connected, but you shouldn't suffer if something goes wrong. Consult financial and legal advisors before signing any legal documents.

» Reflect on how your individual personality traits affect how you spend money.

» Budget money to support causes that give meaning to your life. Giving it away is fun, rewarding, and can heal your soul.

» Volunteering your time to a cause you feel passionate about can actually energize you and make you healthier.

» Giving back allows you to learn new skills, practice skills you need at work, or simply feel good about helping people and more grateful for what you have.

Conclusion:
Becoming a Millionaire . . .
Your Own Way

D o you have what it takes to become a millionaire or multimillionaire? You should have a better idea about that now, having read this book. But one thing should be perfectly clear: Almost anybody can achieve breakthrough success—millionairedom—no matter where they started in life. You just need to want it, very much.

Almost none of our *Millionaire Mystique* women were born into money. Most of them are true self-made women, who rose to the top through their own efforts. A good number of them experienced significant setbacks and traumas in their early lives. Nevertheless, they responded to a mysterious alchemy that determined whether someone will want to be financially successful. And, for the most part, it is that fire in your belly that makes the difference. You'll be willing to sacrifice a lot, and work incredibly hard, if you decide that being successful and wealthy is important to you.

Of course, luck plays a part in where you end up in life. In their book *Luck Is No Accident*, career development psychologists John Krumholtz, Ph.D., and Al Levin, Ed.D., encourage people to "take advantage of chance events, to keep your options open and to make the most of what life offers."[1] Even if what life offers, sometimes, is failure. "Unexpected events are inevitable. But if you are alert, you can make the most of them when they happen."

You can't overlook the fact that even the wealthiest people in the *Millionaire Mystique* study failed, sometimes repeatedly. They persisted, they tried again, they found champions, and they worked their social networks until they succeeded. Careful planning, good money management, and a determination to capitalize on their personality traits helped them to become millionaires and multimillionaires on the strength of their efforts alone. And then they gave back, generously, to help others as they had been helped. Trust me, these are some of the most satisfied people you will ever meet and not just because they have money. I hope you will join us soon.

Appendix:
The Research Behind the Book

A s the examples in this book have shown, women and men can achieve the same level of stellar career success, with the right preparation, education, determination, and conscientiousness. The gender differences we once thought prohibited women from advancement can be parlayed into what we have found to be the most effective tools in building an organization—trust, communication, and relationship building.

Fifty-one percent of the 103 *Millionaire Mystique* women were millionaires and 49 percent were multimillionaires—a truly unique group of women who had traversed multiple obstacles to succeed. Their average annual income was $307,000. They were business owners, corporate executives, CEOs, CFOs, and senior partners in a variety of industries, from sales and marketing to finance, health care, and architecture. In addition to having wealth, they reported that their overall life satisfaction was higher than the normal population and their health was very good to excellent. This appendix has been created to provide you with more specific details about this unique group of women.

Family Socioeconomic Backgrounds

Surprisingly, the family socioeconomic backgrounds of the women we studied were not remarkable. Most of our *Millionaire Mystique* millionaires and multimillionaires were from middle-class and lower-middle-class backgrounds, which may have induced their drive to "prove themselves" and improve the socioeconomics of their lives.

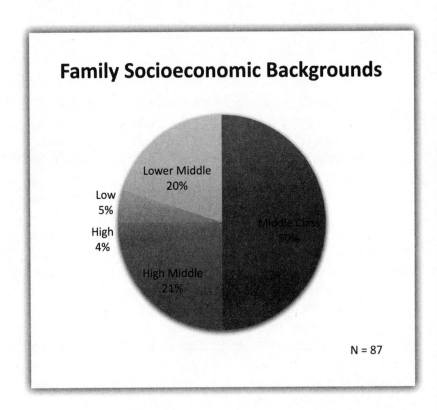

Childhood Challenges

The *Millionaire Mystique* women also had their share of difficulties in childhood. Most of them had childhoods that included two to eight serious and painful events, an average of two per person. This group was not protected from "real life" difficulties; rather, these successful adults may have developed hardiness and an ability to manage problems at an early age, which then helped them later in life to be resilient and overcome personal and career adversities.[1]

Childhood Adverse Events	Women Millionaires (N = 89)
Serious illness for self or family member(s)	36%
Death of family member or close friend	35%
Alcohol or substance abuse of parents	22%
Divorce or separation of parents	21%
Victim of abuse (physical or emotional)	20%
Witness of abuse (physical or emotional)	18%
Low income or poverty	17%
Moved frequently	10%
School problems	8%
Added family siblings	7%
Other	9%
Average number of total events per person	2

Educational Achievements

The *Millionaire Mystique* women's educational achievements are worth noting, as this group is far more educated than the average American woman. There is a strong link between education/intelligence and higher lifetime income and career success.[2] This data speaks to the importance of being fully prepared for the career you choose.

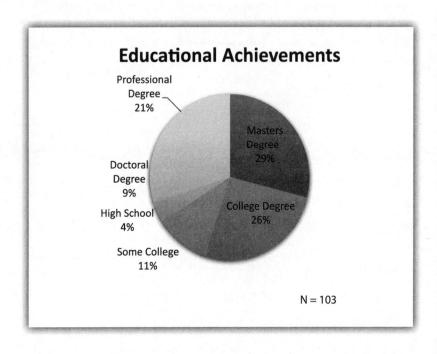

Parents' Accomplishments

The parents of *Millionaire Mystique* women also had educational and business accomplishments worth noting. Their mothers and fathers were far more educated, on average, than the U.S. norms, even if they were in lower- or middle-class socioeconomic groups. These parents modeled the importance of both attaining a college education and entrepreneurship, which instilled in their children values of education, appropriate risk taking, and independence in business.

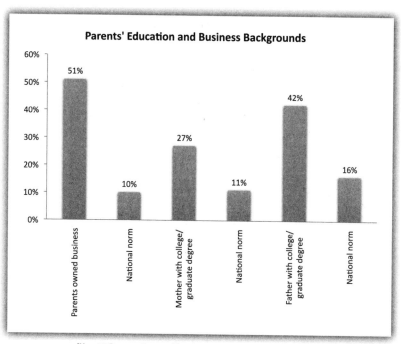

(N = 61 Parents' owned business; N = 81 Parents' educational attainment)

Overall Life Satisfaction

The *Millionaire Mystique* women's breakthrough career success increased their overall life satisfaction, although this was not necessarily tied to making money or creating wealth. Rather, these women found that being successful and having a passion for their life's work contributed to their overall sense of well-being.[3]

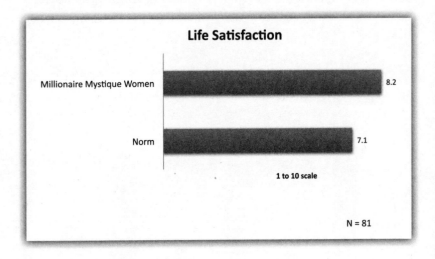

Personality Characteristics of Super Successful Women

Understanding and developing the personality characteristics that lead to success can be a great asset in your personal and work life. Researchers who have studied highly successful professionals report that the personality characteristics shown here in bold in column 1 are critical to success. In addition, a low level of neuroticism and and average amount of self-esteem can increase focus on achieving goals by reducing "background noise" and producing a higher level of positive feelings. Other research links a positive core self-evaluation with occupational status, pay level, and job satisfaction.[4]

Personality Characteristics

Women Millionaires HIGHER than Norms	Women Millionaires LOWER than Norms	Women Millionaires SIMILAR to Norms
Conscientiousness **Agreeableness** **Resiliency/flexibility** Extraversion Openness	Neuroticism	Positive Core Self-Evaluation

Bold print reflects a large statistical difference from the norm.

The Importance of Owning a Business

A significant majority of our high-achieving millionaires currently owned businesses or had owned them in the past (70 percent). On average, in the U.S., far fewer people in general own businesses—just 10 percent. Owning a business seems to be a significant indicator of potential for breakthrough success.

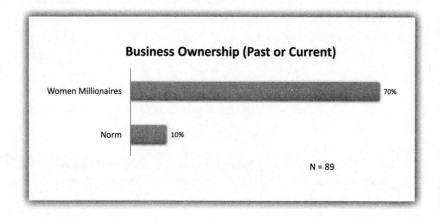

The Work Styles of Millionaires and Multimillionaires

The work styles of high achievers are different from those of average people ("the norm") in three dimensions: work engagement, flexibility, and social engagement.

First, the *Millionaire Mystique* women were committed to and passionate about their work. Higher work engagement is linked to higher job performance and higher quality of work output.[5]

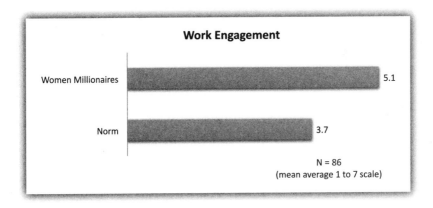

Second, millionaire women adopted a flexible and agreeable style at work as a way to develop cohesive teams and accomplish goals. They found changes in routine interesting and challenging.

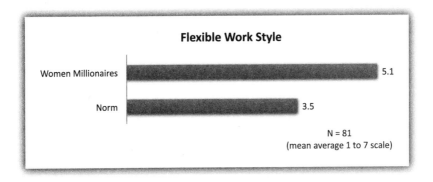

Third, the *Millionaire Mystique* women used highly developed interpersonal skills to understand and positively influence others. In other words, they practiced being politically astute. They easily developed good rapport with people and communicated easily and effectively with others. Research shows that high social influence skills are also associated with less social stress at work.[6]

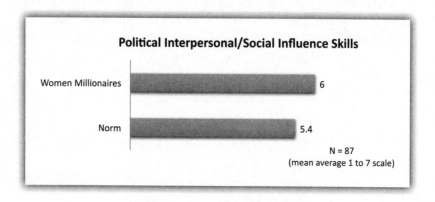

Mixing Masculine and Feminine Behaviors

The *Millionaire Mystique* women used a mix of what have been considered feminine and masculine behaviors at work—including relationship building and assertiveness techniques—to accomplish the job. Flying in the face of stereotypes, very few of these women expressed only behaviors that are considered as masculine at work.

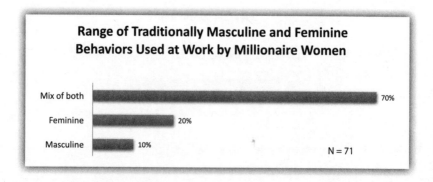

On the other hand, 35 percent of our research participants stated they deliberately toned down their traditionally feminine style at times in professional settings.

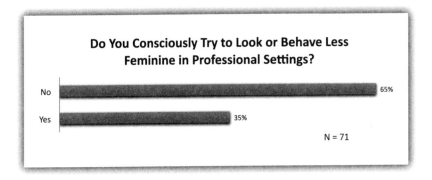

Skills for Handling Conflict

High-level executives encounter work problems that often do not have easy resolutions. This necessitates being comfortable with conflict, having assertiveness skills, and not personalizing debates. While past research cites women's difficulties in negotiating conflict, over half of the *Millionaire Mystique* women were comfortable arguing a point to closure and had been told by others that they were argumentative. Learning conflict negotiation skills is important for women on the road to success.

Comfortable with Conflict	
Willingness to argue a point to closure	51%
Others have told me I am argumentative	62%
	N = 80

Relationship-Building Skills

The *Millionaire Mystique* women were competent and valued building relationships through authentic acquaintances and friendships. Their networks facilitated professional activities and enhanced their careers.

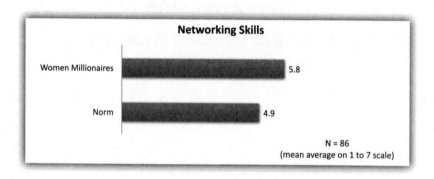

Networking Skills

Women Millionaires — 5.8

Norm — 4.9

N = 86
(mean average on 1 to 7 scale)

"Tend and Befriend" Work Style

The women and men in the *Millionaire Mystique Study* were similar in that they were friendly at work, but had clear boundaries. But, there were differences in how many social activities and close personal work relationships they participated in.

	Women	Men
Participate in work social activities	60%	36%
Have close work personal relationships	57%	44%
Friendly, but don't share too much personal information	73%	71%
		N = 126

The Value of Seeking Out Mentors

Sixty-six percent of the *Millionaire Mystique* women had mentors with senior work experience and knowledge who provided support and guidance.

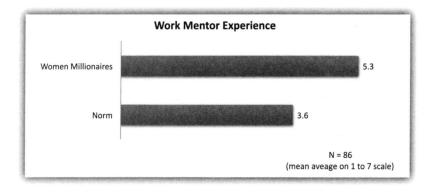

The Foundations of Breakthrough Success

The male and female millionaires and multimillionaires reported similar fundamental career experiences that were foundational to their success.

Recommended Foundational Career Experiences
(in descending order of importance, but all rated highly important)

Networking with others

Diversity of jobs throughout career

Challenging positions/assignments

Operational/line experience

Management experience

Start your own business

Create your own positions

Work for good organizations with good managers

Education/licensure/certifications

N = 125 Millionaire Mystique female and male millionaires

Detours on the Way to the Top

Seventy-four percent of the *Millionaire Mystique* women stated they had career detours and cited the following challenges to attaining success. Career detours were common. If you expect to take detours from your own path, you should plan for them in advance whenever possible.

Career Path Detours

1	Childbearing/childcare/family	41%
2	Job change	26%
3	Started own business	24%
4	Relocated for spouse	20%
5	Personal illness	17%
6	Marriage	17%
7	Back to college/grad school	15%
8	Illness/other	13%
9	Divorce	10%
10	International travel	8%
11	Bankruptcy	4%
12	Trauma/abuse	1%
		N = 64

Gender Differences in the Personal Lives of Male and Female Millionaires

While the personality traits and work behaviors were similar for wealthy women and men, there were gender differences in their rates of marriage, children, salaries, career detours, and rate of discrimination.

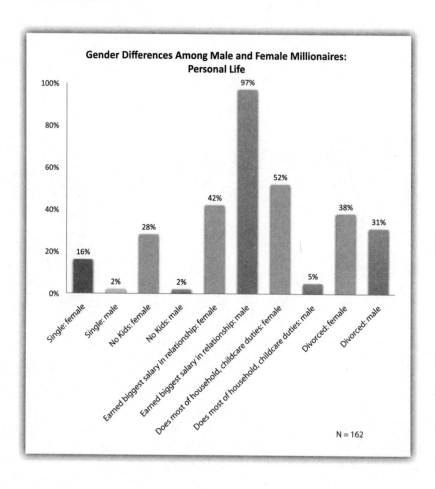

Gender Differences in the Career Progression of Male and Female Millionaires

Millionaire and multimillionaire women were less likely to experience work failures than men. They were more likely to experience career detours and prejudice that affected their upward trajectory, despite ultimately making it to the top anyway.

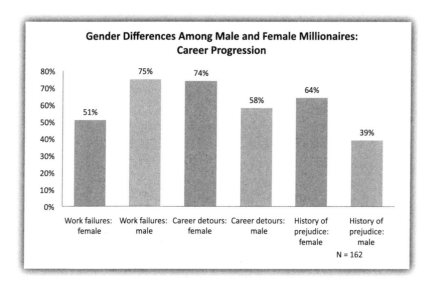

What Both Genders Say about
Obstacles for Women

The *Millionaire Mystique Study* also gave the successful men who were bosses, business owners, fathers, and husbands the opportunity to anonymously tell us what they observed about women in general at work. Almost *nine out of every ten men* stated that women had obstacles to their career success due to their gender. And, an astonishing 98 percent of *Millionaire Mystique* women say that obstacles to success still exist for women today.

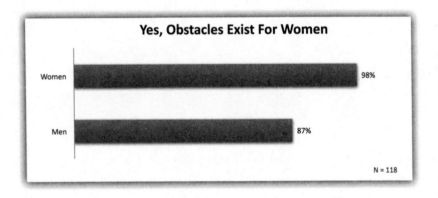

Here is a list of the specific work obstacles for women noted by both male and female *Millionaire Mystique* participants.

Specific Work Obstacles Faced by Women (Rank order)

1. Women are responsible for child and family care needs.
2. Women face stereotypes and sexism from others.
3. Women are excluded from men's professional networks.
4. Women lack self-confidence and assertiveness.
5. Women lack mentoring.
6. Women lack pay equity.
7. Women are expected to act like male leaders.

With that in mind, the *Millionaire Mystique* women gave very valuable advice about how they overcame obstacles to continue on their road to success.

Steps to Overcome Obstacles (N = 50)

Work Orientation

- Be passionate and tenacious about your product/services.
- Have a vision, be creative, and maintain the inspiration to lead.
- Focus on achieving measureable/definable goals.
- Take risks, be focused, be decisive, and work hard—put in the needed hours.
- Create a family-friendly work environment in your own business.
- Continuously develop your industry knowledge and join professional associations—attain specialty licenses and degrees.
- Take management and leadership development courses.

People Skills

- Develop great communication skills to create teamwork built on trust.
- Know your values and strive to maintain them—proactively create a culture.
- Build a strong network of friends, colleagues, and mentors.
- Use your compassion to understand others—be authentic, kind, generous, and make male and female friends at work.
- Believe in yourself; improve your self-esteem and assertiveness skills.
- Choose a supportive partner and balance family, work, and spiritual beliefs.
- Make yourself interesting, read good books, and be knowledgeable about current events.
- Remove emotions from decision making—don't make conflict personal.

Gender Differences in Leadership Experiences, Challenges, and Styles

The *Millionaire Mystique* men *and* women acknowledged that leadership is different for women in many ways.

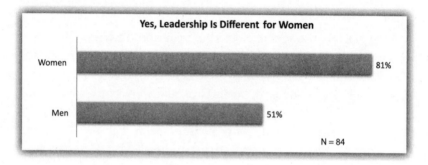

Then, a larger group of Millionaire Mystique male and female leaders (N=120) told us specifically how they thought leadership was different for women.

Challenges to Women in Leadership

1. Women leaders must be more competent than men.
2. Women leaders walk a fine line between being competent enough to be taken seriously and yet also feminine enough to avoid social backlash.
3. Women leaders are expected to have characteristics and behaviors like male leaders.
4. Leaders are assumed to be men.
5. Women leaders are expected to be or actually are better at communicating with others than men.
6. Women leaders are penalized interpersonally for their success and competence.
7. Women leaders who express anger are judged more harshly than men.
8. Subordinates are less comfortable with and less friendly toward leaders who are women.

Preferred Leadership Style: Transformational

The *Millionaire Mystique* women and men are senior leaders (average age fifty-seven) in the world of work and in their communities. The leadership style they overwhelmingly recommend is the transformational style—94 percent of female millionaires and multimillionaires agreed. The transformational style includes demonstrating respect, trust, pride, cooperation, and facilitating employees' individual development.

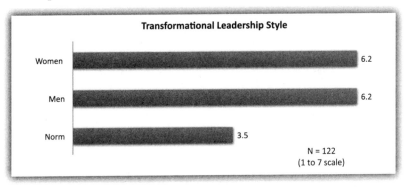

When It's Needed: Autocratic Leadership Style

Perhaps surprisingly, the *Millionaire Mystique* women and men both recommend sprinkling a little pepper with the salt when the transformational style isn't working: autocratic leadership. In other words, sometimes, both men and women agree, it is necessary to make a command decision for the group. But, the most successful people would prefer to try other methods first.

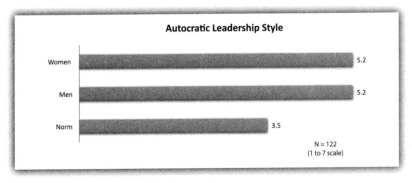

Attributes of Effective Leadership

The *Millionaire Mystique* women and men were in complete agreement about the leadership attributes that led to their success. These are listed in rank order by the number of times they were mentioned by the millionaires and multimillionaires.

Communication skills (oral and written)
Managerial competence
Integrity and honesty
Self-confidence
Strategic vision
Team-orientation
Dedication and hard work
Emotional intelligence
Motivating others
Decision-maker
Intelligence, knowledge
Humility
Respect
Sense of humor

N = 123

Effective Ways to Handle Discrimination

The *Millionaire Mystique* women and men both acknowledge experiencing discrimination and prejudice in the workplace—women at a higher rate than men. But, unless the behavior is illegal, they recommend using interpersonal tools available to you to get around, over, or through it.

Recommendations for Dealing with Discrimination (N = 30)

- Take any opportunity that is being offered—even if you lose that battle, you can win the war.
- Ignore it, work hard, earn respect, outperform others, and succeed.
- Start your own business or look for a new opportunity.
- Befriend those who are jealous and forge positive relationships.
- Use interpersonal skills to demonstrate your intelligence and competence—be assertive, calmly firm, and humorous when appropriate.
- File a complaint with your Human Resources Department if other actions don't work.

Create and Manage Your Wealth

The *Millionaire Mystique* women suggested the following actions to increase your wealth. They were remarkably consistent in what they recommended regarding the right way to handle your money, if you want to achieve the millionaire or multimillionaire category. Yes, it is that simple.

Tips for Managing Your Wealth (N = 50)

- Determine your goals and proactively manage your money.
- Establish a wealth creation plan early with a trustworthy financial advisor at a reputable institution.
- Do not live beyond your means and save heavily.

- Delay gratification.
- Pay off credit cards each month, avoid loans, and do not take on debt.
- Create well-informed business plans, and if you fail to meet your goals, revise your strategy and consider new options.
- Pursue education as a key to your earning capacity.
- Avoid the "princess syndrome" and the "love syndrome" and do not sign a prenuptial agreement if you are going to have children.
- Invest in profit-sharing plans, stock options, 401K plans, and/or equity stake in a business.
- Own your own company, sell it at the right time, and use that money to wisely invest.
- Invest conservatively, possibly in real estate, land, or stock.
- Become knowledgeable about investing and finances; watch the economy and sell before a recession.
- If someone asks about your salary expectations, don't be timid about negotiating your compensation package.

End Notes

Introduction

1. BMO Private Bank, "Changing Face of Wealth Study: Two-Thirds of Nation's Wealthy Are Self Made Millionaires," privately published by BMO Financial Group at bmo.com, June 13, 2013. The term *millionaire* in this study and in this book refers to people with investable assets of $1 million or more, excluding home value.
2. Friedan, Betty, *The Feminine Mystique, with an Introduction by Anna Quindlen*, New York: W.W. Norton, 2001, p. 5.
3. Covert, Bryce, "Number of CEOs at Major Companies Jumps by 4 Percent," ThinkProgress.com, July 8, 2013.
4. Burke, Jude Miller, and Attridge, Mark, "Pathways to Career and Leadership Success: Part 1—A Psychosocial Profile of $100k Professionals," *Journal of Workplace Behavioral Health*, Vol. 26, 2011, pp. 175–206. Phases 1 and 2 of the study were published in this journal. Phases 3 and 4 are currently unpublished. See also, Burke, Jude Miller, and Attridge, Mark, "Pathways to Career and Leadership Success, Part 2: Striking Gender Similarities Among $100k Professionals." *Journal of Workplace Behavioral Health*, Vol. 26, 2001, pp. 207–239.
5. All anonymous quotes from millionaires and multimillionaires were collected in the course of the study; named persons in the book gave permission for their names to be used.
6. Friedan, p. 464.
7. 2013 Results for Optum: http://www.unitedhealthgroup.com/~/media/UHG/PDF/2013/UNH-Q4-2013-Release.ashx

Chapter 1: Living the *Millionaire Mystique* Life

1. Sandy Brue interview, October 23, 2013.
2. Fran Jacques interview, February 3, 2014.

3. Slaughter, Anne-Marie, "Why Women Still Can't Have It All," *The Atlantic Monthly*, July/August 2012, p. 87.
4. Sandberg, Sheryl, *Lean In: Women, Work and the Will to Lead*, New York: Knopf, 2013, p. 15. Sheryl Sandberg should be credited for putting the onus for changing the workplace where it belongs: on corporations and the government. But until the glorious day when that happens, women and men are in charge of their own success.
5. First identified by psychologist Carol Tavris in 1974. It was pretty rare in the workplace even then.

Chapter 2: Were You Born to Be a Millionaire?

1. Both Winfrey and Chan are currently among only nineteen self-made female billionaires in the world. Nineteen is not many but should give us all hope.
2. Karren, Keith, Smith, Lee, Gordon, Kathryn J., and Frandsen, Kathryn J., *Mind/Body Health: The Effects of Attitudes, Emotions, and Relationships, 5th Edition*, San Francisco: Pearson Education/Benjamin Cummings, 2013, p. 336.
3. Gladwell, Malcolm, *David and Goliath: Underdogs, Misfits, and the Art of Battling Giants*, New York: Little, Brown and Company, 2013, p. 46.
4. Chua, Amy, and Rubenfeld, Jed, "What Drives Success," *New York Times, Sunday Review*, Opinion, January 25, 2014.
5. See, for example, Kobasa, Suzanne C., "Stressful Life Events, Personality and Health: An Inquiry into Hardiness," *Journal of Personality and Social Psychology*, 37(1), Jan 1979, pp. 1–11.
6. Pat Petznick and Beverly Stewart, multiple interviews, 2013. Also partially based on Pat's unpublished memoir.
7. Ginsberg, Kenneth, *Building Resilience in Children and Teens: Giving Them Roots and Wings*, Elk Grove Village, IL: American Academy of Pediatrics, 2nd Edition, 2011, p. 23.
8. Harlow, Harry, "The Nature of Love," Address of the President at the sixty-sixth Annual Convention of the American Psychological Association, Washington, D.C., August 31, 1958, *American Psychologist*, 13, pp. 673–685, Available at: http://psychclassics.yorku.ca/Harlow/love.htm.
9. Kohler, S. and Kamp, J. "American Workers Under Pressure" (Technical Report), St. Paul, MN: St. Paul Fire and Marine Insurance Company, 1992.

10. Dement, William C., and Vaughan, Christopher, *The Promise of Sleep: A Pioneer in Sleep Medicine Explores the Vital Connection Between Health, Happiness, and a Good Night's Sleep*, New York: Delacorte Press, 1999.

11. See, for example, Bryant, Jennings, and Zillman, Dolf, "Television Viewing and Physiological Arousal," *Responding to the Screen: Reception and Reaction Processes*, Mahwah, NJ: Lawrence Erlbaum Assoc., 1991.

12. Zhang, J., Zhu Y., Zhan, G., Fenik, P., Panossian, L., Wang, M., Reid, S., Lai, D., and Veasey, S., "Extended Wakefulness: Compromised Metabolics in and Degeneration of Locus Ceruleus Neurons," *The Journal of Neuroscience*, March 10, 2014, 34(12), pp. 4418–4431.

13. Dialectical behavior therapy was developed in the late 1970s by Marcia Linehan and was described in 2007 in *The Dialectical Behavior Therapy Skills Workbook* by McKay, Matthew, Wood, Jeffrey C., and Brantley, Jeffrey, Oakland CA: New Harbinger Publications. See also, Linehan, Marcia, and Dimeff, L., "Dialectical Behavior Therapy in a Nutshell," *The California Psychologist*, 34, 2001, pp. 10–13.

14. Eagly, Alice H., and Carli, Linda L., *Through the Labyrinth: The Truth about How Women Become Leaders*, Cambridge, MA: Harvard Business Review Press, p. 46.

15. Wendy's International LLC, "Dave Thomas: Made in America," Wendy's Canada website, http://www.wendys.ca/dave/davethomas_biography.pdf.

16. Jamie Thorsen interview, September 3, 2013.

17. Conger, R., Conger, K., and Martin., M., "Socioeconomic Status, Family Processes and Individual Development, *Journal of Marriage and Family*, June 10, 2010, 72(3), pp. 685–704.

Chapter 3: The Millionaire Personality

1. See, for example, McCrae, R.R. and Costa, Jr., P.T.,"Validation of the Five-Factor Model of Personality Across Instruments and Observers," *Journal of Personality and Social Psychology*, 1987, 52(1), pp. 81–90.

2. Judge, Timothy A., and Ilies, Remus, "Relationship of Personality to Performance Motivation: A Meta-Analytic Review," *Journal of Applied Psychology*, 87, 2002, pp. 797–807.

3. Angie Hallier interviews, May, June, and July 2013.

4. This quote is most often attributed to Maya Angelou. Angelou acknowledges that she said it on her own website: http://mayaangelou.com/news/13/, but it is also variously attributed to Anonymous and others.
5. Shepherdson, Nancy, "Risky Business," *Illinois Super Lawyers*, January 2014, p. 5.
6. Thorsen interview.
7. Judge, Timothy A., Erez, A., Bono, Joyce, and Thoresen, Carl J., "The Core Self-Evaluation Scale (CSES): Development of a Measure," *Personnel Psychology*, 56, 2003, pp. 303–331.
8. Judge, Timothy A., and Hurst, Charlice, "How the Rich (and Happy) Get Richer (and Happier), *Journal of Applied Psychology*, 93(4), July 2008, pp. 849–863.
9. Judge, Timothy A., "Core Self-Evaluations and Work Success," Abstract, *Current Directions in Psychological Science*, 18, February 2009, p. 58.

Chapter 4: The Millionaire Work Style

1. Crabtree, Steve, "Northern America Leads the World in Workplace Engagement," www.gallup.com, Gallup, Inc., November 4, 2013.
2. Kahn, W.A. "Psychological Conditions of Personal Engagement and Disengagement at Work," *Academy of Management Journal*, 33, 1990, pp. 692–724.
3. Csikszentmihalyi, Mihaly, *Flow: The Psychology of Optimal Experience*, New York: Harper & Row, 1991, p. 5.
4. Csikszentmihalyi, Mihaly, "The Importance of Challenge for the Enjoyment of Intrinsically Motivated, Goal-Directed Activities," *Personality and Social Psychology*, Bulletin 38, 2012. See also: *Creativity: Flow and the Psychology of Discovery and Invention*, New York: Harper Collins, 1996, p. 122.
5. Macey, W., and Schneider, B., "The Meaning of Employee Engagement," *Industrial and Organizational Psychology: Perspectives on Science and Practice*, 1, 2008, pp. 3–30.
6. Robert Bohannon interview, January 4, 2014.
7. Archelle Georgiou interview, November 14, 2013.
8. Rhoades, Ann, and Shepherdson, Nancy, *Built on Values: Creating an Enviable Culture That Outperforms the Competition*, San Francisco: Jossey Bass, 2011, pp. 58–70.

9. McCauley, Cynthia D., *Developmental Assignments: Creating Learning Experiences without Changing Jobs*, Greensboro, NC: Center for Creative Leadership, 2006, pp. 3, 7–8.
10. King, Eden, and Knight, Jennifer, *How Women Can Make it Work: The Science of Success*, Santa Barbara, CA: Praeger, 2011, p. 174.
11. Eagly and Carli, pp. 148–49.
12. Hill, Napoleon, *Think and Grow Rich*. The latest edition is a deluxe version published by Capstone in 2010. First edition published in 1937.
13. Seligman, Martin, *Learned Optimism: How to Change Your Mind and Your Life*, New York: Vintage Books, 1998, p. 15.

Chapter 5: Are You a Social Influencer?

1. Ferris, G.R., Treadway, D.C., Kolodinsky, David, Hochwarter, Wayne, Kacmar, Charles, Douglas, Ceasar, and Frink, Dwight, "Development and Validation of the Political Skills Inventory, *Journal of Management*, 31, 2005, pp. 126–152.
2. Eagly and Carli, pp. 87–90.
3. Kantor, Jodi, "Harvard Case Study: Gender Equity," *New York Times*, September 8, 2013.
4. Tannen, Deborah, *Talking from 9 to 5: Women and Men at Work*, New York: William Morrow, 2001, p. 300.
5. Brescoll, Victoria, "Can an Angry Woman Get Ahead? Status Conferral, Gender, and Expression of Emotion in the Workplace," *Psychological Science*, 19(3), 2008, pp. 268–275. Victoria Brescoll is an assistant professor of organizational behavior at the Yale School of Management.
6. Practical guides to argumentation and conflict resolution include: Morrow, David, and Weston, Anthony, *A Workbook for Arguments: A Complete Course in Critical Thinking*, Cambridge, MA: Hackett Publishing, 2011; and Cloke, Kenneth, and Goldsmith, Joan, *Resolving Conflicts at Work: Ten Strategies for Everyone on the Job*, San Francisco: Jossey-Bass, 2011.
7. Interview with former Ambassador Barbara Barrett, October 25, 2013.
8. Ferris, Gerald R., Treadway, Darren C., Brouer, Robyn L., Douglas, Ceasar, and Lux, Sean, "Political Skill in Organizations," *Journal of Management*, 32(3), June 2007, p. 307; also, Ferris, Gerald R., Davidson, Sherrie L., and Perrewe, Pamela L., *Political Skill at Work: Impact on Work Effectiveness*, Palo Alto, CA: Davies-Black Publishing, 2005, p. 113.

9. Burt, Ronald S., *Brokerage and Closure: An Introduction to Social Capital*, New York: Oxford University Press, 2005, Section 1.2.2.

10. Sara Dial interview, December 27, 2012.

11. Candyce Williams interview, November 19, 2013.

12. Cialdini, Robert, *Influence: Science and Practice*, 5th Ed., Boston: Pearson, 2009, p. 19.

13. Taylor, Shelley E., Klein, Laura Cousino, Lewis, Brian P., Gruenewald, Tara L., Gurung, Regan A.R., Updegraff, John A., "Biobehavioral Responses to Stress in Females: Tend-and-Befriend, not Fight-or-Flight," *Psychological Review*, 107(3), 2000, pp. 411–29.

14. Ferris, et. al., *Journal of Management*, June 2007, p. 306.

15. Allen, Tammy D., Poteet, Mark L., Eby, Lillian T., Lentz, Elizabeth, and Lima, Linette, "Career Benefits Associated with Mentoring for Protégés: A Meta-Analysis," *Journal of Applied Psychology*, 69(1), 2004, pp. 127–136.

16. Ibid., pp. 132–3.

Chapter 6: The Millionaire Way: Leading with Grace

1. The Honorable Sandra Day O'Connor interview, December 12, 2013.

2. Chapman, Steve, "Sandra Day O'Connor Speaks," *Chicago Tribune, Minority of One blog*, articles.chicagotribune.com, April 26, 2013.

3. Lowney, Chris, *Pope Francis: Why He Leads the Way He Leads*, Chicago: Loyola Press, 2013, p. 2.

4. Goleman, Daniel, *Focus: The Hidden Driver of Excellence*, New York: Harper, 2013, p. 226.

5. Bohannon interview.

6. Mandela, Nelson, *Long Walk to Freedom*, Boston: Back Bay Books, p. 22.

7. Hill, Linda, "Becoming the Boss," *Harvard Business Review OnPoint*, hbr.com, p. 3.

8. Rhoades, p. 52.

9. Miller-Burke, Jude, and Attridge, Mark, "Pathways to Career and Leadership Success, Part 1: A Psychosocial Profile of $100K Professionals," *Journal of Workplace Behavioral Health*, Vol. 26, 2011, pp. 175–206.

10. Thorsen interview.

11. Cialdini, p. 184.

12. Goleman, p. 225.

13. Eagly and Carli, p. 160.
14. Ibid.
15. Heilman, Madeline E., and Okimoto, T.G., "Why Are Women Penalized for Success at Male Tasks? The Implied Communality Deficit," *Journal of Applied Psychology,* 92(1), 2007, pp. 81–92.
16. Bonnie Morcomb interview, December 18, 2013.
17. Bridges, William, *Managing Transitions: Making the Most of Change,* 3rd Edition, Cambridge, MA: DaCapo Lifelong Books, 2009, p. 151.
18. Miller-Burke, Jude, Attridge, Mark, and Fass, P.M., "Impact of Traumatic Events and Organizational Response: A Study of Bank Robberies," *Journal of Occupational and Environmental Medicine,* March 1999, 41(2) pp. 73–83.
19. Woodyard, Chris, "Who Is Mary Barra, the Next CEO of GM?" *USA Today,* December 10, 2013.
20. Hirsch, Jerry, "Next GM CEO Enjoys Industry Competition," *Chicago Tribune,* December 12, 2013, Section 2.
21. Jacque Sokolov interview, November 13, 2013.
22. Kruse, Kevin, "What Is Leadership?" forbes.com, April 26, 2013.

Chapter 7: Choose to Be Resilient

1. Hallier interviews.
2. Southwick, Steven M., and Charney, Dennis S., "Enhance Your Resilience" [originally entitled "Ready for Anything"], *Scientific American Mind,* July 2013.
3. Adriana Holy interview.
4. Tannen, Deborah, *Talking from 9 to 5: How Women's and Men's Conversational Styles Affect Who Gets Heard, Who Gets Credit, and What Gets Done at Work,* New York: William Morrow, 1994, p. 60.
5. Edward Bergmark interview, April 15, 2013.
6. See, for example, Ury, William, and Fisher, Roger, *Getting to Yes,* just republished by Random House Business Books in 2012. It has never been out of print since first published in 1981.
7. Maddi, S.R., "The Story of Hardiness: Twenty Years of Theorizing, Research, and Practice," *Consulting Psychology Journal,* 54(3), 2002, pp. 165–183.
8. Taylor and Shelley, pp. 411–429.
9. Dial interview.

Chapter 8: Great Kids, Great Work Life: The New American Dream?

1. Groysberg, Boris, and Abrahams, Robin, "Manage Your Work, Manage Your Life: Zero in on What Really Matters," *Harvard Business Review*, March 2014, p. 60.
2. Bing, Elizabeth, Coleman, Libby, and Stern, Daniel, *Laughter and Tears: The Emotional Life of New Mothers*, New York: Holt Paperbacks, 1997, p. 30.
3. Parker, Kim, and Wang, Wendy, *Modern Parenthood: Roles of Moms and Dads Converge As They Balance Work and Family*, Washington, DC: Pew Research Center, March 14, 2013, pp. 19–24.
4. Quoted in Alpert, Emily, "Moms More Exhausted Than Dads at Work, Home and Leisure, Study Says," *Los Angeles Times*, October 8, 2013.
5. Eagly and Carli, p. 49.
6. Goodman, Cindy Krischer, "10 Workplace Trends That Affect the Way We Work," *Miami Herald*, October 29, 2013.
7. "Family-Friendly Companies," ParentingWeekly.com, December 2013.
8. Halpin, John, and Teixeira, Rudy, "Battle of the Sexes Gives Way to Negotiations: Americans Welcome Women Workers, Want New Deal to Support How We Now Work and Live Today," in *A Woman's Nation Changes Everything*, by Maria Shriver and the Center for American Progress, edited by Heather Boushey and Ann O'Leary, October 16, 2009, pp. 412–13.
9. Sokolov interview.
10. Holy interview.
11. Interviewed and quoted in Weigel, Jennifer, "The Balance Myth: Expert Advice on Rethinking Your Work Life Formula," *Chicago Tribune*, November 10, 2013, Section 9.
12. Williams interview.
13. Shipman, Claire, and Kay, Katty, *Womenomics: Write Your Own Rules for Success*, New York: Harper, 2009, pp. 37–38.

Chapter 9: The Unspoken Obstacles for Millionaires

1. Merchant, Nilofer, "Being a Woman Is the Least Interesting Thing about Mary Barra, New CEO of GM," *Time: Ideas*, December 10, 2013.
2. Moore, Martha T., "Focus on Hillary Clinton's Appearance Sparks Criticism," USAToday.com, May 10, 2012.

3. Krugman, Paul, "Can Yellen Lead the Fed? So Far, Critics Firing Blanks," *The New York Times*, August 3, 2013.

4. See, for example, Wenneras, Christine, and Wold, Agnes, "Nepotism and Sexism in Peer-Review," *Nature*, 387, 1997, pp. 341–43.

5. See, for example, Forsyth, D. R., *Group Dynamics*, New York: Wadsworth, 2009.

6. Newport, Frank, and Wilke, Joy, "Americans Still Prefer a Male Boss: A Plurality Report That a Boss's Gender Would Make No Difference," *Gallup: Economy*, Princeton: Gallup, November 11, 2013.

7. Merchant, *Time: Ideas*.

8. Steele, Claude M., *Whistling Vivaldi: And Other Clues About How Stereotypes Affect Us*, New York: W.W. Norton, 2010. Dr. Steele also has several good videos on YouTube explaining the importance of this issue.

9. Kahneman, Daniel, *Thinking Fast and Slow*, New York: Farrar, Strauss, Giroux, 2011.

10. Williams interview.

11. Georgiou interview.

12. Bohannon interview.

13. Sandberg, pp. 27–28.

14. Georgiou interview.

15. Steele.

16. Stroessner, Steve, and Good, Catherine, on their website reducingstereotypethreat.org.

17. Brzezinski, Natalia, "Values-Based Leadership and Empowering Women: Interview with CEO of IKEA Group," *Huffington Post Business*, December 20, 2013.

18. Eagly and Carli, pp. 38–39.

19. King and Knight, pp. 103–04.

20. Sandberg, pp. 145 and 149.

Chapter 10: You're in the Money: Earning Satisfaction

1. Leah Hoffman interview, several dates in September, October, and November 2013.

2. Stanley, Thomas J., *Millionaire Women Next Door*, Kansas City: Andrews McMeel Publishing, 2004, p. 21.

3. Petznik and Stewart interviews.

4. William O'Brien interview, January 1, 2014.

5. Jenkinson, Caroline E., Dickens, Andy, Jones, Kerry, Thompson-Coon, Jo, Taylor, Rod, Rogers, Morwenna, Bambra, Clare, Lang, Iain, and Richards, Suzanne, "Is Volunteering a Public Health Intervention? A Systematic Review and Meta-Analysis of the Health and Survival of Volunteers," *BMC Public Health*, 13, 2013, p. 773.
6. Szalavitz, Maia, "Helping Others Helps You to Live Longer," healthland .time.com, August 23, 2013.
7. Lyubomirsky, Sonja, and Della Porta, Matthew D., "Boosting Happiness, Buttressing Resilience: Results from Cognitive and Behavioral Interventions," in J.W. Reich, Zautra, Alex J., and Hall, John Stuart (Eds.), *Handbook of Adult Resilience: Concepts, Methods, and Applications*, New York: Guilford Press (published online at sonjalyubomirsky. com).
8. Klar, Malte, and Kasser, Tim, "Some Benefits of Being an Activist: Measuring Activism and Its Role in Psychological Well-Being," *Political Psychology*, 30(5), October 2009, pp. 755–777.

Conclusion: Becoming a Millionaire . . . Your Own Way

1. Krumholtz, John D., and Levin, Al S., *Luck Is No Accident: Making the Most of Happenstance in Your Life and Career*, Atascadero, CA: Impact Publishers, 2010, p. 7.

Appendix: The Research Behind the Book

1. Maddie, pp. 175–183.
2. Day, J.C., and Newberger, E.C., "The Big Payoff: Educational Attainment and Synthetic Estimates of Work-Life Earnings," *Current Population Reports*, 2002, pp. 23–210; U.S. Census Bureau, retrieved from www.census.gov/prod/2002pubs/p23-210.pdf; Schmidt. F.L., and Hunter, J., "General Mental Ability in the World of Work: Occupational Attainment and Job Performance," *Journal of Personality and Social Psychology*, 86, 2002, pp. 162–173; Zagorsky, J.L., "Do You Have to Be Smart to Be Rich? The Impact of IQ on Wealth, Income and Financial Distress," *Intelligence*, 35(5), pp. 489–501.

3. Diener, E, Suh, E.M., Lucas, Richard, and Smith, Heidi, "Subjective Well-Being: Three Decades of Progress," *Psychological Bulletin*, 125(2),1999, pp. 267–302.
4. Judge, T.A., and Bono, J.E., "Relationship of Core Self-Evaluation Traits—Self-Esteem, Generalized Self-Efficacy, Locus of Control, and Emotional Stability—With Job Satisfaction and Job Performance: A Meta-Analysis," *Journal of Applied Psychology*, 86(1), 2001, pp. 80–92; this was not demonstrated in the *Millionaire Mystique* women.
5. Attridge, Mark, "Measuring and Managing Employee Work Engagement: A Review of the Research and Business Literature," *Journal of Workplace Behavioral Health*, 24(4), 2009, pp. 383–398.
6. Johnson, W., and Krueger, R.F., "Attenuating the Effects of Social Stress: The Impact of Political Skill," *Journal of Occupational Health Psychology*, 12(2), 2007, pp. 105–115. For higher job performance ratings: Harris, K.J., Kacmar, K.M., Zivnuska, S., and Shaw, J.D., "The Impact of Political Skill on Impression Management Effectiveness," *Journal of Applied Psychology*, 92(1), 2007, pp. 278–285.

Acknowledgments

I moved to Arizona from Minneapolis in 2000 and met many successful people who had grown up via the school of "hard knocks" and went on to create beautiful families and business success. The juxtaposition of their childhoods to their adult lives was the impetus for this research project and subsequent book. I admire and respect them and, as a psychologist, I wanted to know how they did it.

To paraphrase F. Scott Fitzgerald, this book took one year to write, a couple of minutes of curiosity to conceive, and a lifetime of experience to understand and explain to others. I hold all of the people I studied and interviewed in the highest regard. I am very fortunate to have met them and been allowed to see into their lives. The very fact that (at this point) several hundred people allowed me to research their lives speaks to their interest in helping others be successful. This is a group of people who wants the best not only for themselves but others in our society.

At this stage of my life, the one contribution I wanted to make was to take the information I found from these "big successful kids from the school of hard knocks" and translate it into a roadmap for those that may be having a little bit harder time thriving in our very challenging society today. Hopefully, this book will provide guidance not only for you, but for your daughters and sons as well.

First, I want to thank Dr. Mark Attridge of Attridge Consulting. I worked with Mark at UnitedHealthcare and, when I called him in 2010 to help me design, implement, and statistically analyze the research results for the *Millionaire Mystique* project, he was eager to do so. He ensured the integrity of the research and became a dear friend.

Second, I want to thank Nancy Shepherdson for her help in writing this book over the past year. We have spent many hours together analyzing, writing, rewriting, and encouraging one another. She was able to take sometimes dense psychological research and make it understandable and useful for everyone. She also helped me see how much practical advice I had to offer to people who wanted to follow in the footsteps of our millionaires and multimillionaires.

Third, thank you to our agent, Linda Konner, Linda Konner Literary Agency, for her initial excitement and interest in the book. Her determination is inspiring.

Finally, I want to thank Nicholas Brealey and all of his colleagues at the publishing company, Nicholas Brealey Publishing, for having faith in this book.

There were also many, many friends and colleagues who have encouraged me, filled out research surveys, and provided extensive interviews on their personal and professional lives. Thank you to: **The Honorable Sandra Day O'Connor**, retired U.S. Supreme Court Justice; **The Honorable Barbara Barrett**, former Ambassador to Finland; **Pat Petznick**, cofounder of Fresh Start Women's Foundation; **Jamie Thorsen**, former Global Head of Foreign Exchange Products, BMO Capital Markets; **Sandy Brue**, former Owner & CEO, Sandicast; **Robert Bohannon**, former CEO, Viad Corporation; **Jacque Sokolov**, M.D., CEO, SSB Solutions; **Edward Bergmark**, Ph.D., former CEO, Optum UnitedHealthcare; **Sara Dial**, Owner, Sara Dial & Associates; **Archelle Georgiou**, M.D., former Chief Medical Officer, UnitedHealthcare and Fox News Health Commentator; **Candyce Williams**, M.D., Medical Director Spinal Cord Injury Rehabilitation, St. Joseph's Medical Center; **Adriana Holy**, M.D., Owner, The Center for Advanced Dermatology; **Angie Hallier**, J.D., Managing Partner, Hallier and Lawrence Family Law; **Bonnie Morcomb**, Director, Coventry Workers' Compensation; **Fran Jacques**, Vice President of Marketing and Public Relations, West Hills Hospital and Medical Center; **Leah Hoffman**, Vice President, R.W. Baird; **Teresa and Rene Romero**; **Michelle**

Mitnick; **Melissa VanDolah**; **William O'Brien**, CEO, J Bio Anti-
Aging; **Jamie Hines**, M.D., Arizona Cardiology Group; **Tom Kull**,
Ph.D., W.P. Carey School of Business, Arizona State University;
Jeffrey Wincel, D.Min., Sr. Director, Honeywell Aerospace; **Lisa
Galper**, Psy.D., Clinical Psychologist; **Phillip Welp**, VP Business
Development, WinCraft, Inc.; **Mitzi Krockover**, M.D., Consultant,
SSB Solutions; and, **Pat St. Claire**, St. Claire Design Studio.

A huge thank you, too, to my three children, Ian, Shannon, and
Brendan, for patting me on the back while they ran in and out of the
house saying over and over again, "I'm proud of you, Mom. You can
do it." And, so I did. As the Beatles said: "I get by with a little help
from my friends"—and family.

Index

A

"A Players," 116
Absorption, 72–73
Acceptance, of childhood, 24–25
Accomplishments, 152
Action taking, 25–26
Active listening, 29–30
Adversity, childhood, 20
Agnefjall, Peter, 203
Agreeableness, 47–48, 53–55, 61, 119, 121, 229
Allen, Tammy, 104
Ambition, 8, 38, 217
Analytical thinking, for problem solving, 33
Angelou, Maya, 53
Anger, 98, 124–125
Appearance, 200
Arizona Center for Neurosurgery, 101
Assertiveness, 65–66, 97–98, 115, 118, 125, 146, 148, 232
Assessment, of family behaviors, 24
Atlantic Monthly, The, 6
Attitudes
    comfort, 87–88
    description of, 84–85
    engaged, 86
    enthusiasm, 86
    optimism, 85
    passion, 85–86
    positive, 145

Attractiveness, 200
Attridge, Mark, xvi, 117
Authenticity, 111
Authoritarian leadership, 114
Autocratic leadership style, 243
Automatic thinking, 193
Awareness, of family behaviors, 22–24

B

Balance Myth: Rethinking Work-Life Success, The, 179
Barra, Mary, 131–133, 189, 192
Barrett, Barbara, 99
Barriers, 7–10
"Beat," 56
Behavioral modeling, 17
Benevolent sexism, 192
Bergmark, Edward, 81, 148
"Big," 66
Bing, Elizabeth, 170–171
Bohannon, Robert, 74, 115, 198
Bowles, Barbara, 132
Bragging, 8, 14
Breaking the rules, 118
Brescoll, Victoria, 98
Bridges, William, 128–130
Brue, Sandy, 1–3, 5, 10–13
Budgeting, 212
Building of relationships, 10–12, 14, 84, 99–100, 147, 155, 234

Building Resilience in Children and Teens: Giving them Roots and Wings, 22
Built on Values: Creating an Enviable Culture That Outperforms the Competition, 78, 116
Burt, Ronald S., 99–100
Business line managerial skills, 77–78
Business ownership, 230

C

Calmness, 145
Career detours, 166–167, 237
Caring, 27–28
Carli, Linda, 36, 84, 123, 173, 204
Cash, 212–213
Center for Advanced and Aesthetic Dermatology, 145, 178
Challenging positions, 83
Character, 117
Charisma, 28–29
Charney, Dennis, 142
Childcare, 182
Childhood
    acceptance of, 24–25
    adverse events during, 19–20, 148, 152, 225
    challenging experiences in, 19
    creativity in, 40–41
    curiosity in, 41
    dysfunctional, 19
    research data on, 225
    "rotten," 18–20
    tenacity development in, 42
Chopra, Deepak, 109
Chua, Amy, 19
Cialdini, Robert, 119
Cigna, 76
Clients, honoring of, 11
Clinton, Hillary, 190
Cognitive abilities, 149–151
Coleman, Libby, 170–171
Comfort, 87–88
Commanding presence, 29–30

Communication
    anger in, 98
    assertiveness in, 97–98
    biases in, 95
    enhanced, 94–98
    gender differences in, 95–96, 124
    interpersonal, 114
    by leaders, 117
    persuasive, 79
    self-assessment of, 90
    social, 115
    speaking style used in, 96
    style of, 96
Compassion, 111, 113
Compassionate accountability, 127
Competence, 117, 124
Competitive spirit, 118
Conflict, 118–119, 145–149, 233
Conflict resolution, 90, 147–149
Conger, Rand, 40
Connectedness to others, 155
Connections
    building of, 67
    developing of, 86–87
Conscientiousness, 47, 49–51, 55, 60, 119–120, 179, 229
Consent, leadership by, 115
Continuing education, 39–40
Coping with stress, 9, 141
Core self-evaluation, 62, 183
Corporate board members, 132–133
Corporate flexibility, 174
Corporate path, 81–84
Creativity, 40–41, 56–57, 121
Csikszentmihalyi, Mihaly, 73
Curiosity, 41–42

D

Danks, William, 215
David and Goliath, 19
DBT. *See* Dialectical behavior therapy
Debriefing of stress, 64–65
Debt, 212
Decision making, 33

Dedication, 72
Delegation, 10, 14
Deliberate reaction, 88
Deliberate thinking, 193
Dell, Phil, 81
Dement, William C., 32
Depression, 217
Detours, career, 166–167, 237
*Developmental Assignments: Creating
    Learning Experiences Without
    Changing Jobs*, 81
Dial, Sara, 100, 157–158
Dialectical behavior therapy, 35
Dimensions of success
    emotional discipline, 31–35
    integrity, 36–39
    moral values, 36–39
    outsmarting the world, 39–42
    social connection. *See* Social
        connection
Directness, 29
Disagreement, 147
Discrimination. *See also* Prejudice
    description of, 7
    gender-based, 190–191
    identifying of, 205
    overcoming, 198–202
    personalizing of, 201
    racism and, 194–195
    reduction of, 205
    research data on, 245
    steps for handling, 196–197, 199–
        201, 245
    termination for, 197
    walking away from job, 197,
        201–202
Dolesji, Jan, 78
Dress, 69
Dysfunctional childhood, 19

E

Eagly, Alice, 36, 84, 123, 173, 204
Early life experiences, 17
Ease, 87–88

Education
    continuing of, 39–40
    research data on, 226
Einstein, Albert, 53
Elbert, Angela, 57
Emotion(s)
    dealing with, 149–150
    denying of, 150–151
    description of, 9
    managing of, 34–35, 88
    thought and, integration between,
        120
Emotional crises, 34–35
Emotional discipline
    description of, 31
    energy levels, 31–32
    managing emotions, 34–35
    problem solving, 32–34
Emotional intelligence, 34
Employee(s)
    caring about, 27–28
    engaged, 72
    leadership affected by, 116
    mistakes by, 12
    motivating of, 82–83
    problem employees, 126–131
    rewarding of, 12
Employee assistance programs, 78,
    81
Energy levels, 31–32
Enthusiasm, 86
Entrepreneurship, 178
Ethnic prejudice, 194–195
Extraversion, 47, 51–53, 60, 119, 229
Extroverts, 47, 51–52

F

Failure, 222
Family. *See also* Parents; Work-
        family/life balance
    behavioral modeling by, 17–18
    decision making by, 33
    dysfunctional, 19
    emotions in, 33

Family *(Cont.)*
   as microculture, 26
   teachings from, 17–18
Family behaviors
   action taking, 25–26
   assessment of, 24
   awareness of, 22–24
   escaping from, 42–43
   influential, 23
   negative, 24–25
   positive, 24
Family values
   creativity, 40–41
   curiosity, 41–42
   description of, 26
   education, 39–40
   emotional discipline, 31–35
   honesty, 37
   humility, 37–38
   integrity, 36–39
   moral values, 36–39
   respect, 38–39
   social connection. *See* Social
      connection
   tenacity, 42
Fear of failure, 145
Feedback, 11
Feminine behaviors, 232–233
Feminine Mystique, The, x
Ferris, Gerald, 99
Ferris, Ronald, 103
Fighting, 145–149
Financial advisors, 213–214
Flexibility, 148, 173–176
Flow, 73, 75
Flow: The Psychology of Optimal
      Experience, 73
Focus, 86, 180
Focus: The Hidden Driver of
      Excellence, 115
Foundations of success, 236
Fox News, 198
Fresh Start Women's Foundation, 20,
      216, 218
Friedan, Betty, x, xiii, 7, 165

Friendships, 99, 101–102, 155

G

Gallup Inc., 72
Gates, Bill, 69
Gender
   career progression and, 239
   communication differences based
      on, 95–96, 124
   leadership and, 122–125, 191,
      242–243
   obstacles based on, 240–242
   personal lives and, 238
   prejudice and discrimination based
      on, 190–191
   stereotypes based on, 7–8, 202
Gender-specific relationships,
      102–103
General Dynamics, 3
General Electric, 199
Georgiou, Archelle, 75–76, 198
Ginsburg, Kenneth, 22
Giuliani, Rudy, 130
Giving back, 216–219
Gladwell, Malcolm, 19
Goals
   clarifying of, 67
   setting of, 154
Goleman, Daniel, 115, 120
Good, Catherine, 203
Goodman, Cindy Krischer, 174
Graceful leadership, 111–116,
      126–131
"Grit," 42
Grounded, 65
Growth mindset, 13
Groysberg, Boris, 170

H

Hallier, Angie, xiv, 51–52, 139–140,
      143
Happiness, 169
Hard work, 201

Hardiness, 20
Harpo Productions, 16
Having it all, 5–6
Health, 9–10
Heilman, Madeline, 124
Hidden agendas, 88
High core self-evaluation, 62, 183
High-stakes positions, 83
Hill, Linda, 115
Hill, Napoleon, 85
Hoffman, Leah, 210
Hoffman and Hock Group, 210
Holy, Adriana, 145, 178, 182
Home scheduling system, 181
Honesty, 37, 55, 117
Honeywell, xviii, 72, 77, 80–81, 101, 104, 147, 151
Honoring clients, 11
Hope, 156–158
Hospira, 132
How Women Can Make It Work: The Science of Success, 205
Humility, 37–38
Humor, 9, 30–31, 51, 66, 200
Hurst, Charlice, 63

I

IKEA, 203–204
Imposter syndrome, 66
Impulse control, 19–20
Impulses, respecting of, 56
In Search of Excellence, 189
Influence: The Psychology of Persuasion, 119
Inner chatterbox, silencing of, 64
Inner circle of friends, 101
Inner voice, xiii
Insecurity, 19
Integrity, 36–39, 117
Interpersonal communication, 114
Interpersonal skills, 232
Intrinsically motivated people, 73
Introverts, 47, 51–53

Investment diversity, 213
Islands of competence, 22

J

J Bio Anti-Aging, 217
Jacques, Fran, 3–5
"Jangling of nerves," 58–59
Jenkinson, Caroline, 217
Jobs, Steve, 53, 69
Jones, Audie Foster Dryer, 216
Journal writing, 150–151
Journaling, 59
Judge, Timothy, 63

K

Kahn, William, 72
Kahneman, Daniel, 193
Karren, Keith J., 17
Kasser, Tim, 218
Kay, Katty, 184
King, Eden, 84, 205
Klar, Malte, 218
Knight, Jennifer, 84, 205
Kobasa, Suzanne C., 20
Kremer-Sadlik, Tamar, 171
Krugman, Paul, 190
Krumholtz, John, 221
Kruse, Kevin, 133

L

Laissez-faire leadership, 113
Laiwa, Chan, 15
Lapp, Joni, 80
Laughter and Tears: The Emotional Life of New Mothers, 170
Leader(s)
    admitting mistakes, 112
    agreeableness of, 121
    authentic, 112
    case examples of, 131–133
    compassionate, 113
    conscientiousness of, 120

Leader(s) *(Cont.)*
  extraversion of, 120
  gender considerations, 122–123
  listening by, 115
  neuroticism and, 122
  openness to new experiences by,
      55, 121–122
  performance issues handled by,
      126–131
  personality of, 119–122
  power of, 122–123
  problem employees and, 126–131
  skills of, 116–119
  social influence used by, 114–115
  terms used to describe, 204
  transparency of, 12
  vulnerability of, 112
  women as, 122–125, 131–133
Leadership
  in adverse situations, 130–131
  attributes of, 117, 244
  authentic, 111–112
  authoritarian, 114
  autocratic style of, 243
  challenges to, 242
  by consent, 115
  in corporate board positions,
      132–133
  factors that affect, 110–111
  gender and, 122–125, 191, 242–
      243
  graceful, 111–116, 126–131
  laissez-faire, 113
  readiness assessments, 134–135
  self-assessments, 133–135
  social influence used in, 114–115
  transactional, 113
  transformational, 113–114, 131,
      204, 243
  in transitions, 128–130
Leadership ambition gap, 6
Lean In, 6, 200, 205
Learned optimism, 85
Learned passivity, 95
Learning from mistakes, 145

Levin, Al, 221
Life satisfaction, 217–218, 228
Linehan, Marcia, 35
Listening, 29–30, 115
Logical animated arguments, 146
"Love syndrome," 214–215
Lowney, Chris, 111
Luck, 221
Lyubomirsky, Sonja, 217

M

Madi, Salvatore, 153
"Male boss preference bias," 124
Management principles, 78–79
Managerial competence, 117
Managerial skills, 77–78
Managing emotions, 34–35
*Managing Transitions: Making the
      Most of Change,* 128
Mandela, Nelson, 115
Masculine behaviors, 232
McCauley, Cynthia, 81
Meaning, sense of, 156
Mentor/mentoring, 103–106, 235
Merchant, Nilofer, 192
Millionaire Women Next Door, 215
Millionaires
  female versus male, 13–14
  statistics about, x, xvii, 223
  upbringing of, 16
*Mind/Body Health: The Effects of
      Attitudes, Emotions, and
      Relationships,* 17
Mindfulness, 35, 46, 149, 182
Mistakes, 12, 112, 145
Money management, 210–215,
      245–246
Mood, 217–218
Moral values, 36–39
Morcomb, Bonnie, 125–126
Mother Teresa, 53
Motivating of employees, 82–83
Motivations of others, 88
Motorola, 3

Myths
  case example of, 10–13
  description of, 7–10

N

Negative emotions, 9
Negative family behaviors, 24–25
Negative humor style, 30
Negative talk, 64
Negotiation, 149, 183, 201
Nervousness, 87
Networking, 98–103
Neuroticism, 48, 57–59, 61, 119, 121, 229
Neutral zone, 129
"No", 13, 199–200

O

O'Brien, William, 217
Obstacles
  discrimination. *See* Discrimination
  gender-specific, 240–242
  overview of, 189–192
  prejudices. *See* Prejudice
  research data on, 240–242
O'Connor, Sandra Day, 109–110
Online e-tailing, 177
Openness to new experiences, 48, 55–57, 61, 119, 121–122, 141, 229
Operational managerial skills, 77–78
Opportunities, 82
Optimism, 85
Optum, xvii–xviii, 9, 37, 80–81, 129, 175
Outsmarting the world, 39–42
Overworking, 54

P

Parents. *See also* Family
  accomplishments of, 227
  behavioral modeling by, 17–18

education level of, 39–40
Passion, 85–86
Passive language, 97
Performance issues, leader's handling of, 126–131
Perseverance, 6–7
Persistence, 140–143, 200
Personal control, 153–155
Personal lives, 238
Personal relationships, 12
Personal satisfaction, 218
Personality
  description of, 45
  female characteristics, 204
  of leader, 119–122
  self-assessment of, 89
Personality traits
  agreeableness, 29, 47–48, 53–55, 61, 119, 121
  case studies of, 59–62
  changing of, 46
  conscientiousness, 47, 49–51, 55, 60, 119–120, 179, 229
  extraversion, 47, 51–53, 60, 119–120, 229
  neuroticism, 48, 57–59, 61, 119, 121, 229
  openness to new experiences, 48, 55–57, 61, 119, 121–122, 141, 229
  positive, 46
  research data on, 229
  success and, 19
Personalizing, xiii
Persuasive communication, 79
Pessimism, 149
Peters, Tom, 189–190
Petznick, Pat, xiv, 20–22, 38, 209, 216
Physical appearance, 200
Platform for success, 74–81
Political skills, 99
Pope Francis, 111
Pope Francis: Why He Leads the Way He Leads, 111
Positive expectations, 156–158

Positive family behaviors, 24
Power, 122–123
Prejudice. *See also* Discrimination
  description of, 7
  ethnic, 194–195
  gender-based, 190–191
  overcoming, 198–202
  sexism, 191–192, 194, 196–197
  subtle, 192, 194
  thinking methods and, 193
Prenuptial agreements, 214
Priorities, 39
Problem solving, 32–34, 144
Profit sharing, 211–212
Purpose, sense of, 156

Q

"Queen Bee Syndrome," 10

R

Racism, 194–195
Random acts of kindness, 55
Rapport talk, 95–96
Reactions, managing of, 88
Reciprocity, 102, 105
Relationships
  building of, 10–12, 14, 84, 99–100,
    147, 155, 234
  friendships, 99, 101–102, 155
  gender-specific, 102–103
  healthy, 6
  mentoring, 104
  with outside stakeholders, 83–84
  personal, 12
  "tend and befriend" style, 102–103,
    155, 234
  toxic, 66
Report talk, 95–96
Research data, 223–246
  business ownership, 230
  career progression, 239
  childhood, 225
  conflict, 233

detours, 237
discrimination, 245
educational achievements, 226
family socioeconomic
    backgrounds, 224
foundations of success, 236
gender differences, 238–239
leadership, 242–244
life satisfaction, 228
masculine and feminine behaviors,
    232–233
mentors, 235
obstacles, 240–242
parents' accomplishments, 227
personal lives, 238
personality characteristics, 229
relationship-building skills, 234
"tend and befriend" works style,
    234
wealth management, 245–246
work styles, 231–232
Resiliency
  assertiveness and, 146, 148
  case example of, 139–140
  conflict and, 145–149
  connectedness to others and, 155
  core principles of, 152–158
  definition of, 142
  emotions and, 149–151
  fighting and, 145–149
  hope and, 156–158
  importance of, 140–143
  personal control and, 153–155
  planning ahead and, 132
  positive expectations and, 156–158
  self-assessments, 158–162
  sense of control and, 143–145
  sense of meaning and purpose, 156
  socialization effects on, 144
  in subordinates, 158
  success and, 143–144
  values and, 151–152
Respect, 38–39, 120
Rewarding of employees, 12
Rhoades, Ann, 78, 116

Risk taking, 80–81, 149
Role conflicts, xiii
Role models, 203
Rubenfeld, Jed, 19
Rule of 72, 213
Rule of reciprocity, 102
R.W. Baird, 211

S

Sandberg, Sheryl, 6, 200, 205
Satisfaction, 217–218, 228
SBB Solutions, 132
Scheduling, 145
*Science of Mastering Life's Greatest
	Challenges, The*, 142
Self-assessments
	leadership potential, 133–135
	personality, 89
	resiliency, 158–162
	social influence, 107
	work–family/life balance, 185–186
Self-awareness, 34, 112
Self-belief, 62–67
Self-blame, 58
Self-compassion, 65
Self-confidence
	benefits of, 93
	of leader, 117
	techniques for improving, 64–67
Self-control, 149
Self-employment, 79–80
Self-esteem, 18, 38, 64
Self-fulfilling prophesies, 65
Self-leadership, 112
Self-reliance, 18
Self-talk, 64
Seligman, Martin, 85
Sense of control, 143–145
Sense of meaning, 156
Sense of purpose, 156
Sexism, 7, 191–192, 194, 196–197, 205
Shipman, Claire, 184
Shriver, Maria, 175
Silencing of inner chatterbox, 64

Silos, 83
Sincere caring, 27–28
Slaughter, Anne-Marie, 6
Sleep, 32
Social communication, 115
Social connection
	caring, 27–28
	charisma, 28–29
	commanding presence, 29–30
	humor, 30–31
	overview of, 26–27
Social influence/influencers
	communication, 94–98
	description of, 93–94
	mentoring, 103–106
	networking, 98–103
	research data on, 232
	self-assessments, 107
	transformational leadership and,
		114–115
Socialization, 144
Socioeconomic backgrounds, 224
Sokolov, Jacques, 132, 176
Southwick, Steven, 142
Spending, 215
Sponsors, mentors as, 106
Stakeholders, 83–84
Stanford University, 202
Stanley, Thomas, 215
Starting your own business, 79–80,
	166–167, 176
Steele, Claude, 202
Stereotype threat, 202–203
Stereotypes, 7–10, 193, 202–203
Stewart, Beverly, 20–21, 216
Stock options, 80, 211–212
Straw man argument, 98
Strengths, 76, 113, 133
Stress
	coping with, 9, 141
	debriefing of, 64–65
	neuroticism and, 58
Stroessner, Steve, 203
Success, xii
	behavioral modeling effects on, 17

Success *(Cont.)*
dimensions of. *See* Dimensions of
success
factors involved in, 70
platform for, 74–81
resiliency and, 143–144
traits associated with, 19
Superiority complex, 19
Support systems, 50, 170–171
Szalavitz, Maia, 217

T

Talking from 9 to 5, 146
Tannen, Deborah, 146
Taylor, Shelly, 155
Taylor, Teresa, 179–180
Teasing, 30
Tenacity, 42
"Tend and befriend" work style,
102–103, 155
Think and Grow Rich, 85
Thinking, 193
Thinking, Fast and Slow, 193
Thomas, Dave, 37
Thorsen, Jamie, xiv, 59–62, 118
*Through the Labyrinth: The Truth
About How Women Become
Leaders*, 36, 84
Time, 213
Title, 119
Toxic relationships, 66
Traits, personality. *See* Personality
traits
Transactional leadership, 113
Transformational leadership, 113–
114, 131, 204, 243
Transitions, graceful leadership
during, 128–130
TripleTree, 75
Trust
building of, 54, 130
conscientiousness effects on, 120
as relationship foundation, 77
Truth telling, 37

U

UnitedHealthcare, 9, 16, 37, 57,
75–76, 80–81, 125, 156
Upbringing. *See* Childhood
Utrecht Work Engagement Scale, 72

V

Values
alignment of, 151
family-based. *See* Family values
resiliency and, 151–152
Viad Corporation, 74, 115, 199
Vigor, 72
Visibility, 76
Volunteering, 217–218
Vulnerability, of leaders, 112

W

Weakness(es)
acknowledging of, 65
publicly sharing of, 76
self-awareness of, 113
Wealth management, 245–246
Well-being, 28
Wendy's, 37
Williams, Candyce, xiv, 101, 183,
194–195
Winfrey, Oprah, 15–16
*Womenomics: Work Less, Achieve
More, Live Better*, 184
Work behaviors, 89
Work effort, 72–74
Work engagement, 72–74, 89, 231
Work hard, 4
Work styles
assessment of, 89–90
changing of, 71
description of, 70
flexible, 231
platform for success in business,
74–81
research data on, 231–232

"tend and befriend," 102–103, 155, 234
Work-enhancing opportunities, 79–80
Work–family/life balance
childcare, 182
company flexibility, 173–176
defining of, 168–169
home scheduling system, 181
male involvement in, 171–172
negotiations with partner, 171–172, 183
part-time work, 173
personality traits, 179–184
recommendations for, 178–179
self-assessments, 185–186
starting your own business, 176–179
strategies for, 182
support system for, 170–171
tips for creating, 168–173
work scheduling, 181

Y

Yellen, Janet, 190
Y.E.S. crisis hotline, 71, 73, 77